Crisis and Creativity

African Dynamics

Editorial Committee
Dr Piet Konings (African Studies Centre, Leiden)
Dr Paul Mathieu (FAO-SDAA, Rome)
Dr Adebayo Olukoshi (CODESRIA, Dakar)
Prof. Deborah Posel (University of Witwatersrand, Johannesburg)
Dr Ruth Watson (Birkbeck College, University of London)

VOLUME 5

Crisis and Creativity

Exploring the Wealth of the African Neighbourhood

Edited by
Piet Konings
Dick Foeken

BRILL
LEIDEN · BOSTON
2006

This book is printed on acid-free paper.

Library of Congress Cataloging-in-Publication Data

A C.I.P. record for this book is available from the Library of Congress.

ISSN 1568–1777
ISBN 90 04 15004 8

© Copyright 2006 by Koninklijke Brill NV, Leiden, The Netherlands
Koninklijke Brill NV incorporates the imprints Brill Academic Publishers,
Martinus Nijhoff Publishers and VSP.

All rights reserved. No part of this publication may be reproduced, translated, stored in
a retrieval system, or transmitted in any form or by any means, electronic,
mechanical, photocopying, recording or otherwise, without prior written
permission from the publisher.

Authorization to photocopy items for internal or personal
use is granted by Brill provided that
the appropriate fees are paid directly to The Copyright
Clearance Center, 222 Rosewood Drive, Suite 910
Danvers, MA 01923, USA.
Fees are subject to change.

PRINTED IN THE NETHERLANDS

Contents

Figures *vii*
Maps *vii*
Tables *vii*
Photographs *viii*

1 The African neighbourhood: An introduction *1*
   Piet Konings, Rijk van Dijk & Dick Foeken

2 Surviving in the neighbourhoods of Nakuru town, Kenya *22*
   Samuel Owuor & Dick Foeken

3 'Bendskin' drivers in Douala's New Bell neighbourhood:
   Masters of the road and the city *46*
   Piet Konings

4 Intimate strangers: Neighbourhood, autochthony and the
   politics of belonging *66*
   Basile Ndjio

5 Neighbourhood formation process: Access to housing land
   in Kamwokya, Kampala, Uganda *88*
   Emmanuel Nkurunziza

6 Urban space, gender and identity: A neighbourhood of
   Muslim women in Kano, Nigeria *119*
   Katja Werthmann

7 Maps of what matters: Community colour *142*
   Deborah Pellow

8 Not quite the comforts of home: Searching for locality
   among street youth in Dar es Salaam *163*
   Eileen Moyer

9 Togolese cartographies: Re-mapping space in a
   post-Cold War city *197*
   Charles Piot

10   Neighbours on the fringes of a small city in post-war Chad   *211*
     Mirjam de Bruijn

11   Neighbourhood (re)construction and changing identities in
     Mauritania from a small town perspective   *230*
     Kiky van Til

List of authors   *251*

Figures

5.1	Date of plot acquisition	*101*
5.2	Attraction to neighbourhood	*107*
5.3	Plot use at acquisition	*111*
6.1	The longest row of houses in the barracks	*125*
7.1	'Map' drawn by a 30-year-old Grunshie male carpenter	*154*
7.2	'Map' based on the instructions of a 60-year-old female Hausa trader	*155*
7.3	'Map' drawn by a 25-year-old female Fante store clerk	*156*

Maps

2.1	Nakuru town, Kenya	*25*
3.1	The New Bell quarter of Douala	*51*
4.1	The Ngodi quarter of Douala	*68*
5.1	Kamwokya neighbourhood	*91*
5.2	The hills of Kibuga/Mengo and Kampala	*100*
6.1	Metropolitan Kano	*121*
7.1	Sabon Zongo and Accra, Ghana	*145*
9.1	Lomé, Togo	*202*
10.1	*Secteur Quatre* in Mongo, Chad	*216*
11.1	Mauritania	*234*

Tables

5.1	Methods of land access in Kamwokya	*104*

Photographs

2.1	Generating income in a Nakuru town neighbourhood	*23*
2.2	Rita in her *sukuma wiki* garden in Nakuru town	*31*
3.1	A modern bendskin in action	*48*
3.2	An early example of a Cameroonian motorized taxi	*54*
3.3	Bendskin drivers waiting for passengers	*54*
5.1	The land acquisition/development process	*112*
5.2	Reclaimed and settled area in Kisenyi II zone, Kamwokya	*112*
6.1	Aerial view of the police barracks	*122*
6.2	A street in the barracks	*126*
6.3	Kitchen vents used for peeping out into the street	*128*
6.4	Three old friends: Inna, Barira and Yalwa	*135*
7.1	A roof-top view of Sabon Zongo	*147*
7.2	One set of public toilets in Sabon Zongo	*147*
8.1	'Don't Spy My Life' minibus in Dar es Salaam	*170*
8.2	'Don't Mind' minibus in Dar es Salaam	*171*
8.3	*Karibu Uswazi* by Hassani Mwanyiro	*172*
10.1	Children are often left alone during the day	*218*
10.2	A typical street in Mongo	*218*
11.1	A pastoral-urban mix with camels	*237*
11.2	Grass being brought to town by a local Haratin	*240*

1

The African neighbourhood: An introduction

Piet Konings, Rijk van Dijk & Dick Foeken

Introduction

'Neighbourhood' research goes back to the 1920s with the work of the sociologists of the Chicago School. Urban space, they found, was segregated in 'neighbourhoods' based on the cultural background of immigrants. It was thought that this segregation would disappear as immigrants and their offspring assimilated in American culture. However, subsequent researchers found that urban space remained segregated, not based on cultural background but on class and race. Researchers found that the attachment to particular neighbourhoods also depended on various other aspects as well. They became more heterogeneous, yet their names and boundaries remained the same, thus maintaining their distinctiveness *vis-à-vis* other neighbourhoods.

This raises the question as to what constitutes a neighbourhood. Or what defines this 'distinctiveness' other than just a name and a boundary? Geographers have many definitions, all of which can be grouped according to explanations that describe neighbourhoods as (1) homogeneous areas sharing demographic or housing characteristics; (2) areas that may have diverse characteristics but whose residents share some cohesive sense of identity, political organization or social organization; (3) housing sub-markets in which homes are considered close substitutes; and (4) small spatial units that do not necessarily have any of the above characteristics (Megbolugbe *et al.* 1996: 1787). In modern, western geography, it is particularly the second definition that has gained ground, i.e. that a neighbourhood shows a certain degree of social cohesion[1] and is a source of social identity.

Yet as social networks have increasingly become city-wide, national, international and even virtual (thanks to the Internet), one would, according to

---

[1] See Kearns & Forrest (2000) for a discussion on the various dimensions of social cohesion.

Forrest and Kearns (2001: 2129), expect that 'as a source of social identity the neighbourhood is being progressively eroded with the emergence of a more fluid, individualised way of life'. On the other hand, they argue that 'as globalising processes (...) which bear down upon us seem to be increasingly remote, local social interaction and the familiar landmarks of the neighbourhood may take on greater significance as sources of comfort and security'. Therefore the local neighbourhood remains important as a source of social identity, but 'there are many other sources partly dependent upon our individual and collective time-geographies and action-spaces within the urban areas' (Ibid.: 2130, see also Castells 1997: 60).

Here, we are in the middle of the different views on the concept of 'neighbourhood' between geographers on the one hand, and anthropologists on the other. This discussion is not new. In the 1960s, the sociologist Webber (1964) made a distinction between 'community of place' and 'community of interest'. Neighbourhoods were initially primarily seen as 'communities of place' because of their spatial boundaries. However, the existence of social networks and interactions, not being geographically bounded, allowed the possibility of looking at neighbourhoods as 'communities of interest'. For instance, Sennet and Cobb (1972) stressed that social ties within urban neighbourhoods were declining in favour of relations within the city as a whole as urban areas became more heterogeneous and the divide between home and work increased.

The two perspectives are not incompatible, and indeed most urban neighbourhood scholars adopt a more fluid understanding of neighbourhoods, synthesizing the two approaches. That is also clear from the various contributions in this book. It was not easy to group the chapters under meaningful sub-headings but a rough division into two has been made. The first concerns the chapters where the neighbourhood as a spatial unit (or 'community of space') is the starting point, while the perspective of the chapters in the second half of the book primarily concerns the neighbourhood in terms of social networks and interactions (or 'community of interest'). Although most of the literature on neighbourhoods relates to western urban areas (particularly the United Kingdom and the United States), the general processes described above, and hence the distinction between the two perspectives, are applicable to any urban situation including those in Sub-Saharan Africa. The next two sections of this introductory chapter deal with the two approaches, respectively, even though the various contributions in this volume are linked to a number of theoretical reflections.

The geographical approach to the African neighbourhood

Like many other researchers of African city life, a number of the contributors to this volume have tended to perceive the neighbourhood as a geographical domain in which people are engaged in a variety of socio-cultural, economic and political activities to advance their material and immaterial well-being. They have been inclined to focus on disadvantaged African neighbourhoods and to examine how the residents are coping with the current economic crisis and the processes of economic and political liberalization. They argue in particular that the urban poor have been among those most seriously affected by the economic crisis and structural adjustment, as evidenced by massive retrenchments, job insecurity and falling real wages in the formal sector, rising costs of living, a serious deterioration in urban infrastructure and basic services, and the painful withdrawal of public welfare provision (cf. Rakodi 1997, Tripp 1997, Zeleza & Kalipeni 1999, Simone 2004).

What is most striking in the geographical approach to urban space is its emphasis on the fact that the majority of the residents in disadvantaged African neighbourhoods have not passively watched conditions deteriorate. On the contrary, they appear to behave as active agents, devising alternative strategies to shape their livelihoods and, in some cases, even to accumulate capital. Since the start of the economic crisis and economic liberalization, they have been more or less obliged to find a livelihood within the rapidly expanding informal sector. Informality, in fact, has become a vital facet of African urban life in the sense that it is predominantly driven by informal practices in such areas as work, housing, land use, transportation and a variety of social services (cf. Tripp 1997, Lourenço-Lindell 2002, Hansen & Vaa 2004, Simone 2004).

Residents of urban neighbourhoods often display a remarkable degree of creativity and imaginative innovation in eking out an existence in the informal sector, while taking advantage of the 'opportunities', 'resources', 'assets' or 'capitals' available (Rakodi 2002, de Haan & Zoomers 2005). Besides conventional assets such as land, livestock and equipment, capital includes various elements of human and social capital. Several authors have highlighted the importance of creating social networks based on class, occupation, gender, kinship and generation (cf. Lourenço-Lindell 2002). The current growth of associational initiatives have been well documented, even if some of these initiatives are induced and driven by external agents such as NGOs (Tostensen *et al.* 2001, Leimdorfer & Marie 2003). Less visible forms of collaboration, albeit less documented, are of no lesser importance for survival in the city. These refer to networks of personal ties that people construct for mutual support, for accessing resources and for the exchange goods and services (Hansen & Vaa 2004).

While the geographical approach has a tendency to concentrate on urban life within the more or less well-defined boundaries of the neighbourhood, it mostly acknowledges that the explicit activities and networks of its residents are not confined to this urban space. More than ever before, links with the wider world stretch to other parts of the city, the rural areas, across the nation's borders and even the global world. Obviously, these links tend to maximize sites of opportunities and resources (Tostensen *et al.* 2001, Simone 2004).

In line with this geographical approach and on the basis of intensive empirical research, several contributions in this volume explore the creativity of residents in different African neighbourhoods during the current crisis and the processes of economic and political liberalization. In their contribution, Owuor and Foeken (Chapter 2) examine the livelihood sources of residents in three neighbourhoods in the Kenyan town of Nakuru. Their findings appear to be relevant to coping strategies in most other disadvantaged neighbourhoods in Africa (cf. Zack-Williams 1993, Bangura 1994, Meagher 1995, Potts 1999, Lourenço-Lindell 2002). Using five detailed case studies, they show that low-income households in Nakuru are engaged in multiple livelihood activities, seizing any opportunity to diversify their sources of income. Some are completely dependent on sources of livelihood in the informal economy, but most of them try to combine formal and informal employment, continuously straddling the formal-informal divide (cf. King & McGrath 1999, Niger-Thomas 2000). Formal-sector jobs provide a degree of security for often highly vulnerable informal-sector activities. Depending on the character of these informal activities, the maintenance of wage-labour jobs can provide opportunities for private work, inputs for one's business, subsidized housing, and access to a telephone, transport and clients (Simone 2004). Among the multiple livelihood sources in Nakuru, urban agriculture has significantly expanded, as has been the case elsewhere in Africa (cf. Obudho & Foeken 1999, Zeleza 1999, Page 2001). Interestingly, while Owuor and Foeken do not discuss its possible political implications, Page (2001) argues that urban agriculture in Cameroonian towns has been opportunistically encouraged by the regime in power to act as a safety valve against social unrest.

Although the majority of livelihood sources in Nakuru are still neighbourhood-bound, some have become multi-spatial. According to Owuor and Foeken, Nakuru residents are currently inclined to revive or strengthen rural linkages to provide themselves with access to land in the rural areas for farming purposes and rural networks (see also Gugler 1997, Beall *et al.* 1999, Satterthwaite & Tacoli 2002, Owuor forthcoming). There is, however, proof that access to such urban-rural links have sometimes become problematic in Africa. Tacoli (1998) mentions that some urban residents have become marginalized from urban-rural networks, which prevents them from pursuing multi-spatial strategies of assistance and income generation. In his study of Kitwe on the Zambian Copperbelt, Ferguson (1999) even found an intensification of antagonism between urban and rural kin as urbanites were forced to turn to their rural relatives for help in order to survive the economic crisis. Many urban workers had neglected their rural kin and the latter then utilized their new-found power to make additional demands on the shrinking resources of their urban relatives. Urbanites, in turn, viewed these demands as unfair. Ferguson discusses how, in the context of economic decline, urban workers' ideas of the rural areas changed from being a haven of reciprocity and solidarity to being a locus of selfish, greedy, parasitic demands and even vindictive acts.

Like other researchers (Tripp 1997, Lourenço-Lindell 2002), Owuor and Foeken stress women's increased responsibilities during the economic crisis to compensate for declining incomes in the household as well as decreasing social services. Women are particularly engaged in neighbourhood-bound activities and have created women's groups for mutual support, such as rotating credit associations, sometimes with the help of NGOs.

In their contributions to this volume, Konings and Ndjio (Chapters 3 and 4) both deal with the survival strategies of young people in Cameroon. The youth has emerged as one of the central concerns of African studies (de Boeck & Honwana 2000, Abbink & Van Kessel 2005), and scholars appear to be extremely worried about the occupational and livelihood opportunities as well as the future of African youth, referring to a 'lost' or 'abandoned' generation (Cruise O'Brien 1996). While admitting that many young people find it hard to survive in Cameroon, both Konings and Ndjio relate how some young people in New Bell, one of the most marginalized neighbourhoods of Douala, have invented innovative activities during economic and political liberalization that have enabled them not only to gain a sustainable livelihood but even to accumulate capital. Most of these young people belong to the Bamileke ethnic group, which is known in Cameroon for its high degree of mobility, dynamism and entrepreneurial spirit.

Konings describes in some detail how Bamileke youth in New Bell have become involved in what is called 'bendskin' in Cameroon – the use of motorbikes as taxis. He emphasizes the significance of bendskin to neighbourhood development: not only does it offer a reasonable and secure income to its drivers, it also provides a form of transport that is well adapted to the poor state of the neighbourhood's road network and its residents' low-income levels. In addition, it stimulates growth in other local economic activities, particularly those that provide services in one way or another to bendskin itself. Konings shows that bendskin drivers are inclined to organize themselves in small groups based on ethnic and friendship bonds. Each group has its own parking space at a strategic position in the neighbourhood and its members demonstrate a large degree of solidarity both during working hours and in their leisure time. While these various groups are usually in competition with each other, they appear nevertheless to be capable of overcoming group boundaries, and rally round in defence of common interests against 'outsiders', such as other road users and, more particularly, government authorities and the police.

Ndjio describes how Bamileke youth from New Bell, like some of their counterparts elsewhere in Africa, have created transnational criminal networks extending from Africa to other continents (Malaquais 2001, Bayart *et al.* 1999, Shaw 2002). Their activity is usually designated as *feymania* in Cameroon and the *feymen* groups are involved in various criminal activities, including the international trafficking of drugs, diamonds, arms, human organs and young girls for organized prostitution, the counterfeiting of banknotes, credit cards and passports, swindling and smuggling. As a result of these and other criminal activities, they have been able to amass fabulous wealth in a short space of time. Ndjio explains why the local population is inclined to question the supposedly mysterious origins of the *feymen*'s sudden wealth, often associating it with sorcery and witchcraft.

Several authors have pointed out that access to land for housing has become increasingly difficult for a growing proportion of the African urban population, claiming that informal channels of urban land delivery and neighbourhood formation are now the dominant feature in African cities (cf. Amis & Lloyd 1990, Rakodi 1997, Hansen & Vaa 2004). In Chapter 5, Nkurunziza examines the process of land acquisition for housing in Kamwokya II, a densely populated informal settlement in Kampala. He shows that even in such unplanned settlements, access to land is neither haphazard nor spontaneous but instead follows certain procedures that are usually well known and adhered to by the actors involved. The key actors in the process actually appear to borrow pragmatically from different normative orders, including customary and state regulations. Nkurunziza also highlights the importance of social networks, especially those based on kinship and friendship, in informal land access. They form a pivotal avenue to information about land availability, the reduction of transaction costs in land and the enforcement of non-state rules within the neighbourhood. Although Kamwokya, like other African informal settlements, is characterized by poor-quality housing and rudimentary infrastructure, land acquisition in the neighbourhood is, according to Nkurunziza, of great benefit to low-income households as it provides shelter and space for generating income by renting out part of the premises and conducting home-based activities.

There is extensive evidence that residents of disadvantaged urban neighbourhoods are inclined to contravene existing administrative and legal regulations concerning their informal activities, land occupation and subdivision, and house construction (cf. Tripp 1997, Hansen & Vaa 2004). In some cases, this leads to confrontations with local government authorities and the police. Hansen (2004) analyzes the contests over public spaces in Lusaka, Zambia between street vendors and local government authorities. Street vending had been illegal since the colonial period but continued to grow in contravention of existing regulations. A new city market was opened in 1997 but remained nearly empty for several years because traders claimed that fees were too high, and the congestion of the streets continued. In early 1999, the City Council, with the help of the police and paramilitary personnel, razed the temporary stalls and chased thousands of vendors off the streets. Hansen mentions that vendors returned to the streets after some time, although not in such large numbers as before. Since 2000, they have been facing periodic crackdowns and the daily enforcement of new laws that prohibit buying and selling outside designated markets. In his contribution to this volume, Konings (Chapter 3) shows that New Bell bendskin drivers also ignore all administrative and traffic regulations. Due to their sheer numbers and ability to mobilize so rapidly, they constitute a powerful force in Douala, where they have been successful in contesting police authority and establishing control over the road. In protest against persistent police harassment and extortion, they have on certain occasions even taken control of the city by chasing the police from the streets and bringing traffic to a total standstill.

In most cases, however, residents are inclined to employ more peaceful strategies towards local government authorities and the police so as to be able to proceed with their illegal activities unhindered. In their case study of a female-headed household in Nakuru, Owuor and Foeken (Chapter 2) illustrate one of these strategies: a female head who was engaged in the illegal brewing and selling of *chang'aa* (a local brew) had made an 'arrangement' with the local police. By regularly offering them a tiny share in her profits, she was able to avoid fines or imprisonment and to continue her business. In his study of the informal Kamwokya settlement in Kampala, Nkurunziza (Chapter 5) demonstrates that its residents were able to avoid being punished for violating the city's formal planning and building regulations by establishing patron-client relations with their political godfathers.

Significantly, in addition to potentially hostile relations between residents of disadvantaged urban neighbourhoods and the state, one can also observe a growing polarization between residents themselves within these neighbourhoods during economic and political liberalization. Several authors have noted the emergence of tensions between autochthons and allochthons within African neighbourhoods, with the former fearing a loss of identity and preferential access to local resources, such as land and employment opportunities (cf. Geschiere & Nyamnjoh 2000, Konings 2001, Leimdorfer & Marie 2003). The xenophobic obsession with autochthony tends to be instigated or fuelled by political entrepreneurs and is likely to surface in a situation where the so-called 'indigenous' population feels dominated in demographic, economic and political terms by 'strangers' or 'settlers', albeit often long-standing migrants of the same nationality. Konings and Ndjio (Chapters 3 and 4) show that the highly mobile and entrepreneurial Bamileke have become the dominant force in Douala, the economic capital of Cameroon – a development that is deeply resented by the 'native' Duala people. Ndjio describes in some detail how the settlement of a Bamileke *feyman* in Ngodi, one of the exceptional Duala-dominated neighbourhoods in Douala, triggered off severe confrontations with the autochthonous population. He shows that Duala residents have been effectively using witchcraft accusations against young Bamileke entrepreneurs in their determined efforts to maintain control over their neighbourhood's resources and to safeguard its ethnic and cultural homogeneity.

The anthropological approach to the African neighbourhood

In anthropology, the study of African cities developed through the pioneering work of members of the Manchester School who, from the 1940s to the 1960s, conducted research in Southern Africa. Prior to this time, the region was already marked by a spectacular growth in urban and industrial areas, resulting largely from the massive labour migration of young men from the countryside to the region's expanding cities. Cities in newly emerging industrial areas such as the Copperbelt or the South African mining complexes took on large numbers of migrant workers from remote rural areas, encouraging the mobility of many across large distances of the colonial territories of this part of Africa. The seminal works of Gluckman (1960), Mitchell (1969), Epstein (1981, 1992), Mitchell & Epstein (1959) and Kapferer (1972), among others, explored the dynamics, causes and consequences of this process of migration and urbanization in social and cultural terms. While their paradigmatic point of departure was the village and its underlying structures of kinship, ethnicity, authority and religious life, they did not maintain the rural as the natural habitat for anthropology but were quick to realize that anthropology should move into the city so as to offer an understanding of the genesis of African urbanity in these newly emerging conditions. Studying the often detrimental effects of the massive out-migration for the social and cultural structures of village life was certainly an important aspect of their work. However it required an anthropology that would allow them to understand the ways in which these structures changed, became adapted to or mitigated the experiences of living a city life. Was the rural-urban migrant to be studied as a displaced villager, a perpetual stranger to urban life and someone who therefore felt the need to maintain kinship and ethnic relations as a way of survival? Was the village in fact transplanted to the city such that urban neighbourhoods formed the natural continuation of village structures of sociality, authority and livelihood?

Studies by the Manchester School began to highlight the new urbanites' creativity and agency in the way they incorporated elements of their rural backgrounds in the multi-ethnic and multi-cultural composition of life in these cities. This process was not simply one of 'de-tribalization' as if the blending of the many ethnic and cultural backgrounds to which these migrants belonged would lead to an unavoidable loss of cultural identity (Gluckman 1960). Nor was this process one by which these migrants were alienated, and only partially or remotely involved in city life, thereby remaining highly dependent on the rural places from which they had originated. Instead, the insights gained by the Manchester School demonstrated many more subtle processes in the creation of urban life, which was neither fully dependent nor dictated by the local, the rural and the village, nor fully westernized as if the African city was no more than a copy of its western counterparts. These studies aimed to show that the African was as much a villager as a townsman and that there was flexibility in the way in which new social and cultural formations came about in these expanding cities, entirely adapted to urban conditions. One important element in this exploration was an investigation of how kinship structures were transformed under conditions of urban life into larger networks that enabled the inclusion of relations with people of very different cultural and ethnic backgrounds (Boswell 1969, 1975). The method of network analysis allowed for an understanding of the extent to which class and occupational identities were crosscutting ethnic identities and kinship structures, and provided room for the transformative nature of the urban social fabric (Epstein 1961, Mitchell 1969, Boswell 1969, Boissevain & Mitchell 1973, Kapferer 1972). Network analysis showed that, after arriving in the city, migrants were initially dependent on kinship relations but, over time, needed to affiliate with communities and neighbourhoods where kinship relations were still relevant but where they were also able to build networks of support, mutual help and trust that increasingly were less dictated by kinship ideology (Boswell 1975).

Network analysis thus became a well-engrained anthropological method capable of dealing with levels of social interaction that went beyond the study of tight-knit communities, which for so long had formed the basis of the discipline's approach to African social life. These studies also fed into research on the rise of voluntary associations (Tostensen *et al.* 2001: 21-22). While the development of associations could initially be perceived as a continuation of ethnic or tribal organizations from the 'home village' in the city, the ethnic marker eventually became less and less relevant for migrants' identity, membership and functioning. Instead, these forms of social capital, of mutual help and support, which often took the form of burial societies, home-town associations or small-credit organizations, came to be organized much more along class, occupational and gender divisions and less along ethnic lines. Ethnic solidarity appeared to become only one of the many opportunities or assets that a migrant could negotiate for organizing relations of reciprocity (Peil 1981).

Interestingly, these studies did not stress an exclusive community type of approach to the exploration of migrant situations in African cities. Networks and associations were not bound by geographical borders, which a community approach often presupposes. In fact, a community-based approach to African urban life developed much more in another field of anthropology, namely that of the study of ideological systems – religion and politics in particular. Of these two, it appeared that religion provided for the kind of overarching identity through which a sense of community of people from very different backgrounds could be created (Van Binsbergen 1981, Daneel 1987, DeVisch 1996). One important process was that, through the spread of the world religions of Christianity and Islam, a more unifying cosmology could be produced that was capable of incorporating all sorts of local religious traditions, rituals and symbolism which were relevant for the urban situation. In many parts of Africa, so-called prophet-healing churches were established, in most cases as urban innovations, in which Christian elements were combined with African traditions of healing and ritual life. For many migrants, these churches provided a kind of homecoming in the way their practices and symbolism appeared to refer to the historic forms of religion these migrants knew from their places of origin (Van Binsbergen 2000). On the other hand, the merging with Christian elements such as the Bible, hymns, and clothes introduced in the cities by European missionaries provided for a much wider cosmological horizon and for an encompassing identity above and beyond all sorts of local traditions (Comaroff & Comaroff 1991). These prophetic-healing or African Independent churches became immensely popular in urban areas and grew rapidly in numbers from the 1930s onwards (Peel 1968, Bond *et al.* 1979). Often founded by a charismatic and healing prophet, communities of followers emerged who, within the urban context, organized places to meet and worship, to conduct healing ceremonies and to establish centres for the production of objects to sell at urban markets (Dillon-Malone 1978). These healing churches had a profound impact on urban life because of their sheer numbers and also because they demonstrated that the urban had become a place for religious innovation and experimentation (see, for example, Scarnecchia 1997). In some cases, religion also played a part in demarcating a particular section of the city as a bounded geographical neighbourhood (DeVisch 1996, Englund 2001). In West Africa, certain quarters of cities in southern parts of, for example, Ghana and Nigeria where migrants from Sahelian areas had settled became known as *zongo* locations specifically reserved for 'strangers' and known for their preponderance of Muslims (see Chapter 7).

The city as a place of ideological innovation became important when Marxist anthropology emerged as a dominant discourse in the study of Africa. While the Manchester School and its new anthropological methods were capable of describing the emergence of networks, associations and ideological innovations, it had few means of conceptualizing the motors of change. It successfully exploded the notion of the African as a victim of urbanization, as being estranged, de-rooted and displaced while living a city life, but it was not equipped to provide an explanation for the direction the changes, adaptations and innovations took in the hands of the new urbanites. Marxist anthropology, however, presupposed a historical process of articulation of modes of production by which encroachment and exploitation of one particular political economy was perceived as the ultimate causative factor of changes in ideological and social systems. As Ferguson (1999: 90) demonstrates, this Marxist anthropology critically approached the dualism of the Manchester School that perceived of the rural and the urban as two very distinct life worlds and instead perceived of both as being encapsulated within a single comprehensive socio-economic and exploitative capitalist system. Rural-urban migration was one of these particular forms of the articulation of modes of production, whereby dominant economic power relations at the centre encroached upon the hinterland and made the rural subject to its project. The growth of industrial urban centres in Africa and the massive rural-to-urban migration it produced were to be perceived as one phase in the growing dominance of a capitalist and colonial mode of production engendered in the West. Authors such as Van Binsbergen (1981) and Ranger (1979) perceived of the new religious forms and communities that emerged in the cities as super-structural innovations, meaning that they largely resulted from and were nothing but reflections of the structural inequalities these migrants suffered in the process of becoming engulfed in capitalist forms of labour. The study of inner-city religious, ethnic or political communities received attention as migrants tried to cope with situations of capitalist exploitation and alienation. Often these communities were viewed as forms of resilience, creativity and resistance to an outer world where capitalist labour relations were seen as dominant and alienating, but belonging to a community of this nature provided a comforting environment (Comaroff 1985). These religious communities were neither to be viewed as extensions of a rural society nor as a product of an urban life world, as Marxist anthropology refused to perceive of the rural and the urban as two totally separate and exclusive cultural systems. In fact, Marxist anthropology came to emphasize less the idea of a transition between the rural and the urban as super-structural innovations occurred both in situations in which massive rural-urban migration and the formation of urban religious neighbourhoods created an important element in the way people coped with the encroachment of capitalist systems of the market, labour and industrial production.

A new anthropology, which questioned the modernist assumptions of all the approaches discussed so far, was starting to become popular by the mid-1980s. Characterized as being 'postmodern', it was far less united around one singular paradigm, such as agency or modes of production, but was organized around a set of questions (Gupta & Ferguson 1997). These questions had in common a focus on the exploration of modernity and the kind of dichotomies and distinctions the 'products' of modernity, such as the state or science or the Christian mission, appeared to produce. The question became what meaning such distinctions and dichotomies – such as the modern versus the traditional, the religious versus the materialist, the past versus the present, faith versus superstition, the subject versus the citizen, the rural versus the urban, the West versus the rest – meant for the people concerned (Hannerz 1987, Comaroff & Comaroff 1993, Piot 1999). What are people's own understandings of modernity and to what extent are their actions informed by the distinctions that modernity produces in the guise of academic science, state policies, citizenship, law and education? Earlier approaches in the urban anthropology of Africa uncritically embraced the idea that whereas the city must be modern, the rural must be traditional, and that while the city was transformative of social relations and culture, the rural was, in fact, the domain of time-honoured rootedness in culture. Africa was perceived as a patchwork of essentially and analytically distinct cultures and ethnic groups (tribes) (see Gupta & Ferguson 1997) and the modern city was, therefore, the place of either existential confusion or the place where networks and associations resolved the incompatibilities that multi-culturalism brought about.

For postmodern anthropology, however, the question became how people themselves experienced the distinctions that modernity had created for them and whether they were actually meaningful. Through the work of Ferguson (1999), Weiss (2002, 2005) and de Boeck & Plissart (2004), for example, a much clearer picture emerged of the expectations and anxieties of urbanites for whom, as an imagined community, the city held promises of connecting to a larger world, of taking part in Western wealth, prosperity and consumption and of being able to overcome the limitations, restrictions and tribulations of tradition and custom. Dealing with second-, third- or even fourth-generation urbanites, anthropologists became interested in studying the consequences of the failing dreams modernity had made city-dwellers believe in for so long: namely, that the urban could be separated from the rural, that traditions are not meant for the city, that archaic rituals and witchcraft should belong to the village, that the townsman is a citizen and not a subject of traditional authority, that employment is reserved for the city, and self-sufficiency is the fate of the rural (Geschiere & Nyamnjoh 1998, Mamdani 2000, Van Dijk 2003). While the state, systems of law, Christianity and education all contributed to these modernist dreams of African urbanity, reality proved much harder, making the pursuit of such clear-cut distinctions a troublesome and often virtual endeavour. For postmodern anthropology, the question remained as to whether there was a real rural-urban divide, or whether it was a figure of speech and a way in which people created a sense of reality in their minds (Ferguson 1999: 92). If so, why are such divides being proclaimed, and by whom? Likewise, if the city is divided into communities and neighbourhoods, who is producing these distinctions and what is the meaning of maintaining or overcoming such divisions in the hearts and minds of the people concerned?[2] The inspiration to explore these questions was not only drawn from Lefebvre's 'social production of space' (1991) but also from Appadurai's 'production of locality' (1996). They demonstrated that the 'local' could not be taken for granted but that people construct ideas of localness by using a plethora of ideological, material and cultural ideas and artefacts, even if this notion of locality embraces an entire city (Hannerz 1987). Locality has thus come to be regarded as a product of all sorts of social, cultural, political and economic relations and their meaning in human interaction.

The anthropological contributions to this volume deal with the question of the social construction of locality and its meaning in social interaction. All underline the importance of this approach to the understanding of African urban life, even though each takes a different angle in demonstrating how and in reference to which context a production of locality (not necessarily a geographical neighbourhood) is realized. The contributions by Werthmann (Chapter 6) and Pellow (Chapter 7) deal with situations in which a locality at first sight appears to be produced on the basis of clear geographical borders and demarcated physical structures. Werthmann describes a location – known as the police barracks – in the city of Kano in Nigeria that exemplifies a highly patterned structure and physical lay-out, which sets it apart from the rest of the city. A clear case of a geographically determined neighbourhood, so it seems, but the question is whether the people living in this area perceive of it as a neighbourhood in social and cultural terms and reproduce it as a locality for their social relations, their systems of mutual support and help, and their belonging and identity. By focusing on the lives of women, often wives of the policemen stationed there, Werthmann analyzes how subtler processes are at work in the way they negotiate the structure of this locality. Much of the women's social behaviour and their identity is given shape and meaning by the way in which they try to circumvent and negotiate the rigid physical lay-out in which they

---

[2] See Zeleza & Kalipeni (1999) for a discussion of similar questions.

live. They attach great meaning to the ways in which they deal with the walls, doors and small streets that seem to force them into a very secluded, indoor lifestyle. Contesting this seclusion is what unites them, producing a neighbourhood sociality that opposes precisely the geographical neighbourhood in which they live and that, in accordance with public norms and social values, threatens to limit their conviviality with other women and households in the area.

Pellow's contribution (Chapter 7) on one of the *zongo* in Accra, Ghana also deals with a clearly demarcated area in geographical terms but she demonstrates, by using specific forms of mental mapping, that not only *zongos* are marked by certain socio-cultural features such as the presence of migrants from the northern part of Ghana and the subsequent importance of Islam. This mental mapping is part of the production of locality in the way in which it is dependent on the socio-cultural and socio-economic status and position of the one who is producing the mental map of the area, while often being an inhabitant of that area themselves. A market vendor produces a mental map of the locality with different features and markers on a very different basis from a civil servant or a teacher. In the production of locality, mental mapping thus becomes a highly subjective matter, in spite of the geographical markers such as buildings and markets that would appear to possess an objective reality and place on a map.

While these two contributions deal with inner divisions in the city, the articles by Moyer (Chapter 8), Piot (Chapter 9), de Bruijn (Chapter 10) and Van Til (Chapter 11) discuss the problematic of how these distinctions seem to disappear in exchange for perceptions of the city as a place of differential opportunities. Moyer, dealing with youngsters living on the streets of Dar es Salaam in Tanzania, and de Bruijn, describing the lives of marginalized women in Mongo in Chad, develop an understanding of the way in which their interlocutors organize their lives on the basis of notions of where to go and not to go, where opportunities are better, where there are prospects and where hardships and problems can be expected to emerge. Moyer analyzes the ways in which youngsters in Dar es Salaam distinguish one particular area, a street corner, from another location in town on the basis of socio-economic opportunities on the one hand, and play and pleasure on the other. There is a deep sense of agency here in the way in which these youngsters and women produce their notions of locality, an agency that seems to make the city subject to their divisions of neighbourhoods and opportunities, instead of the other way round. While the city is often the place where government agencies and NGOs can be found (and these youngsters and women certainly do not fail to register the activities of aid agencies on their behalf), they remain elusive, only partially included in the programmes these organisations have set up. In other words, these aid agencies and the location of their care programmes are also included in people's production of the city as a place of differential opportunities and localities. De Bruijn demonstrates how, in the war-torn society of Chad in the 1980s, people fleeing to Mongo formed a new neighbourhood of settlement and of social relations around the Red Cross camp on the outskirts of the town. Long after the Red Cross left the city, this area was still known as the place where the poor and destitute go once they arrive in town and enter the set of social and emotional relations that a sharing of utter poverty produces. The definitions of these opportunities and localities, which the groups construct among themselves, such as 'behind the Sheraton' in Dar es Salaam, remain elusive, inchoate, contextual and situational and are often not congruent with any kind of geographical mapping of such urban spaces. But they depend on these definitions and perceptions for their survival.

Van Til (Chapter 11) explores rural-urban linkages in Mauritania by focusing on the migration of nomadic cattle-herding people into town. Investigating this process in the town of Aioun el Atrouss, she demonstrates that this movement and the way in which these nomadic people establish social relations in town are leading to shifts and changes in the social status and social hierarchies that have a long history in this nomadic and pastoral society. The kinds of neighbourhoods these nomadic people create very much depend on the precise nature of their position in the social hierarchy, where the distinction between being a descendant of a noble or a slave family is highly relevant. While this division is and remains relevant for understanding the kind of social neighbourhoods these groups engage in, changes are taking place in terms of their relative socio-economic power and potential. It has become more difficult for the nobility to maintain an aura of nobility amid the socio-economic relations they engender and the economic activities they engage in. A blurring of the boundaries of these neighbourhoods has occurred as a result of urbanization.

Piot (Chapter 9) goes one step further when describing the city of Lomé as a space of differential opportunities in view of the fascination of many Togolese with moving abroad and taking part in the diaspora. While initially Lomé featured prominently in the migration patterns of northern Togolese moving to the south in search of employment and a more prosperous future, it has now become globally connected and serves as an entry point for access to the outside world, the West in particular. This can be seen as a kind of stepping-stone migration on a grand scale whereby from the northern rural areas, Lomé only serves as a springboard to that enticing global world beyond of seemingly endless possibilities and opportunities. What is crucial for the migrant, however, is having or developing a differential perspective of the city in terms of knowing where the localities are that make it possible to access the global world. Where are the embassies and visa departments, the sellers of fake identity documents, the churches that have overseas links and the places where tickets can be bought? Obviously, many get stuck in the city and only a minority succeed in leaving Togo, which turns the city into something of a lottery, a place of chance where perhaps healers, Pentecostal churches and their deliverance rituals, and other religious specialists can help to improve one's luck. With many overseas migrant communities, transnational connections develop, particularly with the city as a place where remittances can be invested, thereby once more obfuscating a clear-cut dichotomy between the local city and the global world. The modern media and means of transport and communication contribute to this imaginary that appears to transmit the notion that, by entering Lomé, one has already set foot in a global world, something that many aspire to do.

To conclude, taken together these contributions show that in the anthropological study of neighbourhoods and localities in African towns and cities, there are many ways of exploring urban people's understanding of the structured versus unstructured spaces that the city represents to them. These spaces primarily take shape through social relations that are produced on the basis of a range of sentiments and identities that revolve around issues of belonging, of a shared history, a shared predicament, gender and age. As was argued extensively in de Bruijn, Van Dijk & Foeken (2001), the neighbourhood – being settled and belonging somewhere – cannot be assumed as the 'natural' and common state of people and society. If the flux of social relations is taken as the paradigmatic point of departure, such as this volume aspires to do, then these urban spaces appear as special conditions, not taken-for-granted condensations in time and space of what this plethora of social relations is capable of constituting (Zeleza & Kalipeni 1999). Even in the most destitute situations, this perspective still allows some agency to the people concerned, particularly in terms of the 'neighbourly' social relations they engender. While they may have little hope of occupying or owning a place, they may still have the capacity to produce social spaces, a matter of growing importance to many facing the urban realities of Africa today.

References

Abbink, J. & I. van Kessel (eds) 2005, *Vanguard or Vandals: Youth, Politics and Conflict in Africa*, Leiden: Brill.
Amis, P. & P. Lloyd (eds) 1990, *Housing Africa's Urban Poor*, Manchester: Manchester University Press.
Andrae, G. 1992, 'Urban Workers as Farmers: Agro-links of Nigerian Textile Workers in the Crisis of the 1980s', in: J. Baker & P.O. Pedersen (eds), *The Rural-Urban Interface in Africa: Expansion and Adaptation*, Uppsala: Nordiska Afrikainstitutet, pp. 200-22.
Appadurai, A. 1996, *Modernity at Large. Cultural Dimensions of Globalization*, Minneapolis: University of Minnesota Press.
Bangura, Y. 1994, 'Economic Restructuring, Coping Strategies and Social Change: Implications for Institutional Development in Africa', *Development and Change* 25 (4): 785-827.
Bayart, J.-F., S. Ellis & B. Hibou 1999, *The Criminalization of the State in Africa*, Oxford: James Currey.
Beall, J., N. Kanji & C. Tacoli 1999, 'Urban African Livelihood Systems: Straddling the Rural-Urban Divide', in: S. Jones & N. Nelson (eds), *Urban Poverty in Africa. From Understanding to Alleviation*, London: Intermediate Technology Publications, pp. 160-68.
de Boeck, F. & A. Honwana 2000, 'Faire et Défaire la Société: Enfants, Jeunes et Politique en Afrique', *Politique Africaine* 80: 5-11.
de Boeck, F. & M.-F. Plissart 2004, *Kinshasa. Tales of the Invisible City*, Ghent/Amsterdam: Ludion.
Boissevain, J. & J.C. Mitchell (eds) 1973, *Network Analysis. Studies in Human Interaction*, The Hague: Mouton.
Bond, G., W. Johnson & S. Walker 1979, *African Christianity: Patterns of Religious Continuity*, New York: Academic Press.
Boswell, D.M. 1969, 'Personal Crises and the Mobilization of the Social Network', in: J.C. Mitchell (ed.), *Social Networks in Urban Situations. Analyses of Personal Relationships in Central African Towns*, Manchester: Manchester University Press.
Boswell, D.M. 1975, 'Kinship, Friendship and the Concept of a Social Network', in: C. Kileff & W.C. Pendleton (eds), *Urban Man in Southern Africa,* Gweru: Mambo Press, pp. 145-97.
de Bruijn, M. R. van Dijk & D. Foeken (eds) 2001, *Mobile Africa. Changing Patterns of Movement in Africa and Beyond*, Leiden: Brill.
Castells, M. 1997, *The Power of Identity*, Oxford: Blackwell.
Comaroff, J. 1985, *Body of Power. Spirit of Resistance. The Culture and History of South African People*, Chicago: University of Chicago Press.
Comaroff, J. & J. Comaroff 1991, *Of Revelation and Revolution. Christianity, Colonialism and Consciousness in South Africa*, Chicago: University of Chicago Press.
Comaroff, J. & J. Comaroff (eds) 1993, *Modernity and its Malcontents. Ritual and Power in Postcolonial Africa*, Chicago: University of Chicago Press.

Cruise O'Brien, D.B. 1996, 'A Lost Generation? Youth Identity and State Decay in West Africa', in: R. Werbner & T. Ranger (eds), *Postcolonial Identities in Africa*, London: Zed Books, pp. 55-74.

Daneel, M.L. 1987, *Quest for Belonging. Introduction to a Study of African Independent Churches*, Gweru: Mambo Press.

DeVisch, R. 1996, '"Pillaging Jesus". Healing Churches and the Villagisation of Kinshasa', *Africa* 66 (4): 555-86.

Dillon-Malone, C.M. 1978, *The Korsten Basketmakers. A Study of Masowe Apostles, an Indigenous African Religious Movement*, Manchester: Manchester University Press.

Englund, H. 2001, 'The Politics of Multiple Identities: The Making of a Home Villagers' Association in Lilongwe, Malawi', in: A. Tostensen, I. Tvedten & M. Vaa (eds), *Associational Life in African Cities. Popular Responses to the Urban Crisis*, Uppsala: Nordiska Afrikainstitutet, pp. 90-106.

Epstein, A.L. 1961, 'The Network and Urban Social Organisation', *Rhodes-Livingstone Journal* 29: 28-62.

Epstein, A.L. 1981, *Urbanization and Kinship. The Domestic Domain on the Copperbelt of Zambia (1950-1956)*, London: Academic Press.

Epstein, A.L. 1992, *Scenes from African Urban Life. Collected Copperbelt Papers*, Edinburgh: Edinburgh University Press.

Ferguson, J. 1999, *Expectations of Modernity: Myths and Meanings of Urban Life on the Zambian Copperbelt*, Berkeley: University of California Press.

Forrest, R. & A. Kearns 2001, 'Social Cohesion, Social Capital and the Neighbourhood', *Urban Studies* 38: 2125-43.

Geschiere, P. & F.B. Nyamnjoh 1998, 'Witchcraft as an Issue in the "Politics of Belonging". Democratization and Urban Migrants' Involvement with the Home Village', *African Studies Review* 41 (3): 69-91.

Geschiere, P. & F. Nyamnjoh 2000, 'Capitalism and Autochthony: The Seesaw of Mobility and Belonging, *Public Culture* 12 (2): 423-52.

Gluckman, M. 1960, 'Tribalism in Modern British Central Africa', *Cahiers d'Études Africaines* 1: 55-70.

Gugler, J. (ed.) 1997, *Cities in the Developing World: Issues, Theory and Policy*, Oxford: Oxford University Press.

Gupta, A. & J. Ferguson (eds) 1997, *Culture, Power, Place. Explorations in Critical Anthropology*, Durham, NC: Duke University Press.

de Haan, L. & A. Zoomers 2005, 'Exploring the Frontier of Livelihoods Research', *Development and Change* 36 (1): 27-47.

Hannerz, U. 1987, 'The World in Creolization', *Africa* 57: 546-59.

Hansen, K. Tranberg 2004, 'Who Rules the Streets? The Politics of Vending Space in Lusaka', in: K. Tranberg Hansen & M. Vaa (eds), *Reconsidering Informality: Perspectives from Urban Africa*, Uppsala: Nordiska Afrikainstitutet, pp. 62-79.

Hansen, K. Tranberg & M. Vaa (eds) 2004, *Reconsidering Informality: Perspectives from Urban Africa*, Uppsala: Nordiska Afrikainstitutet.

Kapferer, B. 1972, *Strategy and Transaction in an African Factory. African Workers and Indian Management in a Zambian Town*, Manchester: Manchester University Press.

Kearns, A. & R. Forrest 2000, 'Social Cohesion and Multi-level Urban Governance', *Urban Studies* 37: 995-1017.

King, K. & S. McGrath 1999, 'Africa's Urban Informal Economies: Between Poverty and Growth', in: S. Jones & N. Nelson (eds), *Urban Poverty in Africa. From Understanding to Alleviation*, London: Intermediate Technology Publications, pp. 27-35.

Konings, P. 2001, 'Mobility and Exclusion: Conflicts between Autochthons and Allochthons during Political Liberalisation in Cameroon', in: M. de Bruijn, R. van Dijk & D. Foeken (eds), *Mobile Africa: Changing Patterns of Movement in Africa and Beyond*, Leiden: Brill, pp. 169-94.

Lefebvre, H. 1991, *The Production of Space*, Cambridge, MA/Oxford: Blackwell.

Leimdorfer, F. & A. Marie (eds) 2003, *L'Afrique des Citadins: Sociétés Civiles en Chantier (Abidjan, Dakar)*, Paris: Karthala.

Lourenço-Lindell, I. 2002, *Walking the Tight Rope. Informal Livelihoods and Social Networks in a West African City*, Stockholm: University of Stockholm, Department of Human Geography.

Mamdani, M. 2000, 'The Politics of Peasant Ethnic Communities and Urban Civil Society. Reflections on an African Dilemma', in: D. Bryceson, C. Kay & J. Mooy (eds), *Disappearing Peasantries? Rural Labour in Africa, Asia and Latin America*, London: Intermediate Technology Publications, pp. 99-111.

Malaquais, D. 2001, 'Arts de Feyre au Cameroun', *Politique Africaine* 82: 101-18.

Meagher, K. 1995, 'Crisis, Informalisation and the Urban Informal Sector in Sub-Saharan Africa', *Development and Change* 26 (2): 259-84.

Megbolugbe, I.F., M.C. Hoek-Smit & P.D. Linneman 1996, 'Understanding Neighbourhood Dynamics: A Review of the Contributions of William G. Grigsby', *Urban Studies* 33: 1779-95.

Mitchell, J.C. (ed.) 1969, *Social Networks in Urban Situations. Analyses of Personal Relationships in Central African Towns*, Manchester: Manchester University Press.

Mitchell, J.C. & A.L. Epstein 1959, 'Occupational Prestige and Social Status among Urban Africans in Northern Rhodesia, *Africa* 29: 22-40.

Niger-Thomas, M. 2000, *'Buying Futures'. The Upsurge of Female Entrepreneurship Crossing the Formal/Informal Divide in South West Cameroon*, Leiden: University of Leiden, Research School CNWS.

Obudho, R.A. & D. Foeken 1999, 'Urban Agriculture in Africa: A Bibliographical Survey', Leiden: African Studies Centre, Research Report 58.

Owuor, S.O. (forthcoming), 'Bridging the Urban-Rural Divide. Multi-spatial Livelihoods in Nakuru Town, Kenya', Leiden: African Studies Centre, Research Report.

Page, B. 2002, 'Urban Agriculture in Cameroon: An Anti-politics Machine in the Making?', *Geoforum* 33: 41-54.

Peel, J.D.Y 1968, *Aladura. A Religious Movement Among the Yoruba*, London: Oxford University Press.

Peil, M. 1981, *Cities and Suburbs. Urban Life in West Africa*, New York: Africana Publishing Company.

Piot, C. 1999, *Remotely Global. Village Modernity in West Africa*, Chicago: University of Chicago Press.

Potts, D. 1999, 'The Impact of Structural Adjustment on Welfare and Livelihoods: An Assessment by People in Harare, Zimbabwe', in: S. Jones & N. Nelson (eds), *Urban*

Poverty in Africa. From Understanding to Alleviation, London: Intermediate Technology Publications, pp. 36-48.

Rakodi, C. (ed.) 1997, *The Urban Challenge in Africa: Growth and Management of its Large Cities*, Tokyo: United Nations University Press.

Rakodi, C. with T. Lloyd-Jones (eds) 2002, *Urban Livelihoods. A People-Centred Approach to Reducing Poverty*, London: Earthscan Publications.

Ranger, T. 1979, 'Developments in the Historical Study of African Religion. Relations of Production and Religious Change in Central Africa', Leiden: African Studies Centre.

Satterthwaite, D. & C. Tacoli 2002, 'Seeking an Understanding of Poverty that Recognizes Rural-Urban Differences and Rural-Urban Linkages', in: C. Rakodi with T. Lloyd-Jones (eds), *Urban Livelihoods. A People-Centred Approach to Reducing Poverty*, London: Earthscan Publications, pp. 52-70.

Scarnecchia, T. 1997, 'Mai Chaza's "Guta re Jehova" (City of God). Gender, Healing and Urban Identity in an African Independent Church', *Journal of Southern African Studies* 23 (1): 87-105.

Sennet, R. & R. Cobb 1972, *The Hidden Injuries of Class*, New York: Vintage.

Shaw, M. 2002, 'West African Criminal Networks in South and Southern Africa', *African Affairs* 101 (404): 291-316.

Simone, A. 2004, *For the City Yet to Come. Changing African Life in Four Cities*, Durham, NC: Duke University Press.

Tacoli, C. 1998, *Bridging the Divide. Rural-Urban Interactions and Livelihood Strategies,* London: International Institute for Environment and Development, Gatekeeper Series No. 77.

Tostensen, A., I. Tvedten & M. Vaa (eds) 2001, *Associational Life in African Cities. Popular Responses to the Urban Crisis*, Uppsala: Nordiska Afrikainstitutet.

Tripp, A.M. 1997, *Changing the Rules. The Politics of Liberalization and the Urban Informal Economy in Tanzania*, Berkeley: University of California Press.

Van Binsbergen, W.M.J. 1981, *Religious Change in Zambia. Exploratory Studies*, London: Kegan Paul International.

Van Binsbergen, W.M.J. 2000, 'Creating "A Place to Feel at Home": Christian Church Life and Social Control in Lusaka, Zambia', in: P. Konings, W. van Binsbergen & G. Hesseling (eds), *Trajectoires de Libération en Afrique Contemporaine: Hommage à Robert Buijtenhuijs*, Paris: Karthala, pp. 223-50.

Van Dijk, R. 2003, 'Localisation, Ghanaian Pentecostalism and the Stranger's Beauty in Botswana', *Africa* 73 (4): 560-83.

Webber, M. 1964, 'The Urban Place and the Non-place Urban Realm', in: M. Webber (ed.), *Explorations into Urban Structure*, Philadelphia: University of Pennsylvania Press, pp. 19-41.

Weiss, B. 2002, 'Thug Realism. Inhabiting Fantasy in Urban Tanzania', *Cultural Anthropology* 17 (1): 93-128.

Weiss, B. 2005, 'Consciousness, Affliction, and Alterity in Urban East Africa', in: A. Honwana & F. de Boeck (eds), *Makers and Breakers. Children and Youth in Postcolonial Africa*, Oxford: James Currey.

Zack-Williams, A. 1993, 'Crisis, Structural Adjustment and Creative Survival in Sierra Leone', *Africa Development* 18 (1): 53-65.

Zeleza, P.T. 1999, 'The Spatial Economy of Structural Adjustment in African Cities', in: P.T. Zeleza & E. Kalipeni (eds), *Sacred Spaces and Public Quarrels: African Cultural and Economic Landscapes*, Trenton, NJ: Africa World Press, pp. 43-71.

Zeleza, P.T. & E. Kalipeni (eds) 1999, *Sacred Spaces and Public Quarrels: African Cultural and Economic Landscapes*, Trenton, NJ: Africa World Press.

2

Surviving in the neighbourhoods of Nakuru town, Kenya

Samuel Owuor & Dick Foeken

This chapter addresses livelihood sources from the perspective of the (urban) livelihood approach in a setting of economic crisis with increasing unemployment and declining purchasing power. Five case studies of low-income households in the Kenyan town of Nakuru are described, showing the multiple sources of their livelihoods. Livelihood sources have become increasingly multi-spatial (rural as well as urban) but as far as urban livelihood sources are concerned, more spatially concentrated as well, namely in one's own neighbourhood. It is particularly women who are engaged in these neighbourhood-bound activities.

Introduction

Urban poverty[1] in Sub-Saharan Africa was 'steadily and frighteningly on the increase during the 1980s and 1990s' (Satterthwaite 1997: 5). Even though, the rural poor in absolute terms still outnumber the urban poor, the latter have been increasing at an alarming rate over the past few decades. Urban areas have been particularly hard hit by declining economies and the resulting structural adjustment policies, the costs of which have been disproportionately felt by the urban poor (Rakodi 2002b). Life in urban areas has become more expensive, while employment in the formal sector has decreased and real wages have not kept up with price increases, or have even declined in absolute terms (Jamal & Weeks

---

[1] The concept of urban poverty is used here in a general way. No attempt is made to delimit a precise meaning of this multi-dimensional concept. For a discussion on the types and dimensions of (urban) poverty, see, for example, Amis (1995), Jones (1999), Satterthwaite (1997) and Wratten (1995).

1988, UNCHS 1996, Simon 1997). In other words, many urban households have been faced with a serious reduction in purchasing power. People have responded in a number of ways, with the diversification of income sources being undoubtedly the most notable (Bigsten & Kayizzi-Mugerwa 1992, Ellis 2000, de Haan & Zoomers 2003, Kaag 2004). A wide range of activities, all in the informal sector, are being undertaken including own food production (urban and/or rural agriculture), manual jobs, petty trade and, especially in the case of the very poor, prostitution and theft. In addition, social networks are being exploited, examples being women's groups, 'merry-go-round' groups, and ethnically-based groups.

Photo 2.1 Generating income in a Nakuru town neighbourhood
(Photo: Sam Owuor)

This chapter deals with such activities from the (urban) livelihoods approach. What is central to this approach is that people should not be viewed as passive victims of adverse circumstances. Instead, they are seen as developing actions and strategies aimed at preserving a certain livelihood level (Chambers 1983, Jones 1999, Rakodi 2002a, de Haan & Zoomers 2003, Kaag 2004). The keyword is 'access', and the crucial question is how far people have access to all kinds of resources (or 'assets' or 'capital'): natural resources, human resources, physical resources, financial resources and social resources.[2] Access is so important that, according to Bebbington (1999: 2022), '[it is] perhaps the most critical resource of all'.

Much can be and has indeed been said about livelihoods, resources and access but in the context of this chapter, two observations in addition to the above-mentioned diversification of income sources are of particular importance. The first is that livelihoods have become increasingly multi-local, i.e. 'large numbers of rural and urban households ... exploit opportunities in different places and therefore live from both agricultural and urban incomes' (de Haan & Zoomers 2003: 358). Yet, at the same time, there seems to be a tendency that, within the urban context, livelihoods have become more localized, i.e. bound to one's own neighbourhood. The second observation is that the choice of activities and strategies depends on a number of household and individual characteristics, one of them being gender (Beall 2002). According to Kanji (1995), several studies have found that women in particular increase their informal income-generating activities in order to cope with their household's declining purchasing power. Moreover, these activities are generally concentrated in or near their urban homes in their own neighbourhoods (see, for example, Wallman 1996). These two aspects are the focus of this chapter, which considers the extent to which livelihood sources are concentrated in residents' own neighbourhoods and discusses the differences between men and women in this respect.

This study was carried out in Nakuru Municipality, Kenya, a town located in the heart of the Great East African Rift Valley, 160 km northwest of Nairobi. The town started to grow up around a railway station on the East African Railway in 1904 and soon developed into an important regional trading centre and market town. The total area of the municipality is today about 300 km^2, of which 40 km^2 is covered by the famous Lake Nakuru National Park (MCN 1999). In 30 years, the population of Nakuru increased fivefold from 47,000 in 1969 (Kenya 1970) to 239,000 in 1999 (Kenya 2000). At present, Nakuru is the fourth largest urban centre in Kenya.[3] The highest growth rates were recorded during the 1980s, with an average annual growth of 6.5%, but this slowed down during the 1990s to an average of 4.3%. In 1997, the prevalence of absolute poverty[4] in Nakuru town was 41%, compared to about 30% three years earlier

---

[2] For more details on these types of resources in an (African) urban setting, see, for instance, Rakodi (2002a) and Brown & Lloyd-Jones (2002).
[3] After Nairobi, Mombasa and Kisumu.
[4] The 'absolute poverty line' is defined as the income needed to obtain the required minimum amount of basic food and non-food items. For urban areas, this was equal to

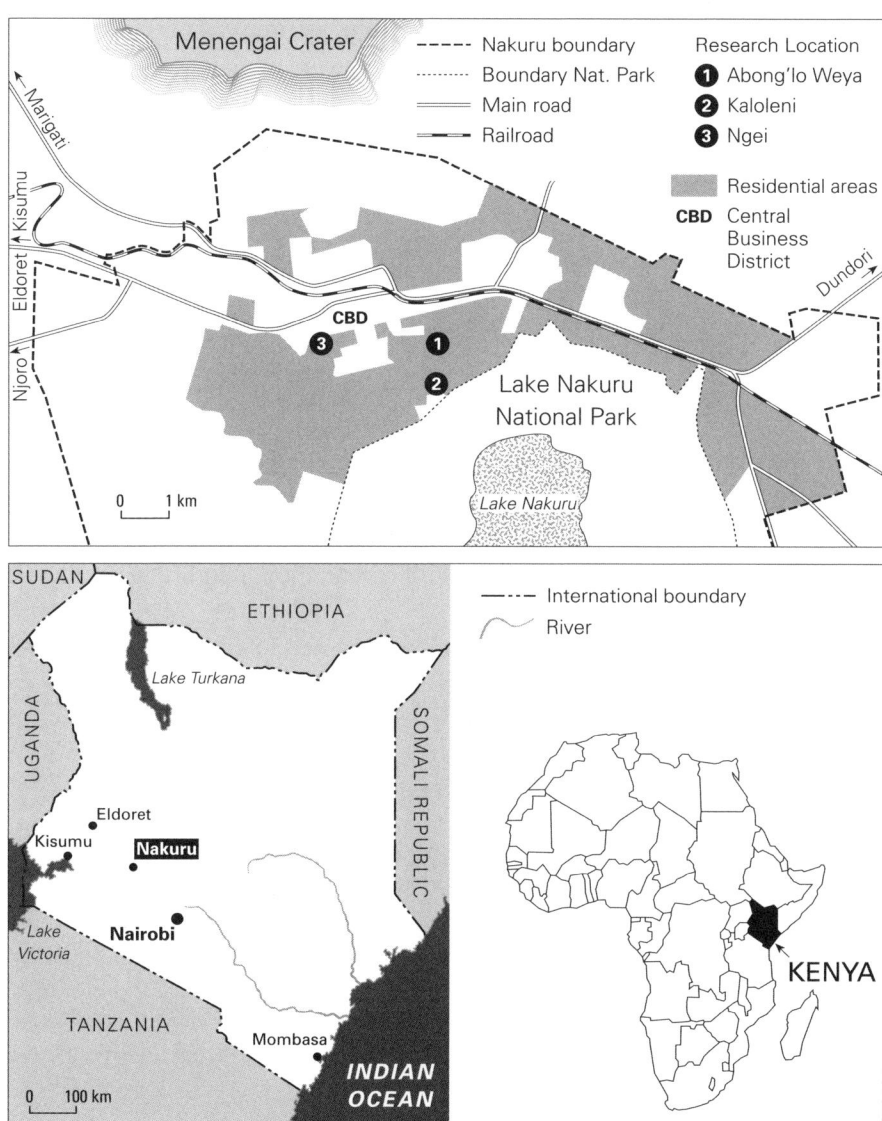

Map 2.1 Nakuru town, Kenya

the official minimum wage as set by the government, which was Ksh 2,648 per person per month in 1997 (Kenya 2001: 11).

(Kenya 2001). This sharp increase was related to the fact that 'only a fraction of the [Nakuru] labour-force is actually employed' (MCN 1999: 62).

This chapter presents five case studies of households in Nakuru, all of which are taken from a larger study[5] carried out in 2001-2003 (Owuor forthcoming). They were selected with an eye on household income (ranging from fairly low to very low), and the sex and age of the household head (roughly indicating the stage in the 'family life cycle'). All five households were visited at least four times during the survey when a great deal of information on livelihood sources was collected. Although the focus of the whole study was on *rural* livelihood sources of these *urban* households,[6] data on (all) other livelihood sources was collected as well.

The five households were all located in three residential areas, namely Abong' Lo Weya, Kaloleni and Ngei. These are densely populated, low-income municipal council housing estates about 0.5 km, 3 km and 2 km from the town centre respectively. Estates are not necessarily geographically defined neighbourhoods but are part of larger, loosely defined areas because people usually refer to a wider region when talking about their neighbourhood. For instance, Abong' Lo Weya and Kaloleni are part of an area called Bondeni, while Ngei belongs to Shabab. It is impossible, however, to clearly delimit these wider areas.

Case 1:   Peter & Priscilla – a retired, medium-to-low-income household

Background

Peter[7] was born in Makueni District in 1946 but moved with his parents to Nakuru where he completed secondary school. He then went to a teachers' training college and was subsequently employed as a primary-school teacher in 1971 and posted to Nakuru Municipality. After that, Peter worked in various primary schools within the municipality until 2001 when he retired. In 1985, he married Priscilla (who had been married before). They had only one child, who was still living with them at the time of the survey although since 1999 a niece, who had dropped out of school due to pregnancy, was also staying with them.

---

[5] We gratefully acknowledge the grant from the Netherlands Foundation for the Advancement of Tropical Research (WOTRO) for this study.
[6] Because of that focus, the first criterion for choosing the households for the in-depth interviews was the presence of a rural plot that was being used as a livelihood source for the urban household. All the cases presented in this chapter have one thing in common: they practise rural farming in one way or another.
[7] The names of the respondents have been changed to preserve their anonymity.

Regular livelihood source (Peter)
1) Pension
Until his retirement, Peter's monthly salary was the household's main regular source of income, and since then he has received a pension from the government.[8]

Livelihood sources in the neighbourhood (Priscilla)
2) Selling milk, charcoal, rice and potatoes
To supplement her husband's income, Priscilla sold fresh cow's milk from a kiosk at the compound gate. She started this business in 1997 because selling second-hand clothes, which she had been doing before, was no longer generating a good return.[9] Priscilla bought milk from peri-urban farmers and later sold it at a profit. She said that she could sell as much as 30 litres a day. The majority of her customers were from the estate, some of whom paid her on a monthly basis.

Since 1996, Priscilla was a member of a local financial institution called Pride Kenya, whose main activity was to help small-scale businesses by offering training and advancing low-interest business loans to its members. It was through this institution that Priscilla got a loan in 2000 to expand her business. She bought a more attractive kiosk and a small freezer to keep the milk fresh. At the same time she diversified her products to include charcoal, rice and potatoes.[10]

3) Urban farming
Priscilla cultivated *sukuma wiki*[11] (kale), spinach, onions and tomatoes in their backyard. She started this practice the year she got married because she wanted her own supply of clean, fresh vegetables. She said she no longer bought these food stuffs, as 'I get them directly from my *shamba*'.[12] Being largely for home consumption, the vegetables were harvested directly from the *shamba* as needed. She claimed that she ate her own vegetables almost every day. The

---

[8] Peter refused to say how much his pension was.
[9] She explained that many people had entered the business and so there was strong competition, in addition to the low purchasing power of the customers.
[10] The amount of money given by Pride Kenya depends on how much one has saved with them and on the member's reliability regarding repayment. On joining the group, a member undergoes a nine-month induction programme, part of which is a mandatory weekly contribution of Ksh 100.
[11] *Sukuma wiki* is a Swahili word that means 'push the week' and, during hard times, you can keep the week going by eating *sukuma wiki*, which is always available, and is relatively cheap and nutritious as well.
[12] *Shamba* is a Swahili word meaning 'plot' or 'field'.

daily rations of *sukuma wiki* and/or spinach would have cost about Ksh 30 in the market, so she was able to save that amount daily.

4) Member of two women's groups
Priscilla was a member of two women's social-welfare groups: Baraka and Genesis. Although the two groups consisted of the same 36 members who all contributed Ksh 500 on a monthly basis to each group, the groups' objectives differed. The Baraka women's group was set up to help members during crises, such as death or illness, and for those not able to repay their Pride Kenya loans. The Genesis group operated on a merry-go-round basis, i.e. each member received the total monthly contribution in turn.

Other livelihood sources
5) Chickens (Peter)
After his retirement, Peter started to keep broilers in their backyard:

> I keep between 50 and 100 broilers that I sell to hotels in town at about Ksh 150 to Ksh 200 per bird. Being retired, this activity keeps me busy most of the time.[13]

6) Rural farming (Priscilla)
Besides their rural home in Makueni, Peter and Priscilla had access to a one-acre plot in Wanyororo, not far from Nakuru town.[14] Priscilla purchased this plot in 1986:

> Though I was already married to Peter, I started thinking about having my own plot after I separated from my first husband. I realized that I had nowhere to turn – I had already left my parents' home and here I was, technically chased from my husband's home. This is when I started saving for this plot and I am proud that I bought it with my own resources, my own sweat and blood. You never know with marriages.

Peter explained that they did not practise rural farming at their rural home in Makueni because of the poor soil and unreliable rainfall (semi-arid climate). For him, farming in Makueni was not worth the trouble, especially because of the distance and the high transport costs involved.

Peter and Priscilla decided to put the Wanyororo plot under crop cultivation to generate additional income for the household. They also got most of their food from this plot. As Priscilla explained:

---

[13] As with his pension, Peter declined to give any details about his earnings from his chicken business.
[14] Wanyororo is along the Nakuru-Nyahururu road, about 70 km from Nakuru town.

From the time I stopped working in 1994, we have depended on this plot as an additional source of money and food to supplement what we get from our businesses and most recently, the pension Peter receives. The income from this plot also helps me to offset the labourers' wages, buy fertilizers and sometimes repay my loans. I never forget to save something small for any eventuality. In terms of food, I hardly buy maize, beans and potatoes in this house. We are almost self-reliant regarding our food requirements.

Case 2: Reuben & Rita – a low-income, multi-spatial household

Background
Reuben, the household head, was born in 1965 in Nakuru Municipality where he completed his secondary-school education. Three years later he was lucky enough to find a full-time job and that year he married his first wife, Akinyi, who gave birth to four sons. In 1998 he married a second wife, Rita, after which Akinyi went to live at the rural home where Reuben's stepmother as well as his brother and sister-in-law were living. Unfortunately, in 2003 both Reuben's brother and Akinyi died, followed in 2004 by his brother's wife, leaving the stepmother alone with two small children from Reuben's brother's marriage.[15]

At the time of the interviews, the urban household consisted of two adults and five children, the latter being Reuben's four sons (ranging from 6 to 16 years of age) from his marriage to Akinyi and a daughter (3 years old) from his marriage to Rita. Despite the high costs of living and education in Nakuru, Reuben decided that all the children would stay in the urban area and go to school in Nakuru because he believed that 'schools in town offer higher quality education than those at home where facilities are lacking'.

Regular livelihood source (Reuben)
1) Full-time employment as a cook
Since 1986, Reuben was employed full-time as a cook at the Sarova Lion's Hill Lodge in Lake Nakuru National Park. At the time of the interview, he was earning a monthly salary of about Ksh 10,000.

---

[15] According to the information available, all these deaths seemed to have been AIDS-related, but without medical reports it was not possible to confirm this.

Livelihood sources in the neighbourhood (Rita)
2) Selling *mboga* (vegetables) and fish
Less than a year after they got married, Rita started a business selling *sukuma wiki*, tomatoes, onions, ripe bananas and *omena*,[16] primarily to supplement her husband's income but also 'to engage in some economic activity instead of just staying at home looking after the children and relying wholly on my husband'. She bought the vegetables from wholesalers and later sold them at a 50% profit along the roadside near her house. With vegetables of a value of up to Ksh 300, she made a profit of about Ksh 150 three times a week.[17] In addition, in 1999 she made some money by selling fish as well. She brought *omena* from her home area near Lake Victoria to sell in Nakuru. Between August and October *omena* is abundant in the local markets around Lake Victoria and very low in price. Rita stopped her businesses selling vegetables and fish in 2000 just before her first child was born.

3) Growing *sukuma wiki* and *kunde*
In front of Rita's house was a well-tended *sukuma wiki* garden that, from 1999 onwards, supplied her household with *sukuma wiki* almost all year-round.[18] The *sukuma wiki* was harvested for about four months before planting new plants. During dry periods, the *sukuma wiki* was watered with tap water. By getting her *sukuma wiki* from this small plot, she saved about Ksh 25 daily from May to July, when there is plenty of rainfall, and twice the amount from January to April when it is dry and *sukuma wiki* is more expensive. She also planted *kunde* (cowpeas) that she used for consumption in the house, again throughout most of the year. Like *sukuma wiki*, the *kunde* was harvested straight from the *shamba* when needed for consumption. Having ready access to a plot was a blessing for Rita because she was able to 'feed her large family from the *shamba*' and therefore spend less on food.

4) Part-time home-based hair-plaiting business
In line with her belief in economic independence, Rita started plaiting ladies' hair for a small fee in 2001. She did this in her free time in her house or on the estate, mainly for her friends and neighbours. Her charges were quite modest, ranging from Ksh 20 to Ksh 50 depending on the style. She concentrated on this activity at weekends where she could get 'one or two customers a day'. She explained that business was usually good during the Christmas holidays 'when

---

[16] *Omena* is a species of small (finger-size) fish.
[17] Averaging about Ksh 2,000-2,500 per month.
[18] Rita took the *shamba* over from Akinyi who in turn had taken it over from Reuben's parents.

Photo 2.2   Rita in her *sukuma wiki* garden in Nakuru town
(Photo: Sam Owuor)

most ladies want to look smart'. For the rest of the year, her customers were mainly children whose parents wanted simple hairstyles and could not afford the commercial rates charged by well-established salons. Rita claimed that, by knowing how to plait, she was just helping her friends and neighbours in her free time. She used the little money she got from plaiting for her own 'personal items'.

5) Trainee nursery-school teacher
At the time of the interviews in 2003, Rita was enrolled as a trainee nursery-school teacher in a nearby private school. She worked half-days during term time and attended in-service teaching courses during the holidays. She hoped that after graduating she would be a full-time teacher and get permanent employment in the formal sector like her husband.

6) Member of a women's group
Rita pointed out that on the estate they had a merry-go-round group which most of the women were members of 'for their own mutual benefit'. They were 15 women who each contributed Ksh 200 weekly. The total amount from the participating members, i.e. Ksh 3,000, was given to them on a merry-go-round

basis, meaning that approximately every four months each of them received Ksh 3,000. Rita talked about what she did with her money:

> The money I get from the merry-go-round has helped me buy myself and the children clothes and kitchen utensils. You can even see this 70-litre water dispenser. The other items I have purchased are at home. When I do not have money to pay, I ask to be given some time so that I can pay in the course of the week. When one of us has a serious problem that requires money, then she can be given priority instead of waiting for her turn.

Other livelihood sources
7) Rural farming
Reuben and Rita had access to two rural plots, one at his rural home in Siaya District, while the other was a plot rented annually in Rongai, Nakuru District. The three-acre rural plot at his home in Siaya was still family land, which was shared between Reuben, his stepmother and his sister-in-law (who was still alive at the time of the visit). Despite the fact that Reuben and Rita were living in Nakuru, they believed that having a rural home was important, especially for them as Luos.[19] It was a place to fall back on if necessary as well as a place to be buried. Although the family land could not be considered as a source of food and/or income for the urban household, the plot nevertheless saved Reuben the money he would otherwise have had to spend on providing his rural family members with food.

In 2001, Reuben managed to rent four acres of land in Rongai, some 20 km from Nakuru town. They decided to do this because of the increased costs of living (and because they were encouraged by Reuben's sister, Mama Jairo, who had already lived in Rongai for many years and who was the one supervising the work on the Rongai plot). The plot was a source of both food and income: all the maize and beans for the urban household came from it, while the sale of the rest was a valuable source of income. In 2001, 40 bags of maize were harvested, of which five were consumed by the urban household, one by Mama Jairo's household, one bag was given to the Siaya household (to sell) and the remaining 33 bags were sold. Three bags of beans were harvested as well, of which half were consumed and the other half sold.

---

[19] Luo is one of the biggest of Kenya's 42 ethnic groups.

Case 3: Alfred & Alice – a low-income, multi-spatial household

Background
Alfred was born in Siaya District in 1971. After completing his primary-school education in 1986, Alfred was not able to go to secondary school because his father had passed away a year earlier and there was no money to cover school fees. However, a cousin living in Nakuru offered to train him in carpentry and joinery and Alfred acquired the skills that enabled him to be employed as a carpenter on the Langa Langa Estate. Towards the end of 1989 Alfred married Alice (also from Siaya District) and started his own carpentry business in 1990. After living on two other (low-income) estates, they moved to their current house in Kaloleni in 1996. The house was inherited from his uncle who was retiring and moving to the rural home.

Alfred and Alice had seven children, two of whom died before reaching their first birthdays. At the time of the visits, the family consisted of three daughters and two sons (aged from 4 to 14 years) and two children belonging to relatives (aged 10 and 16). In November 2001, Alice and the children moved to Alfred's rural home because, as she explained,

> ... my husband does not have enough income to support us in town nowadays. His carpentry business has not been doing well for the past few years. This has been his main income source since 1989 when he married me. Since we had access to the rural plot and given that the cost of living is relatively cheaper at home, we decided to go and live there. My husband is living alone in Nakuru.

In 2002, Alfred married a second wife (Alice's younger sister) who joined Alice at the rural home. In the same year, Alfred was joined in Nakuru town by two grown-up nephews.

Regular livelihood source (Alfred)
1) Carpentry business
Alfred was the household's main breadwinner. Since 1989, his carpentry business was the household's main regular source of income. The business involved repairing furniture and making it to sell. Although his workshop was in Freehold, Alfred moved around a lot not only looking for business but also working in his clients' houses. His best years were between 1993 and 1999 when he had many clients and a steady income of between Ksh 4,000 and Ksh 6,000 per month. However after that business had not been very encouraging as competition was intense and it was becoming difficult to find clients. His profit margins were 'nowadays much lower than when I started the business'.

> The returns from my business have declined considerably in the last three years. The situation is so bad that I do not even keep records as I survive from hand to mouth. I rarely find good business to do. I cannot even estimate how much I earned from my business last month.

Livelihood sources in the neighbourhood
2) Selling fried fish and *samosas*[20]
To supplement her husband's income, Alice started selling fried fish and *samosas* on the estate in 1996 (when they had more mouths to feed) until she moved to the rural home. She bought fresh fish from the market and prepared it on the spot in the evenings for customers to buy and also sold *samosas* that she had prepared at home earlier in the day. The business was strategically located along the roadside for passers-by who usually came directly from work. With this business Alice was able to support her family in various ways, particularly by buying food and other household necessities. The work became even more important when her husband's business began to slow down due to a lack of clients and also later when three more children were born. She could make a profit of between Ksh 800 and Ksh 2,000 a month depending on sales. According to her, this activity was an additional source of household income without which she would not have managed to survive in town.

3) Keeping chickens (Alice)
Alice wanted to farm in town but lack of access to urban land and no capital to rent a plot meant that her dream remained unfulfilled. However, she tried her hand at keeping chickens in 2000. Unfortunately, some died and others were stolen, which discouraged her from continuing. However during this period, the chickens were a source of food and, in few instances, a source of income too.

4) Selling maize, potatoes and vegetables (Alfred)
To make ends meet, in 2003 Alfred started selling maize (both dry and green), potatoes and vegetables (cabbages and *sukuma wiki*) to local kiosks in his neighbourhood. He bought at relatively cheap prices from wholesalers and sold at a small profit. This was a part-time activity for when he did not have work in his workshop:

> This business sustains me when my carpentry business does not provide enough. From this business I would earn a profit of about Ksh 100 per sale.

---

[20] A kind of fried snack.

Other livelihood sources
5) Rural farming
Being the only son, Alfred had access to four of the seven acres of family land in Siaya. This was what Alfred and Alice considered their rural home because that was the only (rural) land they had access to. The other three acres had been left to his mother and his (four) sisters. Alfred and Alice started using their land for crop cultivation in 1990 because, according to Alice, 'the urban household at that time consisting of four persons[21] needed an additional source of food and income to supplement the income generated from Alfred's carpentry business'. As the urban household became bigger, the importance of the rural plot became increasingly important. At the time of the interviews, with all Alfred's wives and children living at the rural home, the land provided them with all their food, while it also added to the food requirements of Alfred and his two nephews in town. Moreover, with a good harvest, some of it could be sold to 'pay school fees for the children in school, pay the hired labour, buy fertilizer or help in the house to buy things like sugar, salt and soap'. In 2002, after Alice's seventh child and her sister's first child died in infancy, Alfred was able to 'feed the mourners' thanks to the sorghum they had harvested from the rural plot. In addition to crop cultivation, Alfred also had a bull, a cow, a heifer, four sheep and four goats, which were all taken care of by a brother-in-law in Siaya.

6) Member of a non-ethnic social network of friends (Alfred)
In Nakuru, Alfred was a member of a welfare association called the Young Friends' Association. The group started in 1990 and there were 16 members in total – all men with the same interests. Every Sunday each member saved with the association whatever he could afford. The money was then deposited in a Post Office savings account. Whenever a member had a problem he could be given half of his savings and even take a loan using the other members' share and repay it later. At the end of the year, each member was given the whole amount of money that he had saved over that particular year. It was saving through this association that enabled Alfred to buy his cow and bull but he also admitted that he had on several occasions had a loan from this association or had had to fall back on it due to problems. He explained that his weekly savings had declined considerably, even to the extent that he sometimes had nothing at all to save. As if to console himself, he added that there were many members in a similar position to him in the association.

Case 4: Mary – a low-income, female-headed household

---

[21] Alfred, Alice, a daughter and a relative.

Background
Mary was born in 1946 in a rural setting in Nyeri District (central Kenya). She had never attended school because her father did not see the value of education for girls. She therefore grew up helping her mother in various household chores and farming until 1967 when she married a municipal-council employee in Nakuru. Four years after getting married, Mary followed her husband to Nakuru and later gave birth to two sons and three daughters. Of these, three, aged 10 to 15 at the time of the interviews, were still living with their mother in Abong' Lo Weya Estate. A year after the birth of her last child, in 1992, Mary's husband passed away.

Regular livelihood source
1) Street sweeper
Mary had a job as a street sweeper with the municipal council in Nakuru and this was the household's regular source of income after her husband's death. Before that, she had earned money as a home worker. Despite working for many years, Mary earned a very modest monthly salary of Ksh 4,000 but she considered herself lucky. In the past if an employee passed away, his wife or a child would be offered a job in the same company as a gesture of goodwill towards the deceased's family but the practice has since ceased to exist.

> I was lucky because in the same year my husband died, the Municipal Council of Nakuru offered me a job as a sweeper. This was a very good offer that has made it a bit easier for me to continue caring for our children.

Livelihood sources in the neighbourhood
2) Urban farming
Before her husband's death, Mary engaged in urban farming activities on the estate and in other parts of the municipality. Off the estate, she cultivated various rented plots:

> It was very cheap to rent a plot in the municipality then. With not more than Ksh 5, you could get a sizeable plot to rent on a monthly basis. Nowadays, to rent a plot within the municipality, that is if you are lucky, costs no less than Ksh 6,000 an acre per year. For those who liked farming, renting a plot was a normal and common thing to do in those days.

On these plots, Mary cultivated maize, beans, *sukuma wiki*, spinach and cabbages. She stressed that the produce was basically for home consumption. Most of the time, her husband did not need to buy whatever they harvested on the *shamba*. The vegetables, which did better than the maize,[22] were harvested directly from the *shamba* on an almost daily basis. Some of the produce was also sold to neighbours and other customers.

Mary explained that she was forced to stop her crop-cultivating activities in the municipality by 1993 because of a lack of plots to rent and the high rents demanded for those that were available. Most of the plots she had rented had been taken over by the owners for development purposes. Furthermore, there was constant harassment from the local authorities who slashed crops, especially those of off-plot cultivators. The only urban farming she was able to continue was on a small plot of land just outside her house:

> I just grow *sukuma wiki*, beans and Irish potatoes for my own consumption, just like everybody else on the estate. This *shamba* is an additional source of food in this house.

Besides cultivation, Mary kept some ducks on the estate. She sold the eggs and once in a while the family fed on an adult bird. She also had to sell mature ducks (at only Ksh 30 each) because there was no space to keep many of them. She stopped this activity in 1996 when harassment from the local authority further intensified. Mary remembers how the local authorities put poison in the estate's open drains, which subsequently killed all the ducks that fed in the dirt.

3) Selling basic household goods in front of her house

In front of Mary's house was a temporary shop-like structure where basic household goods such as sugar, soap, cooking fat, matches, salt and tea were sold. She made part of her profit by unpacking the goods and selling them in small quantities to poor households. She did this after doing her designated duties at work. She explained that she swept the municipal streets and one could not do that the whole day. Her day started very early in the morning and by noon she was already back home ready to open up her business. Mary decided to start this business in 2001 for several reasons.

> First and foremost, life is becoming harder and harder and there is the need to do something extra to earn something small on top of the small salaries we get. Secondly, life has become expensive but our pay has never increased and therefore we continue to suffer. Thirdly, these days, as you are aware, the payment of our salaries is frequently delayed. We can go for months without pay. Fourthly, I am

---

[22] Growing maize was not condoned by the municipality. Apart from the fear of her crops being slashed or destroyed by the local authority *askaris* (by-law enforcers), there was also the fear of theft. On the plots far away, the maize could be stolen while it was still green.

now the only breadwinner and therefore forced to look for other sources of income. And fifthly, I am not able to practise urban farming any more the way I did before.

Mary confirmed that she was now able to cope with the frequent salary delays. Whenever they were not paid, she used her limited profits from her business to buy food and other household requirements.

Other livelihood sources
4) Rural farming
Mary's husband was the only son in his family and he inherited a 3.5-acre plot in Nyeri from his father in 1973, acquiring the title deeds almost immediately. After her husband's death, Mary automatically inherited this land without any resistance from her in-laws. Though she lived in Nakuru most of the time, this was what she considered her rural home where she could practise both crop cultivation and livestock keeping. She cultivated coffee, maize and beans to provide additional income and food.

> My rural home is important to me because of the money I earn from the sale of the crops that I cultivate, especially the coffee. The coffee has helped me a lot in terms of bringing up the children and paying for their school fees. (…) during our usual salary delays, more often than not, I depend on sales from coffee. When there is a crisis like a lack of food or income in the house, I fall back on the plot.

Beans were largely grown for consumption, while maize was only sold when it was really necessary to do so. Otherwise, much of it was used for food, both at home and in Nakuru. In 2000 Wanja sold two bags of maize at the local market for Ksh 2,200 to take her daughter to hospital. Mary summed up the importance of rural crop cultivation as follows:

> The maize and beans for *ugali*[23] and *githeri*[24] in this house comes from the *shamba* at home. When the harvest is good, I rarely buy maize and beans in this house. I can therefore use that money for other things. The money from coffee is mainly used to pay school fees. I could not have survived without all this. Life has become so difficult.

In addition, when her husband died, Mary was left with a cow, a calf and three sheep, which in turn had young ones, and others were sold. At the time of the interviews, she had three cows and five sheep. The cows were for milk while the sheep were kept as insurance, to be sold when there was extreme financial need. For example in 2002, she sold two sheep at Ksh 1,100 each to pay for

---

[23] A staple dish made from maize flour.
[24] A meal made of maize and beans boiled together and then later fried.

hired labour to assist her with her coffee cultivation. With the help of a relative at home, Mary's father-in-law took care of the cows and sheep, and assisted in the herding, milking and watering. Mary did not hire any extra labour for this purpose but let them have the milk from the cows in return. This, indirectly, saved her money.

> The cows currently provide my parents-in-law and the relative at home with milk. They also sell the milk to earn some income and this saves me the burden of sending them money every now and then.

Case 5: Sofia – a very low-income, female-headed household

Background
Sofia (44) was born and brought up in Nakuru, where her parents lived. After dropping out of school, working for two years as a prostitute and with a failed marriage, she returned with her two children to Nakuru in 1981. In 1988 she 'inherited' her parents' rented council house on Abong' Lo Weya Estate where she has lived ever since. Since separating from her husband, she remained single but gave birth to another seven children. At the time of the interviews, only the three youngest children (aged 4, 8 and 11) were living with her. Out of her other six children, her oldest daughter was married and living with her husband, two unemployed sons were living together on a neighbouring estate, two other sons were living with Sofia's mother in Turkana District,[25] while another daughter and her newborn baby lived with an aunt. Sofia explained the family's dispersal as follows:

> Being single, things are nowadays difficult for me financially, especially when I have to take care not only of the three children living with me, but also my mother at home and once in a while some of my other children who are living independently but are unemployed.

Regular livelihood source
1) Brewing and selling *chang'aa*[26]

> My main occupation is brewing and selling *chang'aa*. I brew it here in the house and also sell it from right here. My customers come from both this estate and other

---

[25] Turkana District is a large district in the northwest of Kenya. It has a semi-arid to arid climate.
[26] *Chang'aa* is a local brew that is mainly found in the rural areas but it is also brewed and sold illegally in town. It is becoming increasingly popular in cities because of its affordability. Many urban poor can no longer afford bottled beer and often opt for a cheap and strong brand that 'can kill them quick'.

estates in the neighbourhood. I began this work in 1988, taking it over from my parents who were already practising it. That is how I learned how to brew and sell *chang'aa*. Since I had no other job, and being a single parent, this was – and still is – the only way and option for me to earn a living. This is the job that pays my children's school fees, clothing, rent and food.

Brewing and selling *chang'aa* is generally illegal in Kenya but Sofia explained how she deals with that:

> In this business of ours we know how to cope with the police. Every time we make a profit, we give them 'something little' so that they leave us alone. Actually, it depends on how well you are acquainted with them. We know how to talk to the police even before they come. Sometimes we are of course taken to the police station but find our way out afterwards. Sometimes if you are unlucky, you are taken to court and fined. I have never been taken to court.

Livelihood sources in the neighbourhood
2) Urban agriculture
To diversify her food sources, Sofia, like most of her neighbours on the estate, cultivated *sukuma wiki* on the small *shamba* outside her house. This *sukuma wiki* was an important source of food for the household when she did not have money to buy other food at the market. Even when they could afford food, *sukuma wiki* was still included in their daily menu to reduce costs. She cultivated it throughout the year, irrigating the *shamba* during dry periods. The *shamba* saved Sofia about Ksh 30 a day. From time to time and when there was enough rainfall, Sofia also cultivated Irish potatoes and local vegetables (*saget*[27] and *kunde*). Sofia said that she started cultivating vegetables because she needed food and added that she did not actually know how she could have survived without the *shamba*.

She also once tried to keep chickens but stopped after they ate other people's *sukuma wiki* on the estate, which resulted in daily conflicts. Nowadays, most *shambas* are fenced to keep their neighbours' chickens out and to prevent people from stealing their *sukuma wiki*. At the time of the interviews, she kept one or two chickens for food.

> You can never say that you have refused to keep chickens in town. Regardless of how many years one lives in town, it is natural for many of us to have a chicken or two that you can kill for food.

---

[27] A spider plant.

3) Member of a women's group

In 2001, Sofia joined a women's income-generating group in the neighbourhood. Ten members contributed Ksh 20 each per week and with the money they bought tablecloths that they sold on market days. The treasurer kept a record of sales so that at the end of the year they could share the profits equally among themselves. At the end of 2002, they had a profit of Ksh 1,500 each, after deducting their investment of about Ksh 1,000.

Other livelihood sources

4) Rural farming

Sofia was unfortunate in that, since she was separated from her husband, she could not claim access to her husband's home because no dowry had been paid and the marriage had not been formalized or blessed in any way. Therefore, she was not legally or culturally recognized in her husband's home. The only land she could claim access to was her mother's land in Turkana District.[28] The land was given to her mother by her grandmother's[29] clan after her father's death.

> This is the land that I and my mother benefit from. Some of my children and those of my sisters also live at home. According to our clan, no land belongs to a specific member of the family. The land is therefore used communally.

Sofia started rural farming in 1992 after the birth of her sixth child and because life in town had become increasingly difficult.

> With all the six children, life was becoming hard. Their fathers started deserting me and not helping and I was also afraid of having many male friends because of AIDS. These male friends sometimes helped by buying sugar and milk for the children. Even for them, life has become harder. Nowadays men only part with something small. With these problems and changes in life, I decided to join my mother in rural farming so that I could help my family with some little food from there.

According to her, she did not get more than a little food from the *shamba* in this relatively arid region – mainly sorghum and now and then local vegetables. The family also had some livestock at home. Once in a while Sofia benefited from the sale of a goat, specifically to cater for her children's school fees. The goats and sheep were also a source of income during the dry periods or when they had not practised rural crop cultivation.

---

[28] Traditionally, once a girl is married, she should inherit her husband's land. Culturally, girls are not supposed to inherit their father's or mother's land.
[29] Sofia's mother's mother.

5) Food aid
Since 1999, Sofia had received food aid from a Catholic project called Hekima[30] that assists needy households in poor neighbourhoods of Nakuru Municipality, and was recently expanded to include households affected by AIDS.[31] Apart from food, the project also offers medicines and advice to these households. To qualify for this help, a comprehensive evaluation has to be carried out to make sure that only deserving cases are included. Every Tuesday the Catholic church supplies them with 4 kg of maize flour, 2 kg of beans, 2 kg of green grams, 2 kg of rice and one tin of *omena*. Sofia explained how important this food source was for her.

> Despite being poor, we are rarely without food in this house. For the last three years we received rice, *ndengu*,[32] beans, *omena* and *unga*[33] on a weekly basis from Hekima. Oh yes, this is how I survived in 2000 and 2001 when we did not cultivate the rural plot.

6) Financial assistance from foreigners
In addition to the efforts of the Hekima Catholic church missions, some Americans started paying the school fees for Sofia's 11-year-old daughter and other school-related expenses in 1999. Sofia explained that the Americans volunteered to educate poor households' children through the Hekima programme.

7) Commercial sex?
During discussions with Sofia, the interviewer got the impression that she had not yet forgotten her days as a commercial sex worker. Though not always, Sofia vaguely admitted that she 'still keeps in touch with some of her children's fathers for help'. Asked how she continuously gave birth even after separating from her husband, she quickly answered: 'It was just bad luck while I looked for milk for my children'.

Conclusions

The above examples show, first of all, that low-income households in Nakuru Municipality have diversified their livelihood sources, with their number ranging from four to seven and the mode being six (in three of the five house-

---

[30] Hekima Community Centre in Nakuru was founded in 1998 and advertises itself as a 'Love and Hope Centre' by providing all kinds of social services to the needy.
[31] Sofia clarified that her case was purely that of a needy household and was not in any way related to AIDS.
[32] Green grams.
[33] Maize flour.

holds discussed). The poorest household, that of Sofia, was also the one with the highest number of different livelihood sources (seven). This shows that people grab their chances whenever and wherever they see an opportunity to open up a new livelihood source to cope with a situation in which they face declining purchasing power. Although usually limited in extent, they can employ multiple sources, such as land for urban and/or rural farming (natural resources), savings and sometimes a small loan (financial resources), their own labour and qualities like entrepreneurship and acquired skills (human resources), and the exploitation of social relationships, such as women's groups (social resources).

The fact that all the households presented here practised rural farming is evident because access to a rural plot (with the plot being a livelihood source as well) was the major criterion for the selection of the in-depth cases in the larger study. However, for 84% of the households in this larger study, rural farming was *one* of their sources of income (Owuor forthcoming). Of these, two-thirds practised rural farming themselves, while the other third benefited from the farming activities carried out by their relatives back home. All this indicates that multi-local livelihoods are the rule and not an exception in this town (and in many other African towns as well). What is perhaps typical for Nakuru is the buying or hiring of a rural plot outside the municipality but within an easily accessible distance. It is increasingly common to find households in the town doing this as a specific income-generating activity. For Reuben and Rita, for example, this was indeed a major income source. But this applied in fact to all households practising rural farming.

The third major conclusion concerns the importance of the neighbourhood – or one's immediate surroundings – for the livelihood of these (low-income) households. Out of a total of 29 livelihood sources in the five cases, 15 were 'neighbourhood bound'. For instance, all five households except one practised urban farming, either in their backyard or on a small plot near their house. This mostly involved crop cultivation for their own consumption, although some households kept a few (small) animals as well. Trading activities 'from the front door' was also quite common: all households did or had recently undertaken this. The selling of food stuffs such as vegetables and fish, i.e. buying in large and selling in small quantities, was most common, while one household was engaged in selling small household necessities. For Sofia, selling *chang'aa*, an illegal brew, was even her main livelihood source. In one household, the wife had started a hair-plaiting business.

In line with the observations of Kanji (1995) and Wallman (1996), it is mainly women who practise these activities in the neighbourhood. Of the 15 activities, 14 were carried out by women. The only exception was Alfred who started selling agricultural products in 2003 to make ends meet. (His two wives both lived in their rural home.) Many women are members of one or two women's groups in the neighbourhood; of the four households where the wife lived in town, three had joined such a group. This can take various forms, the most common being merry-go-round groups.

The cases presented above also indicate that engaging in so many activities is related to either the household's stage in the life cycle ('more mouths to feed', which also includes school fees) or a decline in purchasing power, or a combination of the two. This leads to the general conclusion that, in a globalizing world, the urban poor in Sub-Saharan Africa have become increasingly dependent on livelihood sources practised by women, i.e. rural farming, on the one hand, and a wide variety of neighbourhood-bound activities on the other.

References

Amis, P. 1995, 'Making Sense of Urban Poverty', *Environment and Urbanization* 7 (1): 145-57.
Beall, J. 2002, 'Living in the Present, Investing in the Future – Household Security among the Urban Poor', in: C. Rakodi & T. Lloyd-Jones (eds), *Urban Livelihoods: A People-Centred Approach to Reducing Poverty*, London: Earthscan Publications, pp. 71-87.
Bebbington, A. 1999, 'Capitals and Capabilities: A Framework for Analyzing Peasant Viability, Rural Livelihoods and Poverty', *World Development* 17 (12): 2021-44.
Bigsten, A. & S. Kayizzi-Mugerwa 1992, 'Adaptation and Distress in the Urban Economy: A Study of Kampala Households', *World Development* 20 (10): 1423-41.
Brown, A. & T. Lloyd-Jones 2002, 'Spatial Planning, Access and Infrastructure', in: C. Rakodi & T. Lloyd-Jones (eds), *Urban Livelihoods: A People-Centred Approach to Reducing Poverty*, London: Earthscan Publications, pp. 188-204.
Chambers, R. 1983, *Rural Development: Putting the Last First*, Harlow: Longman.
Ellis, F. 2000, *Rural Livelihoods and Diversity in Developing Countries*, Oxford: Oxford University Press.
de Haan, L. & A. Zoomers 2003, 'Development Geography at the Crossroads of Livelihood and Globalisation', *Tijdschrift voor Economische en Sociale Geografie* 94 (3): 350-62.
Jamal, V. & J. Weeks 1988, 'The Vanishing Rural-Urban Gap in Sub-Saharan Africa', *International Labour Review* 127 (3): 271-92.
Jones, S. 1999, 'Defining Urban Poverty: An Overview', in: S. Jones & N. Nelson (eds), *Urban Poverty in Africa. From Understanding to Alleviation*, London: Intermediate Technology Publications, pp. 9-15.
Kaag, M. 2004, 'Ways Forward in Livelihood Research', in: D. Kalb, W. Pantsers & H. Siebers (eds), *Globalization and Development. Themes and Concepts in Current Research*, Dordrecht/Boston/London: Kluwer Academic Publishers, pp. 49-74.
Kanji, N. 1995, 'Gender, Poverty and Economic Adjustment in Harare, Zimbabwe', *Environment and Urbanization* 7 (1): 37-55.

Kenya, Government of 1970, *Kenya Population Census 1969, Vol. 1*, Nairobi: Government Printer.
Kenya, Government of 2000, *Economic Survey 2000*, Nairobi: Government Printer.
Kenya, Government of 2001, *Poverty Reduction Strategy Paper for the Period 2001-2004*, Nairobi: Ministry of Finance and Planning.
MCN 1999, *Strategic Nakuru Structure Plan. Action Plan for Sustainable Urban Development of Nakuru Town and its Environs*, Nakuru: Municipal Council of Nakuru.
Owuor, S.O. forthcoming, 'Bridging the Urban-Rural Divide: Multi-spatial Livelihoods in Nakuru Town, Kenya', PhD thesis/ASC Research Report.
Rakodi, C. 2002a, 'A Livelihoods Approach – Conceptual Issues and Definitions', in: C. Rakodi & T. Lloyd-Jones (eds), *Urban Livelihoods: A People-Centred Approach to Reducing Poverty*, London: Earthscan Publications, pp. 3-22.
Rakodi, C. 2002b, 'Economic Development, Urbanization and Poverty', in: C. Rakodi & T. Lloyd-Jones (eds), *Urban Livelihoods: A People-Centred Approach to Reducing Poverty*, London: Earthscan Publications, pp. 23-34.
Satterthwaite, D. 1997, 'Urban Poverty: Reconsidering its Scale and Nature', Paper for workshops on poverty reduction in urban areas organized by the International Institute for Environment and Development (IIED), UK.
Simon, D. 1997, 'Urbanization, Globalization and Economic Crisis in Africa', in: C. Rakodi (ed.), *The Urban Challenge in Africa: Growth and Management of its Large Cities*, Tokyo/New York: United Nations University Press, pp. 74-108.
UNCHS/Habitat 1996, *An Urbanizing World: Global Report on Human Settlements*, London: Oxford University Press.
Wallman, S. 1996, *Kampala Women Getting By: Well-being in the Time of AIDS*, London: James Currey.
Wratten, E. 1995, 'Conceptualizing Urban Poverty', *Environment and Urbanization* 7 (1): 11-36.

'Bendskin' drivers in Douala's New Bell neighbourhood: Masters of the road and the city

Piet Konings

> *The youth of New Bell, one of the largest and poorest immigrant districts in Douala, have invented a new activity: using motorbikes as taxis. This is commonly known as 'bendskin', an activity that is not only securing them a sustainable livelihood during the current economic crisis and structural adjustment but is also making a significant contribution to solving the neighbourhood's critical transport problem. Bendskin drivers are usually organized in small groups along ethnic and friendship lines, and form a social and spatial 'neighbourhood' within the New Bell neighbourhood as a whole. Nevertheless, they have also proved themselves capable of transcending group boundaries and rally round when their common interests or one of their colleagues are threatened by outsiders, such as other road users and, more particularly, the police. Due to their sheer number and ability to mobilize so rapidly, they constitute a powerful force, which has made them the 'masters of the road' and, on certain occasions, even the 'masters of the city'.*

Introduction

It is widely recognized that young people have been among those most seriously affected by the current economic crisis in many African countries and the implementation of structural adjustment programmes (Trani 2000, Konings 2002). Their chances of finding a job in the state bureaucracy or the formal sector have undeniably been drastically reduced by economic liberalization and state withdrawal from the economy. While this has undoubtedly largely circumvented their range of possibilities for securing a sustainable livelihood (Jua 2003), it would nevertheless be an exaggeration to refer to today's youth as a 'lost' or 'abandoned' generation (Cruise O'Brien 1996). Faced with dramatic changes in the Cameroonian labour market, young people have adopted a variety of livelihood strategies, varying from those with a long history in their neighbourhood to recent imaginative innovations. This can be illustrated by a case study of youth in New Bell, one of the largest and poorest immigrant districts in Douala, the economic capital of Cameroon.

Since the start of the economic crisis and economic liberalization in Cameroon (Konings 1996), a growing number of the New Bell's youth have been forced to adopt long-standing livelihood strategies in their community. Most of them have tried to survive by engaging in legal activities such as petty trade and production, and/or various illegal activities such as prostitution, crime or smuggling. A declining number are still able to find permanent or casual work in the public service, the railways, the port, factories and business enterprises. Of late, however, in the wake of political liberalization in the early 1990s, some youths in New Bell have mapped out new trajectories. Most tend to live in the Bamileke-dominated neighbourhoods of New Bell where I carried out my research. The Bamileke ethnic group is known, and often feared, in Cameroon for its assumed dynamism and entrepreneurial spirit (Dongmo 1981, Warnier 1993, Tabappsi 1999).

The first innovative activity is usually designated as *feymania* – a Pidgin English expression meaning 'swindling' (Malaquais 2001, see also Ndjio, this volume). *Feymen* are young men involved in a number of illegal activities, including the international trafficking of drugs, human organs and diamonds, the counterfeiting of banknotes, credit cards and passports, swindling and smuggling.[1] They have also gradually moved into several legal activities such as the sale of second-hand cars and clothing, building and property rentals, and gambling. They can, apparently, count on the support of most of the leading figures in the Cameroonian regime and its security networks. As a result of their activities, they have been able to amass fabulous wealth in a short period of time, and they are not ashamed to display their material success in the form of conspicuous consumption. The attitude of New Bell residents towards this new form of capital accumulation would seem to be ambivalent. The older

---

[1] Although *feymania* is still a predominantly male activity, some young women have also become involved in it.

Photo 3.1   A modern bendskin in action
(Photo courtesy of Bouba Lawal)

generation is inclined to question the supposedly mysterious origins of the *feymen*'s sudden wealth, often associating it with sorcery and witchcraft. In sharp contrast, the younger generation tend to admire their achievements, seeing the *feymen* as role models and national heroes.

The second innovative activity, and the one which is the focus of this study, is somewhat less spectacular than *feymania* and certainly less remunerative: the use of motorbikes as taxis. This is usually called 'bendskin', a Pidgin English term meaning 'bend yourself' (to hold on tightly to the driver). Bendskin is also the name of popular Bamileke music introduced in the 1960s by the famous Bamileke singer André-Marie Talla (Nyamnjoh & Fokwang 2003: 192). According to informants, bendskin originally referred to the first type of motorbike-taxi with a higher backseat, on which the posture adopted by a passenger resembled that of a bendskin dancer. It was only later that the term 'bendskin' came to refer to the entire operation of motorbike-taxis in general.

Surprisingly little interest has been devoted in African Studies to the serious transportation problems facing inhabitants of African cities and the various agencies and actors involved in urban transportation (cf. Godard 2002). Clearly, the idea of bendskin never originated from the offices of the Cameroonian Ministry of Transport or came from international development agencies.

Instead, it was an innovative response by young people to deteriorating urban transport facilities and has been of great significance to neighbourhood development. Firstly, it offers employment and a reasonable, secure income for a growing number of young people in the neighbourhood. Secondly, it provides a form of transport well adapted to the poor state of the neighbourhood's road network and the inhabitants' low income levels. And thirdly, it stimulates growth in other local economic activities, particularly those that provide services in one way or another to bendskin itself.

This chapter discusses how bendskin tends both to divide and unite its drivers. They are inclined to organize themselves in small groups based on ethnic and friendship bonds. Each group has its own parking space at a strategic position in the neighbourhood and its members demonstrate a large degree of solidarity during working hours and in their leisure time. As such, they form a social and spatial 'neighbourhood' within the larger neighbourhood of New Bell.

While these various groups are usually in competition with each other, they appear nevertheless capable of overcoming group boundaries and rally round when their individual and common interests are threatened by 'outsiders', like other road users, government authorities and the police. New Bell residents have always been inclined to resist any controlling efforts of the colonial and post-colonial state and have succeeded in maintaining a considerable measure of autonomy (Schler 2003). New Bell bendskin drivers also ignore all administrative and traffic regulations, and have been successful in contesting police authority and control measures, thus becoming 'masters of the road'. In protest against persistent police harassment and extortion, bendskin drivers have on certain occasions even taken control of the city by chasing the police from the streets and bringing traffic to a total standstill.

New Bell: An immigrant quarter in Douala

Douala is the largest city of Cameroon and has grown rapidly since independence, from 155,000 inhabitants in 1960 to approximately 2 million in 2000. Being Cameroon's economic capital, it attracts between 60,000 and 100,000 migrants every year (Mainet 1985, Bopda 2000). Many of them have sought residence in Douala's main immigrant residential quarter, New Bell.

New Bell was created by the German colonial administration in 1914 as part of an extensive urbanization plan for Douala (cf. Gouellain 1975, Eckert 1999, Austin & Derrick 1999). This plan aimed to reserve the city centre for Europeans by relocating the local Duala and the growing population of African 'strangers' to the outskirts.[2] New African neighbourhoods were to be established a few kilometres inland from the coast, separated from the European areas by a one-kilometre-wide Free Zone. In early 1914, the Germans succeeded in relocating the 'stranger' population to New Bell, before being ousted itself from Douala in September by Allied forces. The French administration, set up in 1916, adopted the German policy.

Migrants from the interior of Cameroon, as well as from other West and Central African colonies started settling in New Bell. Immigrants from within Cameroon were from various ethnic groups, with large concentrations of Beti, Bassa, Haussa and Bamileke. The flux of Bamileke into New Bell increased tremendously over the years and they came to dominate certain neighbourhoods of New Bell as well as other neighbourhoods in Douala, far outnumbering the autochthonous Duala. This is why some people refer to Douala as a 'Bamileke City' (Mainet 1985).

Some of New Bell's 'stranger' population found work within the colonial economy as permanent or casual labourers and junior civil servants, but most earned their livelihood in the quarter's informal economy as artisans and petty traders. New Bell also became known as a haven for prostitutes, smugglers and 'sand-sand' boys – gangs of youth who try to eke out a living by engaging in odd jobs and petty crime (Gouellain 1975, Joseph 1977). But there also emerged a small group of successful large-scale businessmen, especially among the Nigerian, Haussa and Bamileke inhabitants (Mainet 1985).

The French were initially unwilling to make any substantial investment in the urbanization of New Bell, which largely explains why they decided to exclude it from Douala proper when they established the city's formal borders in 1925. This situation lasted until 1944. Benefiting from French *laissez-faire* attitudes, migrants haphazardly created residential areas and neighbourhoods in New Bell. In the early colonial period land was readily available and residents, using their limited resources, simply claimed plots and built houses. As new communities grew and hierarchies of power sprang up, colonially appointed chiefs would claim control over specific tracts of unclaimed land, demanding that newcomers obtain permission to build. But the native chiefs' control was incomplete at best, particularly in the inter-war years when the first chiefs were selected from among the immigrants who demonstrated total loyalty to the regime. Land became increasingly scarce as the population grew, making it hard for new migrants to settle in the area (Schler 2003: 56-57). Faced with minimal standards of living and poor infrastructure, residents often became part of a

---

[2] Douala is used here to refer to the city and the name Duala to the autochthonous ethnic group in the city.

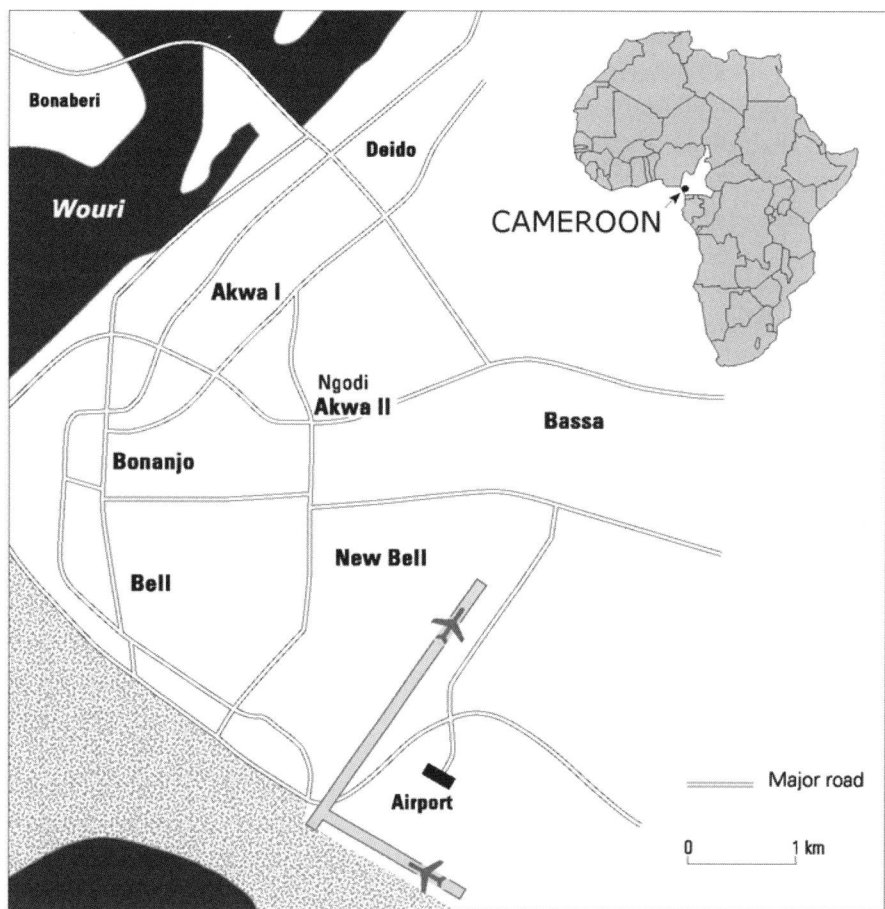

Map 3.1 The New Bell quarter of Douala
(Source: Séraphin 2000: 272)

'floating population', always on the look-out for better options elsewhere and ignoring the city's fluid borders.

When the French eventually initiated plans for urban renewal in New Bell after the Second World War, including renovation of the area's infrastructure, they were immediately met with strong opposition from the autochthonous Duala who claimed ownership of land in the immigrant quarter. It was only after persistent French pressure that the Duala finally, in 1954, authorized the French authorities to carry out limited public works, but a complete and effective renovation and modernization of New Bell's infrastructure was never undertaken (Mainet 1985, Schler 2003). Today's residents live with this legacy:

houses, many of them poorly constructed wooden structures, are packed together; the few paved roads are full of potholes up to a metre in diameter and accessible only via narrow footpaths; open sewers, rats and mosquitoes abound; and many live without running water or electricity. Since the colonial period, the residents of New Bell, with the exception of a few large businessmen and the *nouveaux riches*, have thus continued to experience the history of a space disenfranchised from the narratives of modernity evident in the nearby city centre.

Significantly, residents of New Bell have constantly displayed a remarkable capacity for evading all efforts at state control. They have devised ingenious ways to maintain a large measure of autonomy by simply disregarding any laws or administrative rules aimed at regulating their activities. Schler (2003), for instance, highlights the blatant failure of various colonial attempts at control, such as the introduction of identity cards, pass laws (*laissez-passer*) and well-paid informants. By asserting its autonomy, New Bell's population has been able to engage in a wide range of legal and illegal economic activities that have enabled the community to survive and, in some cases, even to thrive.

Since the end of the Second World War, New Bell has been a hotbed of rebellion against colonial and post-colonial rule. It is mostly the older generation in present-day New Bell that still remembers the main pre-independence political events in its quarter. In September 1945 the New Bell proletariat, organized in newly created militant trade unions, participated in collective strike action against their colonial employers, and its subproletariat, in particular the *sans-travail* and 'sand-sand' boys, staged a riot that destroyed and pillaged property. Soon afterwards, New Bell became the central seat of the *Union des Populations du Cameroun* (UPC), the radical nationalist party. Following the banning of the UPC in 1955, UPC militants patrolled New Bell to protect the party's central seat and regularly clashed with the forces of law and order (Joseph 1974, 1977).

The youngest generation in New Bell, however, still vividly remembers the 1991-1992 *villes mortes* (ghost town) campaign in its quarter. This was essentially a civil disobedience action organized by the political opposition during political liberalization to force the regime in power to hold a sovereign national conference (Konings 1996, Takougang & Krieger 1998). The action aimed to bring the economy to a standstill by calling on the public to stay indoors, boycott markets and offices (except at weekends), and not pay their taxes and public utility bills. People were allowed to come out only during regular anti-government demonstrations. The *villes mortes* campaign was particularly successful in the opposition stronghold of New Bell where there were violent confrontations between demonstrators and the forces of law and order, which resulted in many casualties.

This spirit of disregard for all rules and the rebellion that prevailed in New Bell must have influenced the behaviour of bendskin drivers in the execution of their innovative attempts at solving the serious transportation problems in their underprivileged neighbourhood.

The emergence of bendskin in New Bell

Motorbike-taxis were in existence in some West African countries even before the process of political liberalization started at the end of the 1980s. The so-called *zémidjans* had by then already become the most important means of transport in the urban centres of Benin (Noukpo 2003). Even in Cameroon, the motorbike-taxi was not totally unknown in this period, operating on a relatively small scale in the northern part of the country. As in Lomé, motorbike-taxis emerged in Douala during the general strikes and civil disobedience campaigns at the beginning of the political liberalization process organized by the opposition to force those in power to hold a sovereign national conference (Godard & Ngabmen 2002).

The *villes mortes* campaign in Cameroon aggravated the already-critical transport situation in Douala's various neighbourhoods since the normal means of transport – buses, (ordinary) taxis and private cars – were prohibited from operating on weekdays. There was no similar ban on motorbikes. According to a New Bell motorbike-taxi driver, this state of affairs eventually led to bendskin.

> During the *villes mortes* campaign, owners of motorbikes were regularly requested by colleagues, relatives and friends to assist them in reaching their destinations. Due to growing demand, they started charging for this service. However, the idea of turning motorbikes into taxis and making a living out of them occurred to young people only when it became more and more evident that bendskin could help solve the grave mobility problems in the various neighbourhoods of Douala.

His narrative clearly explains the rapid expansion of bendskin. Although one of the fruits of political liberalization, bendskin emerged as a response to the deteriorating road networks and transport facilities in neighbourhoods.

Like many other African cities (Godard 2002), in the last decade Douala has seen the disappearance of public bus companies that were specifically created by the post-colonial state to meet urban transport requirements. Since its foundation in 1973, the state-owned *Société des Transports Urbains du Cameroun* (Sotuc) had enjoyed a monopoly position in bus transport in Douala.

Photo 3.2 An early example of a Cameroonian motorbike-taxi, a HONDA CG 175 belonging to Haman Daligama
(Photo courtesy of Haman Daligama)

Photo 3.3 Bendskin drivers waiting for passengers at a typical motorbike-taxi parking area
(Photo courtesy of Chehou Abdoul Kadiri)

Understandably, its area of operation remained largely restricted to Douala's paved streets but the company nevertheless used to offer a necessary service for low-income groups in neighbourhoods, including New Bell, because it was able to transport a substantial number of passengers quite cheaply thanks to state subsidies. Its great potential, however, was thwarted by gross mismanagement and the withdrawal of state subsidies during structural adjustment, leading to enormous financial losses. The company was never able to fully recover from the *villes mortes* campaign, during which opposition members threatened to set fire to any bus on the roads (Ngabmen 2002, Séraphin 2000: 69-70), and it was liquidated in 1995. Conscious of the grave consequences of its liquidation for the already critical urban transport situation, the government decided in 1997, in line with its new policy of economic liberalization, to hand over the running of large buses in Douala to a private initiative,. A newly founded Cameroonian company, the *Société Camerounaise du Transport Urbain* (Socatur), was eventually given the monopoly to provide bus services in Douala and it started operations in 2001. At present, it still lacks sufficient buses to carry out its mission satisfactorily.

With the disappearance of public buses, people in New Bell came to depend primarily on taxis although they were not generally satisfied with the services these taxis offered. They claimed that the number of taxis was insufficient to meet popular demand, particularly during rush hour. Mobility at peak times has indeed become a painful experience: one has to wait hours before being able to find a taxi; costs have risen to more than double the official fare; and traffic jams are exacerbated by poor road networks and the deplorable state of the roads. Travelling in the city is, therefore, extremely time-consuming and arrival times at work or at home are highly unpredictable.

People in New Bell also maintain that taxi drivers frequently refuse to go to neighbourhoods that are not easily accessible or are far from the city centre and they often drop passengers somewhere along the road. This is one of the principal reasons for the emergence of non-registered taxis, the so-called *clandos* or *opeps*, in these neighbourhoods (Fodouop 1985). One of my informants aptly described them as 'mobile coffins' on the grounds that they tend not to be roadworthy, are over-loaded, and driven by drivers without a driving licence, leading to frequent accidents. According to him, they continue to operate because their drivers perform the '*countri* fashion' at police checkpoints, i.e. offer *gombo* (bribes) to policemen.

In addition, New Bell residents are increasingly reluctant to use taxis because of the alarming increase in armed robberies in recent years by taxi drivers themselves or their accomplices, particularly at night. They are nevertheless often obliged to risk using taxis in the absence of any alternative.

Despite the introduction of professional badges in 2000, problems regarding personal security still prevail in the taxi business.

Given this situation, New Bell residents have greatly appreciated the emergence of bendskin in their neighbourhood, stressing that it forms a welcome addition to the available means of transport and that it is well adapted to local conditions. In sharp contrast to taxi drivers, bendskin drivers are said firstly to charge reasonable prices that are always negotiable depending on the distance and nature of the terrain, secondly to take passengers into the heart of the neighbourhood dropping them on their doorstep, and thirdly to be able to weave in and out of traffic jams during rush hour, which saves time. However, some New Bell residents appear to have adopted a more ambivalent attitude towards bendskin drivers, claiming that their reckless driving is a frequent cause of accidents.

The number of motorbike-taxis has risen rapidly in New Bell, and Douala as a whole. In 1997, the total number of bendskins in Douala was estimated at 10,000 (Godard & Ngabmen 2002) but their number may well now have tripled.[3] This formidable rise has also promoted local entrepreneurial activities in New Bell and other quarters of the city. Several small and medium-sized enterprises have started selling motorbikes, benefiting from the existence of Douala's port that allows for large-scale formal and informal imports of (second-hand) motorbikes from neighbouring Nigeria, Eastern Europe and South-East Asia. Recently, however, a new enterprise that assembles motorbikes locally, Cocenicam, was set up. Enterprises offering a variety of services to bendskins are also emerging, providing, for example, general motorbike repairs, spare parts, petrol and engine oil. Above all, bendskin provides young men in the neighbourhood with a reasonably good and secure livelihood.

New Bell bendskin drivers: 'Masters of the Road'

Bendskin has offered employment to a growing number of young people in New Bell during the economic crisis and structural adjustment. My informants insisted that the first batch of bendskin drivers were mostly recruited from among the victims of frequent mass dismissals. They were tempted to invest their redundancy pay in this new activity and buy a second-hand motorbike. They were later joined by others who had failed to find employment in the state bureaucracy or formal sector. This group would start bendskin with the financial support of family members or, more often, with their own personal savings

---

[3] A recent study by the Douala municipality estimated the present number of bendskin drivers at over 30,000. See *Mutations,* 26 January 2005.

in formal and informal banking systems, in particular in the *tontines*, the traditional rotating credit associations (Henry *et al.* 1991).

Bendskin has proved to be attractive to young job-seekers, not only because it is perceived as an exciting job with a secure and relatively good income but also because entry into this new sector appears easy. While a long and expensive apprenticeship is required to become a true master, anybody able to acquire a motorbike can start bendskin after a few days' practice.

It did not take long before big businessmen discovered bendskin as a potential form of capital accumulation. They bought up motorbikes in large numbers, sometimes even a few hundred, and employed young job-seekers as drivers. Most of these businessmen were Bamileke, which is unsurprising since transport has always been one of their major routes to capital accumulation. According to Warnier (1993: 19), the Bamileke own 80% of all taxis in Douala and 50% of all the buses and minibuses that run from Douala to other towns in Cameroon. They are also strongly represented in the fields of vehicle maintenance and repair.

Employers offer bendskin drivers contracts similar to those in the taxi business. One common kind is where bendskin drivers hand over a substantial proportion of their daily earnings to their employer, usually around FCFA 4,000, in return for ownership of the scooter or motorbike after two or three years. Bendskin drivers who do not have this type of contract are obliged to hand over a smaller amount of money, usually between FCFA 2,000 and FCFA 3,000 a day.

In 2003 I carried out a survey among more than 100 bendskin drivers in New Bell to explore their main characteristics. All were male and most were quite young (81% were between 15 and 35 years old), single (61%) and had not been in the profession for long (76% had less than 5 years' bendskin experience). They were mostly employed by large entrepreneurs (63%) and did not yet possess a scooter or motorbike themselves. They tended to be relatively well educated: 45% had attended primary school, 43% had a secondary school diploma and 7% were university graduates. Only 5% were illiterate. They had usually been looking for another job before becoming *bendskineur*, and the large majority were Bamileke (79%), which is understandable as I carried out my survey in various Bamileke-dominated neighbourhoods of New Bell. Nevertheless, I was told that, due to their interest in the transport sector, the Bamileke also make up the majority of bendskin drivers in some other parts of the city too. All of the interviewed drivers worked long hours six or seven days a week and earned a monthly income of between FCFA 40,000 and FCFA 100,000 depending on their expenses, and their contribution to their employer. Their monthly income appears to be well above the guaranteed minimum wage in the formal sector, which is still today about FCFA 25,000 (Konings 1993).

While some of them operate on a more or less individual basis, cruising around New Bell and other areas of the city in search of passengers, most appear to operate in groups. Each group constitutes a spatial and social 'neighbourhood' within the neighbourhood of New Bell as a whole. Members of these groups park their scooters and motorbikes at certain strategic places in New Bell, such as at traffic intersections and markets. They consider parking places as spaces reserved for members only, and are inclined to protect them against intruders or competitors. Each group is expected to keep to its zone of operation and competition in this zone is not tolerated. Members form a tight social community and display a large degree of solidarity both during and outside work time. Most of them belong not only to the same ethnic group (Bamileke) but also often to the same family, village or sub-region. The group does not exclude members of other ethnic groups altogether, but non-Bamileke are usually close friends, for example former classmates or ex-colleagues. Members tend to spend their rare leisure time together and frequent the same bars. They often participate in the same *tontines*, which serve not only as savings clubs but also as social gatherings where they enjoy each other's company and, if necessary, settle any conflicts (Henry *et al.* 1991). They also provide moral and financial support in times of sickness, disability or death.

Such spatial and social neighbourhoods tend to create boundaries between bendskin drivers. Nevertheless, they appear to be able to transcend these boundaries and rally round when they see that one of their colleagues or a common interest is being threatened by outsiders. Due to their sheer number and their ability to mobilize rapidly using their scooters and motorbikes to warn their colleagues at different parking places, bendskin drivers form a formidable power in the neighbourhood and the city as a whole. I regularly heard people in New Bell saying: 'Bendskin drivers behave as if they are "masters of the road"'. Evidently, this brings them into frequent conflict with other road users and, above all, with the police. Bendskin drivers are notorious for their total disregard of traffic rules or any state regulation concerning their profession.

The rapid expansion of bendskin led the government to regulate the new activity. In 1996, it issued a series of administrative and fiscal rules. Bendskins should be painted yellow and have a number plate. Both bendskin drivers and passengers are obliged to wear helmets. Every bendskin driver should be in possession of the following documents: a tax certificate showing that the annual tax of FCFA 12,000 has been paid, a road-tax sticker (*vignette*), vehicle insurance, and a driving license for motorbikes. Most bendskin drivers simply ignore these regulations, all the more so because the police are not usually inclined to strictly enforce them, being more interested in extorting money from drivers. 'Why should you bother to obtain these documents', a bendskin driver wondered, 'for even if you have all of them, the police still request a beer.'

Even worse, many bendskin drivers either do not know the most elementary traffic rules or simply flout them. They tend to drive at high speed, ignore red traffic lights, overtake on the left and the right, stop without warning and do U turns in the middle of the road exposing themselves and their passengers to untold dangers. Some bendskin drivers are even convinced that they should always be given priority by other users of the road as they are performing an essential public service. As a result of their reckless behaviour, bendskin drivers cause numerous accidents. The Laquintenie Hospital in Douala has even given the name 'bendskin' to one of its wards that is largely reserved for victims of bendskin road accidents.

Bendskin drivers are characterized not only by their irresponsible driving but also by their aggressive attitude to any other road user who may cross their path or dares to confront them, not hesitating even to attack him physically. I once witnessed how a bendskin driver almost collided with a smartly dressed young man who was about to cross the road. Though being shabbily dressed himself, he shouted: 'Dégagez, fils de pauvre' ('get off the road, you son of a poor').

Bendskin drivers are also often at war with taxi drivers even though both parties have much in common, including their blatant disregard of traffic regulations. Many taxi drivers deeply resent the bendskin drivers' aggressive behaviour and driving style, their 'almost blind solidarity' and their 'misuse of power'. As one of them explained:

> We already submit ourselves too often to their laws, and this is becoming more and more annoying. At the least altercation with one of them, they come and encircle you like bees and attempt to lynch you.

A colleague of his, however, insisted that he was not going to tolerate their 'laws of the jungle' on the road any longer:

> They think that the road belongs to them and that everybody must submit to their jungle laws. But they cannot do so with me. I will not hesitate to drive them into the gutter, even if they are transporting passengers. This will make them understand that they are not safe on their motorbikes.

While bendskin drivers are involved in regular conflicts with other road users, their relations with the police and other state agents are extremely hostile, rooted in a fierce contest for power and control of the road. The police attribute the frequent confrontations between both parties to the persistent refusal of bendskin drivers to submit to government regulations concerning their activities and traffic rules, as well as their lack of respect for police officers. The bendskin drivers, in turn, claim that most confrontations are caused by their refusal to yield to the frequent cash demands of the corrupt police known in Cameroon as *mange mille*.[4] They also stress that the police are quick to pick a quarrel with road users, notably those who assert their rights, and resort too quickly to the use of force. They are therefore inclined to engage in collective action as soon they see that the police are violating the rights of one or more of them. Many examples of such actions can be found in New Bell and other quarters of the city. I will relate here just a few that have attracted a lot of attention in the media.

In early 2001, a heated confrontation between a policeman and a group of bendskin drivers occurred in the district of Madagascar. The group had come to the rescue of a colleague who was being harassed by a policeman. Feeling threatened, the policeman suddenly drew his pistol and at the very moment he wanted to fire, he was pushed from behind by a group member. During his fall he killed himself.[5]

In November of the same year, bendskin drivers occupied the most important traffic intersections in Douala, bringing all traffic to a standstill. They blew their horns continuously and carried placards protesting against the corrupt behaviour of municipal agents charged with collecting taxes from bendskin drivers. According to the demonstrators, these agents were behaving like policemen and gendarmes, demanding not only their tax certificates but also other documents, such as proof of vehicle insurance and a driving license. If they could not produce these documents, the agents threatened to seize their motorbikes unless they paid a substantial bribe of between FCFA 2,000 and FCFA 5,000. The protesters were later received by the Prefect of Wouri, Mr Laurent Mindja, who ordered the municipal agents to restrict themselves to the collection of taxes.[6]

In March 2002, a police vehicle hit a group of bendskin drivers standing at their parking place on the road near Tunnel Ndoketi, killing one of them. In reaction, the group immediately set fire to the vehicle and wanted to lynch the two policemen in it. The latter narrowly escaped by firing several shots into the air.[7]

On several occasions, bendskin drivers have protested against police harassment and extortion by erecting barricades on the Wouri Bridge, which forms the only connection between the two parts of Douala. On 23 February 2003, during one of the frequent demonstrations in the city, they used sticks to chase the police away.[8] It was only a few months later that a renewed incident between

---

[4] This refers to police extortion of money from drivers, amounting to FCFA 1,000.
[5] Cameroon-info.net, 8 October 2003.
[6] *Le Messager,* 26 November 2001, p. 4.
[7] Ibid., 1 April 2002, p. 5.
[8] Cameroon-info.net, 8 October 2003.

the police and a bendskin driver in New Bell gave rise to a violent rebellion in the city.

New Bell bendskin drivers in revolt: 'Masters of the City'

On 9 July 2003, the population of New Bell, and Douala as a whole, witnessed further unrest when bendskin drivers staged an anti-police riot and took control of the city.[9]

A serious incident early in the morning sparked off the trouble. A police control post tried to stop a bendskin driver in Nkolouloun, a Bamileke-dominated neighbourhood in New Bell, but suspecting that he would have to pay a bribe, the bendskin driver attempted to escape. Infuriated by his conduct, one of the policemen hit him on the head with a plank of wood. He fell and died soon afterwards. Bendskin drivers were deeply shocked and news of his death spread like wildfire across the city. Being frequent victims of police harassment themselves, they were not prepared to tolerate the murder of one of their colleagues so they immediately stopped work and started mobilizing.

Some of their representatives went to see the Governor of Littoral Province, Gounoko Haounaye, to demand harsh sanctions against the policemen responsible for their colleague's death. Probably underestimating the gravity of the situation, the Governor refused to meet and negotiate with them. This obviously raised the tempers of the bendskin drivers. They began to erect barricades at the city's main road junctions and on the Wouri Bridge and to burn tyres in the streets, bringing any transportation of goods or passengers to a complete standstill. They then drove in a long procession to the police commissariat in Nkolouloun where the policeman who had caused the incident was posted.

On their arrival, they started attacking the police with sticks, machetes and stones, eventually forcing them to retreat into the building. They then began to throw Molotov cocktails in an attempt to set fire to the building and the police vehicles parked nearby. In response, the police started shooting at the demonstrators to keep them at a distance. A large crowd of New Bell residents watched the scene, applauding any successful actions by the bendskin drivers against the much-hated police. A number of young people, especially the unemployed and some of the criminal element, soon joined the bendskin drivers in their protests, seeing the riot as an outlet to vent their frustrations at the economic crisis and their own harassment by the police. Together with the bendskin drivers, they went in search of policemen in the streets of New Bell

---

[9] This section is based on my own interviews in New Bell and on reports in *The Herald,* 13 & 15 July 2003, and *Le Messager,* 15 July 2003.

and other quarters of the city chanting: 'Policemen, murderers, where are you? Come with your rifles and we shall welcome you with our stones'. Fearing reprisals from the bendskin drivers after the incident, the police had already disappeared from the streets by then, most of them having taken refuge in the various police stations or in their own homes.

Following a number of deaths and injuries, the atmosphere became tenser during the afternoon. The Governor of Littoral Province then finally arrived on the scene and, in an attempt to protect the Nkolouloun police commissariat from further attack, he called upon the demonstrators to walk with him to a neighbouring junction called Shell-New Bell, promising that he would address their grievances on arrival there. He proceeded to request an end to all violent actions, stressing that the administration was already investigating the matter, and assured the bendskin drivers that the policemen responsible for the tragic event were to be arrested and tried in accordance with the law. He subsequently moved to the Wouri Bridge where he appealed to the demonstrators to remove the barricades and allow vehicles to pass.

While the governor's intervention did reduce tensions, it did not bring an end to the riots altogether. Armed with machetes, sticks and stones, groups of bendskin drivers and other young people continued to block traffic at the city's most important intersections. They also set fire to kiosks along the streets and wooden police posts placed at road junctions, and started looting shops and stalls in the market places.

By the end of the day, five people had been killed by police bullets and numerous others wounded, including several policemen. Material damage was also significant: the police commissariat in Nkolouloun was partly destroyed, a number of police vehicles were burnt out, and those involved in the transportation of goods and passengers had suffered huge losses.

A fragile calm was restored in New Bell and the other quarters of Douala the next day. Although the revolt had generated fear in administrative and police circles, no serious attempt was made to resolve the bendskin problem. As a result, drivers continued to operate with total disregard for the law and its custodians, the police. The Prefect of Wouri claimed that no negotiations between state and bendskin drivers could take place as long as it was not clear who the true representatives or leaders of the bendskin drivers were. He urged administrators in Douala to help organize bendskin drivers into trade unions that could serve as intermediaries between the state and the bendskin drivers.

Only two municipal administrators took up the matter, namely the Deputy Mayor of Douala V, Mrs Françoise Foning, and the Mayor of Douala II, Mr Abraham Tchato. Both are Bamileke who, in addition to a number of other entrepreneurial activities, each own a fleet of bendskins. They held a series of meetings with bendskin representatives in their municipalities and during one of these meetings, on 17 July 2003, Mrs Foning signed a 'partnership convention' with a newly created association of bendskin drivers, the Association of Motor-bike Taximen of Douala V (Asmot). Curiously, some of the leaders of this association were her own employees. Other leaders were apparently willing to cooperate because of perceived material advantages. According to the terms of the convention, the municipal council was to take on the responsibility of training bendskin drivers at professional driving schools. The bendskin drivers, for their part, agreed to henceforth seek to resolve all their problems with the police and the administration through peaceful negotiations, as well as to register their organization with the Douala V Council.[10]

This association seems not to have had any significant impact on the behaviour and organization of bendskin drivers. Generally speaking, they continue to mistrust the formation of trade unions, which they view as largely vehicles of state control. Most trade unions in Cameroon, including the taxi drivers' unions, are not yet fully autonomous, their leadership still often being co-opted into the state apparatus (Konings 2003). However, even in the absence of trade unions, bendskin drivers have shown their ability to transcend their internal divisions and mobilize in defence of their interests against their common enemy, the police.

Conclusion

This chapter has attempted to show how young men in Douala's New Bell quarter have taken advantage of the critical transportation situation in their neighbourhood to develop the innovative activity of bendskin driving. It has proved to be advantageous for both the neighbourhood and the bendskin drivers themselves, providing them with a sustainable livelihood at a time when severe economic crisis and structural adjustment have largely excluded young people from finding employment in the state bureaucracy and formal sector.

Bendskin drivers have displayed a remarkable capacity for organizing at several levels and protecting their own interests. They usually organize themselves in small groups based on ethnic and friendship bonds, which protect the interests of each group against others. These groups form tiny social and spatial neighbourhoods within the larger neighbourhood of New Bell. While mutual competition between these groups tends to divide bendskin drivers, they quickly group together as soon as their mutual interests are threatened by outsiders. They share a common disregard for state regulations concerning their profession and traffic rules, which makes them subject to persistent police harassment

---

[10] *The Herald,* 23-24 July 2003, and Cameroon-info.net, 8 October 2003.

and extortion. They have engaged in a series of collective actions to contest police authority, using revolt as a last resort in an attempt to assert their autonomy and their control over the road, and even the city.

References

Austen, R.A. & J. Derrick 1999, *Middlemen of the Cameroons Rivers: The Duala and their Hinterland, c. 1600 – c. 1960*, Cambridge: Cambridge University Press.
Bopda, E. 2000, 'Le Transport par Pousse-Pousse et sa Contribution au Développement dans les Pays du Sud: Le Cas de la Ville de Douala au Cameroun', in: F. Fodouop & A. Metton (eds), *Économie Informelle et Développement dans les Pays du Sud à l'Ère de la Mondialisation*, Yaoundé: Presses Universitaires de Yaoundé, pp. 140-67.
Cruise O'Brien, D.B. 1996, 'A Lost Generation?: Youth Identity and State Decay in West Africa', in: R. Werbner & T. Ranger (eds), *Postcolonial Identities in Africa*, London/New Jersey: Zed Books, pp. 55-74.
Dongmo, J.-L. 1981, *Le Dynamisme Bamiléké (Cameroun)*, (2 vols), Yaoundé: CEPER.
Eckert, A. 1999, *Grundbezitz, Landkonflikte und kolonialer Wandel: Douala 1880-1960*, Stuttgart: Steiner.
Fodouop, K. 1985, 'Les Transports Clandestins autour de Yaoundé', *Les Cahiers d'Outre-Mer* 38 (150): 175-95.
Godard, X. (ed.) 2002, *Les Transports et la Ville en Afrique au Sud du Sahara: Le Temps de la Débrouille et du Désordre Inventif*, Paris: Karthala and Inrets.
Godard, X. & H. Ngabmen 2002, 'Comme Zémidjans ou le Succès des Taxi-Motos', in: X. Godard (ed.), *Les Transports et la Ville en Afrique au Sud du Sahara: Le Temps de la Débrouille et du Désordre Inventif*, Paris: Karthala and Inrets, pp. 397-406.
Gouellain, R. 1975, *Douala: Ville et Histoire*, Paris: Musée de l'Homme, Institut d'Ethnologie.
Henry, A., G.H. Tchenk & Ph. Guillerme-Dieumegard 1991, *Tontines et Banques au Cameroun*, Paris: Karthala.
Joseph, R.A. 1974, 'Settlers, Strikers and Sans-Travail: The Douala Riots of September 1945', *Journal of African History* 15 (4): 669-87.
Joseph, R.A. 1977, *Radical Nationalism in Cameroon: Social Origins of the UPC Rebellion*, Oxford: Oxford University Press.
Jua, N. 2003, 'Differential Responses to Disappearing Transitional Pathways: Redefining Possibility among Cameroonian Youths', *African Studies Review* 46 (2): 13-36.
Konings, P. 1993, *Labour Resistance in Cameroon*, London: James Currey.
Konings, P. 1996, 'The Post-Colonial State and Economic and Political Reforms in Cameroon', in: A.E. Fernández Jilberto & A. Mommen (eds), *Liberalization in the Developing World: Institutional and Economic Changes in Latin America, Africa and Asia*, London/New York: Routledge, pp. 244-65.
Konings, P. 2002, 'University Students' Revolt, Ethnic Militia, and Violence during Political Liberalization in Cameroon', *African Studies Review* 45 (2): 179-204.

Konings, P. 2003, 'Organised Labour and Neo-Liberal Economic and Political Reforms in West and Central Africa', *Journal of Contemporary African Studies* 21 (3): 447-71.
Mainet, G. 1985, *Douala: Croissance et Servitudes*, Paris: L'Harmattan.
Malaquais, D. 2001, 'Arts de Feyre au Cameroun', *Politique Africaine* 82: 101-18.
Ngabmen, H. 2002, 'Libéralisation de l'Exploitation des Transports Collectifs Urbains à Douala: Mise en Oeuvre d'une Nouvelle Approche', Yaoundé: Institut des Transports et Stratégies de Développement.
Noukpo, A. 2003, 'La Diffusion des Innovations: L'Exemple des Zemijans à travers l'Espace Beninois', *Revue de Géographie du Cameroun* 15 (1): 52-67.
Nyamnjoh, F. & J. Fokwang 2003, 'Politics and Music in Cameroon', in: J.-G. Gros (ed.), *Cameroon: Politics and Society in Critical Perspectives*, Lanham: University Press of America, pp. 185-209.
Schler, L. 2003, 'Ambiguous Spaces: The Struggle over African Identities and Urban Communities in Colonial Douala, 1914-45', *Journal of African History* 44: 51-72.
Séraphin, G. 2000, *Vivre à Douala: L'Imaginaire et l'Action dans une Ville Africaine en Crise*, Paris: L'Harmattan.
Tabappsi, F.T. 1999, 'Le Modèle Migratoire Bamiléké (Cameroun) et sa Crise Actuelle: Perspectives Économiques et Culturelles', University of Leiden: CNWS Publications no. 82.
Takougang, J. & M. Krieger 1998, *African State and Society in the 1990s: Cameroon's Political Crossroads*, Boulder CO: Westview Press.
Trani, J.-F. 2000, 'Les Jeunes et le Travail à Douala: La Galère de la deuxième Génération après l'Indépendance', in: G. Courade (ed.), *Le Désarroi Camerounains: L'Épreuve de l'Économie-Monde*, Paris: Karthala, pp. 153-72.
Warnier, J.-P. 1993, *L'Esprit d'Entreprise au Cameroun*, Paris: Karthala.

4

Intimate strangers: Neighbourhood, autochthony and the politics of belonging

Basile Ndjio

> *This chapter explores the wealth of the African neighbourhood with regard to the prevalent autochthony discourse and the politics of belonging that are mediating relationships between autochthonous and allochthonous populations in many regions of Africa. It is argued that, as a result of the autochthony policy that is being promoted by many African leaders, contemporary African neighbourhoods are no longer the so-called 'imagined communities' that exalt a sense of solidarity and harmony among neighbours, regardless of their cultural, ethnic or racial background. Instead, they have become spaces for safeguarding one's ancestral land and sites of exclusion of people who do not 'belong'. The reason is that the native populations tend to consider their 'intimate strangers' as a threat to their native lands and the wealth of their locality, and worry about the latter's economic, political or demographic hegemony. The case study described in this chapter is of Tour de Ville, an allochthonous Bamileke who was accused by his neighbours of being a sorcerer to show that witchcraft charges can be used as a powerful tool in the native population's bid to protect their ancestral heritage and their neighbourhood resources against the greed of strangers.*

During the spring of 2004, the KIT Tropical Museum in Amsterdam organized an exhibition of exotic photos entitled 'Intimate Strangers'. On display were photos of bodies of indigenous people from the Amazon region and the Pacific islands. There was a skinny fisherman with a pale face, a young man whose long phallus might excite any woman, an old lady with dangling breasts, a naked child with a bloated stomach, and an attractive young woman whose wild splendour and sensuality was for many male visitors a vivid depiction of primal passion. But all these heterogeneous bodies shared the same fate of being 'strangers' to their public. In many respects, the models' physical appearance dramatized above all their 'strangeness', although the organizers' objective (I assume) was to make these 'strange folks' the intimates of the predominantly white visitors who were fascinated by this surplus of exoticism. On my way home, I kept asking myself if it was its intimacy that the public was sharing with these strangers, or if it was rather the latter's intimacy that was being violated by the former. What mediated the relationship between these exotic bodies and their 'civilized' audience? Could these dark-skinned foreigners be or become the intimates of these white natives? What would have been people's reactions if one of these *peuples premiers* had decided to settle in a middle-class neighbourhood in Amsterdam or in some other city in the Netherlands? More generally, were the public and its objects of pleasure close enough to blur the racial, cultural and social lines between Blacks and Whites, the West and the non-West, the native and the stranger, the local and the immigrant, the autochthonous and allochthonous, the insider and the outsider?

Exploring the wealth of the neighbourhood, especially in a context dominated by the pervasive autochthony/allochthony debate raises the same question: who should (or should not) be allowed to live with us? Who should (or should not) be granted the legitimate right to enjoy full membership of our locale? These questions can be formulated in a different way: are we open enough to accept foreigners as our neighbours and to share not only our intimacy but also our wealth with people who are racially, ethnically, culturally, sociologically or economically different from us? Can our neighbours be the 'strange' strangers whose dark or brown skins change the colour of our community? Can our intimates be the immigrants who look different, do not speak our language and, much less, share our common values? All these issues are informed by the observation that, in many parts of the world, particularly in post-colonial Africa, the locals' 'imagined community' (Anderson 1991) is now unimaginable with looming hordes of strangers, foreigners, invaders, immigrants, exiles and refugees who, to paraphrase Kristeva (1991: 13), have become the psychotic ghosts that haunt our imagination. More explicitly, the contemporary African neighbourhood has tended to become a space for the *défense identitaire* (Taguieff 1985: 181), a 'locus of categorical purity' (Malkki 1995: 4) and a bastion of exclusion of those who do not belong (Geschiere & Nyamnjoh 2000: 423-52). For native populations have a tendency to consider

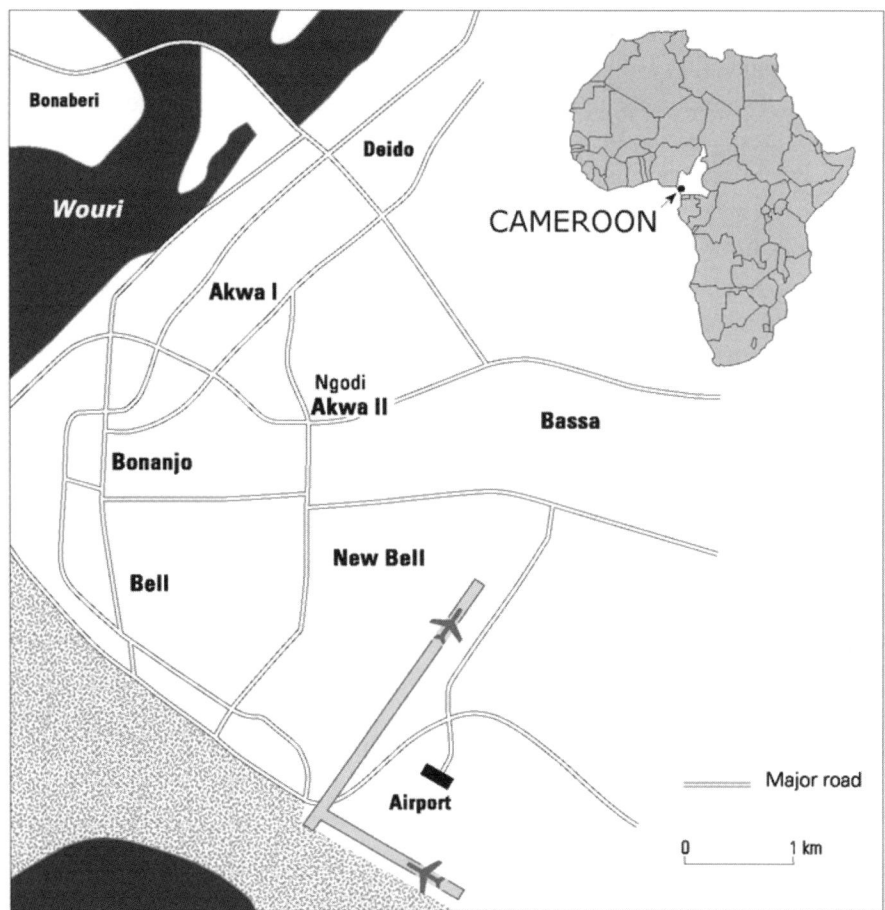

Map 4.1 The Ngodi quarter of Douala
(Source: Séraphin 2000: 272)

'strangers' as a threat to the wealth of their locality, and are anxious about their economic, political and demographic hegemony.

In Cameroon, the autochthony-allochthony question, which is at the heart of our reflections here on the Africa neighbourhood, is inflamed by political entrepreneurs. Indeed, from the start of political liberalization in the early 1990s, local political elites have been making use of what Geschiere & Nyamnjoh (2000: 423-52) call 'autochthony governmentality', a divide-and-rule policy that has so far enabled Cameroonian rulers to maintain their hegemonic position, thanks to the invention or exacerbation of regional, ethnic and cultural differences among their subjects. The Constitution of January 1996, for instance, provides a good illustration of this politics of belonging that the ruling CPDM regime has been promoting since 1991. As Awasom (2001: 22) rightly observes, 'the emphasis of the 1996 Constitution was on the right of "indigenes" and "minorities" against other nationals considered "outsiders" and "strangers". Priority was given to "ethnic", "indigenous" or "autochthonous" citizens, while the concept of national citizenship was relegated to the background.' He explains further that 'this constitution stratified citizenship by starting first with belonging to an ethnic group, district, or province before any national consideration' (Awasom 2001: 22).

As a result of this politics of belonging and its emphasis on ethnic identities and cultural differences, one's admission into a particular neighbourhood, or the way one is perceived as being a good or bad neighbour now depends largely – but not exclusively – on one's status either as an 'autochthon' or 'allochthon', as an 'insider' or 'outsider', or as a 'son of the soil' or an 'invader'. Cameroonians are increasingly sharing their living space or conniving with their village kinsmen or fellow natives rather than with *allogènes* (strangers) or 'foreigners'. What is symptomatic in this respect is the tendency of many urbanites to recreate their village in their hometown, or to withdraw into highly secluded ethnic quarters where they feel more secure among their kin group than in ethnically cosmopolitan neighbourhoods. As is discussed in this chapter, witchcraft accusations can be used as a powerful tool in the natives' bid not only to maintain the ethnic and cultural homogeneity of their locale, but also to protect their wealth and ancestral lands from invasion by strangers. I refer here to the case study of Tour de Ville, a young Bamileke feyman (nouveau riche), to demonstrate how his 'intrusion' in Ngodi, a predominantly Duala neighbourhood in Douala triggered off confrontations with local residents – a conflict that culminated in witchcraft accusations in September 2002.

Popular perceptions of the *feymen*

Since the mid-1990s, *feymen* or Cameroonian swindlers, who through deceit, extortion and other unlawful practices succeed in accumulating an unimaginable fortune in a short space of time, have become the embodiment of success in Cameroon. The stunning prosperity of many of them epitomises their fantastic ways of accruing wealth from nothing that yield incomes without production and value without effort. Popular imagination has awarded this new mode of wealth creation the name *feymania*. In the Cameroonian context that is marked by pervasive economic depression (see Courade 2000) and the *manque d'argent* (Roitman 2005), many people perceive *feymania*-related activities as the only means of achieving their expectations of modernity or what Séraphin (2000: 117) cogently calls the *conquête statutaire* (statutory quest) – the moving from the disparaging status of social juniors to that of respectable social seniors (see also Foko 2000: 177-90). But over time, this practice has proved deceptive for

Cameroonians from other ethnic groups because only young Bamileke from New Bell and Madagascar, the two largest and poorest immigrant neighbourhoods in Douala and Yaoundé, have so far been successful in *feymania*. Indeed, the newly emerging class of young and affluent Bamileke *feymen* has, since 1995, attempted through the construction of extravagant houses and ostentatious display of wealth, conspicuous consumption and social investments to alter and manipulate particular configurations of power, wealth and hierarchy that characterize post-colonial Cameroonian society. The wealthier among them have even managed to gain prestige and popularity, or to support their claims for gaining access to a high social status on the basis of their wealth. One can understand why both disillusioned Duala natives and the Beti elite who hold political power in Cameroon consider *feymania* a 'Bamileke phenomenon', or interpret it as another Bamileke scheme to affirm their economic domination over other ethnic groups. This view deliberately disregards the fact that many young people from other regions of the country are also involved in this activity (see Malaquais 2001: 19).

But, more importantly, non-Bamileke (and some Bamileke as well) tend today to associate the extraordinary promotion of these formerly underprivileged Bamileke youths with what is popularly known in Cameroon as *mokoagne moni* (magic or occult money). This expression was popularized in the mid-1990s by a group of young comedians from Douala (*Les Guignols de Douala*) whose satiric sketches were mostly addressed to *feymen* and were derisively dubbed *mokoagne men*. In addition, the wealth of the *nouveaux riches* was called *mokoagne moni*. Like many Cameroonians, these young artists made use of this term to voice their astonishment at the fantastic social advances made by some of these former slum-dwellers of New Bell and Madagascar who were now driving expensive Italian or German cars, living in luxurious houses or hotels, or distributing money to their destitute neighbours.

People began to equate *mokoagne moni* with wealth obtained by occult means. Moreover, *mokoagne moni* became an all-purpose concept that gave a simple answer to people's perplexity at the mysterious origin of these new riches: the *feymen*'s sudden and inexplicable fortune originated from their alleged connections with mystical societies. For example, one day in Douala I was discussing with some friends the story a local newspaper had reported the previous day about the feats of some Cameroonian swindlers in South Africa and Europe. An old man with whom we were sharing a table in the bar interrupted our discussion to say that he was less than satisfied with the reporter's explanation. He thought that these 'cunning and audacious young men' – as the newspaper described them – had a mystical power that permitted them to perform such unusual exploits. He asked whether a *simple man* (by whom he meant someone who was not a sorcerer) would be able to succeed in cheating 'all these white men in their own countries and come back home unscathed'.

His argument was so riveting that it encouraged a group of middle-aged men who were drinking next to us to join in our conversation, as people often do in Cameroon. All of them thought along the same lines: *feymen* had occult powers that were behind their extraordinary success and remarkable rise in fortune. One of my interlocutors asked:

> 'Can you explain how formerly underprivileged young men can overnight become extremely rich without resorting to magic?' 'You *long crayons* (intellectuals) always find rational explanations for everything, even when it is beyond common knowledge. Believe me or not, but I tell you that these young men *pratiquent* (are involved in occultism). Their fortune is a *mokoagne moni* that is widespread today among the *nouveaux riches* in Douala,' the oldest man in the group added.

What these men were expressing was the widespread belief that the *nouveaux riches* are involved in occult-related practices and that their success or failure rests not so much in their cunning and skill, but rather in their talisman or magical powers. For these people, as for many Cameroonians, you cannot operate successfully in *feymania*-related practices unless you are a sorcerer or a member of a mystical *mokoagne* society.

As appreciated by many of my informants, *mokoagne moni* means the new asocial form of wealth creation (*feymania*) in Cameroon that is not merely illegal or unlawful but also dangerous because *feymania*-related activities allegedly imply the sacrifice of innocent people to *mokoagne* sects in return for instantaneous profits. In the last decade, Cameroon has witnessed a proliferation of alarming rumours about the *nouveaux riches* and their alleged 'magic money', These rumours, which the local media regularly echo, claim that many notorious *feymen* in the country are *mokoagne* sorcerers who offer up not only their kinsmen as sacrificial victims to their mystical organisations but also people with whom they have no blood relations. It is widely believed that *mokoagne* sorcerers attract their prospective victims by offering them generous presents that often turn out to be 'poisoned gifts'. The beneficiaries of such presents supposedly become indebted to the mystical sect and have to pay back their debt with their lives (see Mbunwe-Samba 1996, Bongmba 2001).

Local Ngodi apprehension of the wealthy Bamileke who decided to take up residence in their neighbourhood in 1999 was based on the general distrust of Bamileke *feymen* as people who prosper at their neighbours' expense, for they allegedly live off the traffic of their neighbours' bodies in a global occult market.

Ngodi quarter: A Duala enclave within a Bamileke settlement

What is unusual about the Ngodi neighbourhood in which young Bamileke *feymen* and their families reside is that, unlike the other quarters of Douala that are dominantly populated by allochthonous populations, notably the Bamileke from Western Province of Cameroon, this area is mostly inhabited by Duala autochthons.[1] This group, which inhabits the coastal region of the country, today numbers between 50,000 and 75,000 people. Thus, the Ngodi quarter appears as a Duala enclave whose populations are endeavouring to preserve their ethnic homogeneity and cultural identity in the face of the threat represented by the so-called Bamileke invasion. It is worth stressing that in Cameroon the Bamileke are well known, not only for their dynamism and entrepreneurial spirit (see Dongmo 1981, Warnier 1993), but also for their propensity to settle outside their homeland. It is in this respect that some regions or cities of Cameroon, such as the coastal regions, the fertile zone of Moungo or the city of Douala have been 'colonized' since the German period (1884-1919) by Bamileke who have become the main ethnic group in these 'foreign' territories. The Bamileke's inclination to emigrate to more appropriate lands where they settle has fostered suspicion among the native populations and sometimes aversion to those they generally perceive as potentially dangerous 'strangers'. The disrespectful joke non-Bamileke like to make about Bamileke people is that they use a rubber string to measure the lands of the naïve Duala or Beti who are fond of red wine (see *Le Patriote*, 11 January 1993). Another story is the one which advises the man who catches a snake and a Bamileke in his house to kill first the latter and let the former go, advice that fits with the image of the Bamileke as cunning and clever people who are always ready to deceive those who are foolish enough to trust them. These popular wisecracks also highlight the menace the Bamileke present for others, most notably the autochthonous populations in the localities where they happen to live.

So, like other minority groups in Cameroon, Ngodi natives and the Duala populations at large have always shared the same apprehensions about being outnumbered or deprived of their ancestral lands by 'Bamileke invaders', as has happened in other Duala quarters (see Trani 2000; Séraphin 2000). This collective concern with the loss of their ancestral heritage, especially their survival in a city which is now demographically and economically dominated by *allogènes*, explains why the local populations have done their best to keep 'strangers', who

---

[1] The native Duala accounted for at least 75% of the population of Ngodi, which is estimated to be 12,000 people. This is why Douala city dwellers usually refer to this inner-city area as *le quartier des Duala* as opposed to the whole New Bell district that is generally regarded as the Bamileke quarter (68% according to *La Nouvelle Expression*, 26 September 2002). See also, Séraphin (2000) and Tabapssi (1999).

are generally viewed as a menace, out of the district. It shows too why these people have become more and more reluctant to sell a plot of land to 'foreigners' – notably to the Bamileke who are renown for their 'colonial mentality' and their 'cunning spirit', as Mr Pierre-Roger Ewedi,[2] a Duala kinsman put it.

Indeed during my fieldwork in this quarter, I was surprised to discover that very few Bamileke (who are known for settling everywhere) were living in this neighbourhood, or owned a shop there, although Ngodi was an extension of New Bell that was predominantly populated by people from the western region of the country. The information I received from a number of my informants was that the natives were managing to restrict the access of 'strangers', particularly the Bamileke, to property. For example, I learned from Mr Gaston Kwedi, an elderly Ngodi native, that landlords from the locality had turned down the offers of several non-native businessmen, most notably Bamileke, who wanted to buy plots of land to construct modern buildings or to open a shop in the neighbourhood[3]. As he explained:

> Duala natives were reluctant to sell their land to people who could later turn them into strangers on their own soil, or who could transform their territory into a *Bamilekeland.* I personally have nothing against the Bamileke, but we all know that our 'brothers' from the Western Province have this bad habit of growing like ants wherever they happen to settle. That is why people don't really like them. (Personal communication, 25 November 2002)

The pervasiveness of this opinion among the people I encountered during my fieldwork was proof that, at best, the locals were only ready to rent out their land to Bamileke so as to prevent these settlers from allegedly taking control of their properties. In another discussion I had with him three days later, my informant (quoted above) questioned:

> What would our future have been if our elders had sold off our soil to those people (the Bamileke) who like to accumulate everything even plots of land? We prefer to remain poor with our ground rather than be rich without land, like Duala natives from other localities who have become strangers on their own homeland. (Personal communication, 28 November 2002)

From what I knew about the Duala people and especially their well-established propensity to sell their land at any price, it was surprising to see so many

---

[2] All the names in this chapter have been changed to protect the identity of my informants.
[3] The natives' attitude was paradoxical if one acknowledged the significant numbers of Senegalese, Nigerian, Pakistani or Vietnamese merchants who own a shop in this area.

plots of fallow land in the very heart of the city centre, where a square metre of land alone would cost a fortune. In many ways, this bore witness to the Ngodi natives' serious concern about preserving their ancestral heritage and their awareness of their vulnerability in the face of the demographic and economic threats presented by the Bamileke. This worry accounted for why many preferred to stand for the ruling CPDM party, the only party that could supposedly safeguard their rights and interests against the Bamileke populations that were generally associated with the opposition party, notably the SDF (Social Democratic Front). The support of Duala natives for the ruling CPDM regime was due to the fact that between 1991 and 1996 it had enacted a series of laws that were purportedly and ostensibly designed to protect the 'autochthons' and the 'natives' (Awasom 2001: 22), They allegedly feared being overwhelmed or outvoted by Anglo-Bami[4] settlers in their native region (see also Geschiere & Nyamnjoh 2000: 423-52). For example, the preamble and Article 57(3) of the new Constitution, which was adopted in January 1996, uphold the state's obligation to 'protect minorities and preserve the rights of indigenous populations'. Moreover, this law states that 'the Chairperson of each Regional Council and Local Government region shall be an indigene of the area'.

The SDF's sizeable victory in Douala in the municipal and parliamentary elections in January 1996 and May 1997 – when they (as the opposition party) won almost all the seats and councils in Douala city – bolstered the indigenous population's sense of weakness *vis-à-vis* the allochthons who allegedly added political hegemony to their lengthy economic and financial domination over the former. After the election of Bamileke settlers as mayors on four out of the five councils that made up Douala city, there were mass demonstrations in the streets by Duala natives to protest at what they saw as the Bamileke's hegemonic position in their homeland. Demonstrators carried placards with messages like: 'Let all the tribes vote in their place of origin', 'Mayors should be natives', 'Strangers go home', 'Sawa (another word for the autochthons from Cameroon's coastal region) People Must Stand up Against Bamileke Invaders', 'Yes to Democracy, No to Ethnic Domination', 'A Majority Based on Ethnic Votes is a Sign not of Democracy but of Expansionism', 'No Democracy without Protection for Minorities and Indigenes' (see Geschiere & Nyamnjoh 2000: 430).[5]

---

[4] 'Anglo-Bamileke' refers to the coalition between Grassfields Anglophones from the northwest and Bamileke French-speaking people from the West Province of Cameroon. During the political struggles in the early 1990s, some extremist Beti elites made use of this expression to point out the political alliance between these two ethnic groups who were associated with the SDF, the country's main opposition party.
[5] See also *Cameroon Tribune*, 14 February 1996; *Impact Trib-Une*, April-May-June 1996.

At that time, the Ngodi quarter placed itself as the vanguard of Duala resistance to the alleged Bamileke imperialism and hegemonic project. In this area, many shops or properties owned by Bamileke were attacked or destroyed by young Duala natives. In addition, a number of settlers were forced to leave Duala territory where they were living or ran a business. A local newspaper reported the misfortune of a Bamileke family who had taken up residence in the neighbourhood more than half a century ago, and who was forced into exile after their house was knocked down by autochthons.[6] And young men from the neighbourhood then looted their store, one of the oldest in the area.

But, what lay behind much of the violence against Bamileke businesses was less the hatred of allochthons by the indigenous populations than their common anxiety about the future of their community in a multi-party system that assumes the principle of elective representation but also encourages ethnic competition for the control of power and local resources. It was in the wake of this resentment of 'strangers' and the desire to preserve ethnic homogeneity, that Tour de Ville encountered difficulties when he wanted to make his home in this predominantly Duala neighbourhood.

Tour de Ville: A strange allochthon in an autochthonous neighbourhood

Because of his Bamileke origins, Tour de Ville experienced first-hand Ngodi apprehensions about being overwhelmed by allochthonous Bamileke. Some of his relatives (his wife and two of his brothers) who I interviewed in January and February 2003 confided that he had found himself in a predicament after he purchased a house in the Ngodi quarter in early 1999. His wife revealed in an interview she granted me in the *feyman*'s new residence in Nkolouloum, an overpopulated Bamileke-dominated inner city area of Douala, that:

> I know that the witchcraft accusation against my husband was just the culmination of the Duala's scheme aimed at forcing us to leave their *quartier*, and therefore abandoning our beautiful building, which many of them had always coveted. For example, when a friend of his, a French-based Cameroonian, who was the heir of the Duala family who formerly owned the building, sold him the then old and neglected edifice in 1997, he could neither undertake any work nor move in. This was due to the fact that some Duala elders from the locality were strongly opposed to the deal. A meeting of wise men was even secretly held in the *chef du quartier*'s house in order to decide what legal actions should be taken to invalidate what the elders judged as the treason of a defective and acculturated young village fellow who was

---

[6] See *Le Messager*, 12 March 1997, and especially the article 'La chasse aux Bamilekes à Douala'.

not ashamed of *brader* (selling off) the familial patrimony to a Bamileke. As we heard from our neighbours, some of the attendants even suggested that my husband's property be stonewalled, so as to prevent him from taking possession of his acquisition. (Personal communication, 29 January 2003)

For more than two years after he bought the building, the place was still in a complete shambles, often because Tour de Ville's workers, in his elder brother's words, 'were being driven away from the site by a horde of protesters armed with sticks, machetes and axes, and could no longer stand working at a place where their lives were permanently being put in danger'.[7] Mr Joseph Esso, a middle-aged Duala who had worked in the *feyman'* s compound, also recalled a number of bizarre incidents that occurred there. For example, several times, what my informant described as 'magical objects' (animal heads or blood on the walls, amulets, human excrement, etc.) were found in the vicinity. Moreover, workers were regularly injuring themselves with saws or harmers, or were falling off ladders or the scaffolding. These mishaps eventually forced him and his colleagues to abandon their work. For many people who were aware of the controversy over the *feyman*'s property, there was no doubt that the autochthons, notably the elders, were the masterminds of these manoeuvres, which aimed at 'moving the alleged Bamileke invader away from their locale', as Tour de Ville's wife stated. This belief was confirmed by the assertion that some Duala natives had decided to prevent the *feyman* and his relatives from settling in their quarter at all costs.

In public, Tour de Ville's opponents advocated the illegality of the contract between the *feyman* and the young Duala kinsman. According to some witnesses, the young man had no right to sell the parental house to a non-native without seeking the elders' advice in advance. And by acting in that way, the offender had transgressed the Duala custom that obliges a native to involve his fellow villagers in any land transaction, or to offer then food and drink, since the land belongs to the entire community and not to a single person or family. What was worse was that the agreement was negotiated in Paris between the two partners and sealed in a notary office in Douala. However, from my interviews with Ngodi residents as well as private conversations I held with some of the actors who were directly or indirectly involved in the land polemic, what emerged as the overwhelming explanation of the natives' opposition to this land transaction was the fact that the purchaser of the house was a Bamileke. Moreover, the man got in before a Duala kinsman who was also hoping to buy the same building: the Duala lost the deal because he was not able to pay the asking price of FCFA 30 million (US$ 50,000). Many Ngodi natives, who were displeased with the fact that a village kinsman had sold their ancestral land

---

[7] Conversation, 15 February 2003.

to an *allogène* at a native's expense, still considered themselves the *ayant-droits* (legal claimants) of the now *feyman*'s property, and were determined to get back their 'possession' from the so-called Bamileke usurper.

Faced with all these complications, Tour de Ville finally turned to a bailiff who issued a warning that brought the agitators back to their senses. Thus, it was only when they were threatened with legal action that the Ngodi natives allowed the *feyman* to settle in their quarter in July 1999. But the intervention of the judiciary in favour of the Bamileke did not deter the natives' determination to defend their collective patrimony against a 'Bamileke land-grabber', to use the words of one of my informants.

Although they were forced to 'welcome' an unwanted *allogène* in their midst, the Ngodi natives had never accepted the young Bamileke *feyman* as a fully-fledged member of their community. For example, Tour de Ville was best known in the neighbourhood not as a Ngodi resident but as a Bamileke kinsman. One of his most popular nicknames was 'Bams', which is the diminutive of Bamileke. In addition, his properties, notably his well, house and garage, were associated with his ethnic origin, or were named after his Bamileke background. Even my informants emphasized the *feyman*'s ethnic background.

Despite the successes he had on behalf of his residential area, Tour de Ville was always regarded as a stranger who should be kept outside political, social and economic activities. He experienced this ethnic segregation for the first time during the election for the chairman of the Ngodi Development Committee when a significant number of the elite and natives from this locale gathered together. The chairman of this committee was one of the most influential people in the neighbourhood and some of the association's leaders had used their prominent position in the past as a springboard in their quest for a political position and control over local people and land.[8] Although Tour de Ville was deeply involved in the development of the locality and was the promoter of a handful of cultural and sport activities, most notably youth movements in his locale,[9] he was prevented by some prominent members of the committee from putting himself up as a candidate. The argument his opponents put forward to block his candidature was that it would be inappropriate for a non-Duala native to be chairman of a development committee in a Duala-dominated neighbourhood. Unfortunately, the 35-year-old man was a Bamileke who aspired to the association chairmanship in a locale where many people viewed him as a wolf in sheep's clothing. When questioned about this ethnic exclusionary policy in

---

[8] For instance, one of the former Chairman of the Ngodi Development Committee (André Epessé) had been elected the CPDM sub-section president.
[9] He sponsored the self-defence group who protected the neighbourhood against thieves and burglars assisted financially some destitute people from the quarter.

relation to democracy, which implies everyone's right to stand for any position in one's locale or country, one of the contestants had this answer that he expressed in the form of question: 'Does democracy mean that Bamileke will deprive us of our lands, or that they will dominate us even in our own native land?'

Some of Tour de Ville's rivals also advocated the fact that his application did not comply with the association's rules because the man had been living in the area for only two years. Indeed, it was in the course of 1999 that Tour de Ville left the Bonaberi neighbourhood and moved to the Ngodi quarter. As one of the members of the committee (45-year-old Ebenezer Ngosso), confided to me in an interview,[10] there was a real fear among the local populations, particularly among some autochthonous elites that the committee chairmanship could fall into the hands of a stranger at the expense of the natives who had so far occupied it.[11] The committee chairmanship, the man disclosed, was a Duala preserve that should be protected from 'strangers', most notably the 'greedy Bamileke'. But some progressive Duala elites[12] who took a more pragmatic view argued that the locale needed a wealthy and generous man as the chairman of its development committee whatever his ethnic origins. The financial difficulties the association was encountering due to the scandals that the outgoing committee had been involved in required finding a new candidate who might bail out the committee's coffers. After lengthy discussions and negotiations, people finally agreed on Tour de Ville's candidature.

Nevertheless, as some informants told me, there was great expectation among Ngodi natives that no Duala would risk voting for a *Bosniaque* (another appellation of the Bamileke) against an autochthon. The day before the election, orders were passed to electors to choose the *feyman's* challengers (who were Duala natives). But at the end of the day, Tour de Ville emerged as the winner, much to the surprise of his opponents who pointed out massive fraud and voter corruption. It was alleged that some 'unscrupulous and shameless Duala fellows',[13] to borrow the words of one Ngodi native, had sided with the wealthy Bamileke in order to receive 'some bank notes'. Word had it that the *nouveau*

---

[10] The interview was carried out in one *circuit* (eating house) in the vicinity on the 23rd November 2002.

[11] This assertion was partly true, because it appeared from my investigation that during the last decade three of the five Committee Development presidents were non-Duala fellow: a Bassa and Beti have already chaired the association.

[12] Most of the Ngodi natives who stood for the *feyman* were his close friends or neighbours.

[13] These alleged 'traitors' were mostly young unemployed men from the locale who generally fawned on or buttered up the newly rich. Some Ngodi residents ironically called them Tour de Ville's *chindas* (slaves or brokers).

riche had distributed FCFA 5,000 (some sources advanced FCFA 3,000) to each elector if he would vote for him. Other members of the committee, who pointed to a lack of evidence, turned down the contestants' request to invalidate Tour de Ville's victory. The dispute over the allegedly rigged election finally led to the Ngodi Development Committee splitting into two groups after the launch of another development committee. Those who had stood against the *feyman* during the election led the dissident association, called the Ngodi Development Council (NDC). For example, the chairman of this council was the Duala native who Tour de Ville had beaten during the aforementioned election, while the secretary general was in third position.

Despite his position as chairman of the Ngodi Development Committee, Tour de Ville enjoyed very little support from his neighbours, who were inclined to espouse the Ngodi Development Council's cause. For example, a couple of months after his controversial election, the newly elected chairman convened a general meeting to appeal for popular support for his project to erect a well that could provide the neighbourhood with drinking water. To achieve the project, it was decided that each Ngodi resident would pay FCFA 1,000 as a contribution to the purchase of building materials and the payment for workers' wages. Although the quarter inhabitants were in need of drinking water, very few people turned up at the meeting called by the committee chairman. Moreover, the large majority of neighbourhood dwellers disregarded the request to cooperate. I heard from local people that some local and external elites who were associated with the CPDM ruling party persuaded their fellow natives not to bank on a project that was initiated by a Bamileke who just wanted to deceive them, as one man put it.[14] It was alleged that the government and the Douala Urban Council had released funds to finance the construction of several wells and public fountains in the neighbourhood in order to sort out the water problems many Ngodi residents were experiencing. So, in reaction to what appeared as a challenge to his authority, Tour de Ville decided to have his own well dug in his courtyard. But orders were given to his watchman not to allow any neighbour[15] to use his well for whatever reason, in spite of the fact that many Ngodi residents were experiencing daily water cuts by the SNEC, the national water company. Time and again, local dwellers – particularly the elders – tried unsuccessfully to bring their wealthy colleague back to his senses, or at least to reach a settlement with him. But every time, their efforts met with intransigence.

---

[14] Only FCFA 80,000 out of the expected FCFA 2.5m were collected.
[15] Only a handful of Ngodi residents who were close to the *feyman* were granted permission to use the man's well. They were the members of the development committee board who had backed him during the controversy over the election, and his young protégés (his *chindas*).

So, prior to the outbreak of the witchcraft accusation against Tour de Ville, many Ngodi residents, notably the local elite who were very sensitive to the social and political changes their community was going through, were already convinced that they were dealing with a dangerous Bamileke *allogène*.

The origin of the rumour: A local tragedy

In early September 2002, Tour de Ville's neighbours accused him of witchcraft-related practices. As a reporter of *Le Jeune Enquêteur*, one of the local newspapers that covered the stories explained:

> The speculation that led to physical assault and attempted murder of the accused and his relatives was triggered by the accidental death of six young men (between 18 and 27) from the Ngodi neighbourhood, who fell down a well they were cleaning and died. The well that belonged to Mr Jean-Pierre Feunda, better known in the town as *Tour de Ville*, was in the courtyard of the modern two-storey building where he was living. A few hours after the tragic incident that had all the area in a flutter, the *feyman*'s house was ransacked, while two of his new cars were burnt out by angry populations who likely would have murdered him if he had not been rescued by some of his relatives who helped him to escape from his pursuers in time. Having failed to capture the alleged sorcerer and to put him to death as people were shouting, the assailants turned against all the non-Duala natives in the neighbourhood, especially the *feyman*'s Bamileke kinsmen who endured physical and psychological assaults from excited young men armed with sticks, cutlasses, machetes and spears. These ill-fated people were singled out because of their ethnic ties with the accused, but also because they allegedly sided with the man who was accused of having brought about sorrow and distress in the Duala community. As their properties were sacked and their lives threatened, some Bamileke took refuge in the police station in the vicinity, while others organized themselves in self-defence groups to challenge their 'enemies'. To prevent what could well have degenerated into an ethnic confrontation between the autochthonous and allochthonous populations, a squad of law and order enforcers was sent into the neighbourhood to restore order. But at the sight of riot police, some young agitators began to throw stones at the policemen, who reacted by using tear gas and water to disperse the demonstrators. Intervention by the police led to the arrest of several young men from the neighbourhood.[16] (Author's translation)

According to two of my informants who witnessed the different turns of event, the allegation about Tour de Ville's involvement in the young men's death was motivated by his alleged insouciance when the ill-fated men were stuck in his well. Indeed, it was said that he and his family were having dinner

---

[16] *Le Jeune Enquêteur*, 26 September 2002, p. 5.

upstairs[17] at the time the incident occurred, and did not seem eager to rescue the victims when they cried for help. Even the shrieks of the dismayed crowd that gathered around Tour de Ville's concession did not make him come down and join the rescuers. He reportedly showed up only after the young men had died. As the brother of one of the victims observed, the *nouveaux riches* behaved as if the tragic accident had not occurred on his property. Subsequently, the *feyman* hastened to declare that the tragedy was just an unfortunate mishap that could have happened to anyone, and he paid for the transportation of the bodies of the deceased to the Lanquintinie Hospital mortuary. He even offered to assist the bereaved families in organizing the funerals but the victims' families, with the backing of the crowd, turned down his offer.

Many people were so disconcerted by what they described as Tour de Ville's astonishing attitude, especially his alleged attempt to prevent all speculation about the fatal accident, that they began to question whether he had in fact not been involved in the young men's awful deaths. The pervasive suspicion that surrounded this tragedy later found its expression in insinuating gossip and witchcraft speculation levelled at the *feyman*. In Mr Roger Epouma's accounts,[18] for less than an hour after the terrible incident, what had until then been simple apprehension grew into an intoxicating rumour that spread throughout the Ngodi quarter like wildfire. It was being whispered that Tour de Ville was responsible for his young workers' deaths, and that his attentiveness towards the relatives of the deceased was a subtle way of masking his guilt. All the nail-biting gossip later led to the accusation that the *feyman* had sold his young workers to his *mokoagne* sect and covered up their deaths with fake drownings to mislead people. This allegation was voiced by some of the relatives who publicly accused the young man of having sacrificed their parents for money, and enjoined him to bring his victims back to life, should he not want to be killed too. As soon as they heard from the deceaseds' families that Tour de Ville was the mastermind of the misfortune that affected the whole Ngodi neighbourhood, many of the onlookers began to boo or attack with stones and sticks the man they derisively called a *mokoagne man* (rich sorcerer). 'How many innocent people will you kill to satisfy your lust for money?' shouted an excited crowd.

This tragic incident finally forced the *feyman* and other 'intimate strangers' to seek refuge in their own ethnic quarter in New Bell or Bepanda. When I was

---

[17] This version was rejected by Tour de Ville's wife who explained that she and her husband were playing music at the time, and so could not hear the victims' screams for help (personal conversation, 29 January 2003).

[18] My informant, who was a Ngodi, lost his young brother in this tragic accident.

conducting my fieldwork, Tour de Ville[19] and his relatives were living in Nkoulouloum, a slum in New Bell that is mostly populated by destitute Bamileke.

When I started my research in this populated downtown neighbourhood less than three months after the outbreak of the witchcraft episodes, the story had already lost its excitement and fervour but showed no sign of fading from people's memories. In private as well as in public, especially in bars, restaurants, cafés, *circuits* (popular eating houses) and the market place, people were still talking about the young men's tragic deaths. Their hearts and souls had undoubtedly been touched by the event. Tour de Ville featured prominently in people's comments about witchcraft-related practices, particularly the offering of the six young men to a *mokoagne* sect. One day, while my friends and I were in a bar near the accused's house, I heard a man saying that he had seen the *feyman* who had lived in the quarter, and one of the others asked if he meant the *mokoagne* man who had plunged the whole neighbourhood into mourning.

Tour de Ville: A bad neighbour

In many respects, the criminalization of Tour de Ville as a dangerous sorcerer who thrived at the expense of others was the culmination of his conflictual relationship with his fellow neighbours, a disagreement that went back to the young Bamileke allochthon's decision to settle in a Duala-dominated quarter where the native populations tended to endorse the government-sponsored ethno-politics that denies allochthons and 'strangers' the right to make the most of the wealth of their neighbourhood, while at the same time compelling them to be good neighbours. This meant sharing their riches with their neighbours or using them to promote the development of the locality where they were considered nothing but 'intimate strangers'. For example, the Ngodi autochthons tolerated the presence of the *allogène* Bamileke in their neighbourhood because they expected to be able to profit from them. They even, surprisingly, allowed him to occupy an outstanding position in their neighbourhood, despite their concern about the preservation of their ethnic and cultural homogeneity in the midst of the process of 'allochthonization' of the whole city of Douala, because they viewed his wealth as an opportunity to develop their local area.

Prior to his disagreement with his neighbours, the 'intimate stranger' was generally appreciated as a good neighbour because he lived up to the hopes of others. For example, I learnt from my informants that before Tour de Ville was

---

[19] It is a pity that I did not succeed in getting in touch with the accused (Tour de Ville), who allegedly was at what *feymen* fellows generally call the *front* (the place where they perform their feats or coups) in Indonesia.

at odds with his neighbours, he regularly invited them to lavish parties and celebrations that he liked to organize in his imposing house. These occasions generally offered him the opportunity to compete with his fellow *feymen* in displays of wealth or demonstrations of generosity and munificence. The above-mentioned Mr Gaston Kwedi remembered these events at which Tour de Ville made almost the whole neighbourhood drunk, and the time when he distributed more than FCFA 3m (US$ 5,000) to the dancers and singers who sang his praises. In addition, the Bamileke, who was said to be the most affluent man in the neighbourhood, was the promoter of a handful of cultural and sports activities in his locale, notably youth movements. I was told that he once patronized a local football club (Club Santé) and l'Association des Jeunes de Ngodi (the Ngodi Youth Association) in which involved a significant number of local youth.

However, following his disagreement with his neighbours, the previously good neighbour was cast in the role of the villainous allochthonous Bamileke. Ngodi autochthons spoke evil of Tour de Ville because he had severed his relationships with many of them, especially with those who forced him to step down from his position as chairman of the Ngodi Development Committee. One Ngodi resident described him as someone who had become 'haughty and unfriendly' towards his homeland friends since resigning from the chairmanship of the local committee. As he explained:

> The Bamileke man thought that since he was the wealthiest man of the quarter, he could look down on the people as if they were *des machins* (things). He should not have been disrespectful toward us because after all he was a stranger in our ancestral land.

From another Ngodi native, I learnt that as a result of his conflicts with his neighbours, Tour de Ville had stopped financing development projects in the neighbourhood or promoting youth activities as he had done in the past.

Moreover, the locals who lacked access to drinking water were prevented from using the *feyman's* well despite efforts by the elders to bring their neighbour to his senses. One of my informants related a number of clashes between Tour de Ville and some of the neighbours who had blamed him of depriving them of drinking water. One day, there was a wedding ceremony in the neighbourhood and a group of women who were cooking wanted to get some water from the *feyman's* well but were blocked by his watchman who reminded them that the well was private property and not in public ownership. Some men intervened on the women's behalf by arguing that nobody, especially a Bamileke, had the right to appropriate water on Duala soil and it was suggested they dig their own well if they were *des vrais hommes* (brave men) and not *des simples tonneaux vides qui font du boucan pour rien* (empty vessels which make a lot of noise about nothing). One of the protesters who visibly disapproved of the man's arrogance reportedly called him a 'poor illiterate and upstart who could hardly write his name properly'. The quarrel finally led to a violent altercation between the *feyman* and the young men from the neighbourhood who smashed in the man's door and would have ransacked his house, if the *chef du quartier* (neighbourhood headman) and some elders from the locale had not calmed them down.

Conclusion: Utopian intimates and heterotopian strangers[20]

The view advanced in this chapter is that, in the present age of global ethnopolitics, it is becoming increasingly problematic to get to know strangers or to imagine a community with those whose presence among us makes us become 'strangers to ourselves' (Kristeva 1991), or brings about what Appadurai (1998: 913) cogently calls a 'radical uncertainty about ourselves'.[21] Moreover, the sense of 'deep horizontal comradeship' (Anderson 1991: 7), solidarity and friendship that is generally evident among neighbours is only possible if they share the same ethnic, racial or cultural background. Heterotopian strangers who 'dissolve our myths' and subvert the national or communal 'order of things' (Foucault 1970: xvii-xviii) can only be accepted as utopian intimates or virtual neighbours. In plain language, we tend to 'connive' with strangers only in museums and galleries or in images and pictures that delude us about our great humanism or open-mindedness. How many of us have a representation of a 'stranger' hanging on our living room or bedroom wall? And how many of us are willing to have a 'stranger' as a neighbour?

This chapter has demonstrated the pervasive autochthony/allochthony issue and the politics of belonging that appear as an unexpected conclusion of the political liberalization of the early 1990s. Both are highly relevant today in the study of African city neighbourhoods and their wealth. Contemporary African neighbourhoods have become the spaces for 'safeguarding the ancestral land' (Geschiere & Nyamnjoh 2000: 442-43) and sometimes sites of the violent exclusion of 'strangers' and allochthons who are not ethnically or racially con-

---

[20] By heterotopian strangers, I refer to strangers or foreigners whose presence is experienced by the native people and not imagined. The iconic figure of the heterotopian stranger is the asylum seeker, the immigrant, the exile, the refugee who put our degree of openness towards the Other to the test.

[21] For example, the virility and sensuality of the 'Intimate Strangers' at the KIT Tropical Museum forced the natives of Amsterdam to question their own masculinity and femininity.

nected to the other members of the locality.²² As we have seen, to retain control over the wealth of their neighbourhood, local inhabitants can cast the Other, who is considered a dangerous allochthon, in the role of the villainous sorcerer who prospers at their expense. But one can also question whether people are vilified because of their strangeness or otherness, or rather because they are members of a particular community, ethnic group or race.

The example of Tour de Ville would seem to suggest that foreigners or strangers undergo ethnic or racial discrimination in the place where they reside less because of their ethnic or racial difference with the autochthons than because they are the victims of intolerance. They are associated with a particular ethnic group, race or community that is generally perceived by the locals as a threat to their common values, their ethnic or racial homogeneity, and the wealth of their locality. For example, while the natives of Ngodi were wary of the presence of their Bamileke 'brothers' on their soil, they were, at the same time, hospitable to Senegalese, Nigerian and Asian merchants who run businesses in their neighbourhood, for the latter did not constitute a danger to the integrity and wealth of their locality. They distrusted the former because they embodied, in different ways, the social transformations many were facing with apprehension: loss of control over the local political and social landscape because of the strangers' domination. Moreover, Bamileke allegedly had the habit of 'deceiving those who trust them' or of 'accumulating everything even plots of land', as one of my informants put it. But despite their distrust of allochthonous Bamileke, the natives of Ngodi allowed Tour de Ville to gain a prominent position in their neighbourhood because they expected to make good use of his wealth, or hoped that their wealthy 'intimate stranger' would use his fortune to promote the development of their locality. Unfortunately, the Bamileke *feyman* failed to honour his moral obligation *vis-à-vis* those who were kind enough to accept him in their locale, or to live up to the locals' expectations because he prevented them from profiting from his wealth and used it instead to subjugate or weaken them.

No wonder then that the natives' interpretation of the tragic demise of their neighbours in terms of witchcraft-related practices was part of individual or collective efforts to solve a problem posed by a 'stranger' who had given many the impression of being exploitative or parasitic concerning the human, material and financial resources of their ancestral land. To paraphrase one Ngodi resident, Tour de Ville's 'unfriendly and mischievous demeanour' made the natives rightly or wrongly believe that they had set the Bamileke fox to mind Duala geese. This was because his behaviour allegedly inverted the logic of solidarity

---

²² See also Malkki's interesting study on the ethnocidal violence among social intimates in Burundi in the 1980s (Malkki 1995).

and the ethics of sharing into the selective mechanisms of redistribution. As Marcel Mauss (1985/1950) has shown, within the logic of reciprocity, the 'economy of constipation' (Bataille 1967), or the blockage of flow is seen generally as socially negative or dangerous. Moreover, if the young Bamileke *feyman* was construed as a 'bad man' or a dangerous *mokoagne man* (rich sorcerer) who threatened the very existence of the autochthonous populations, it was because he allegedly made the most of the neighbourhood's wealth at the expense of the native residents who were compelled, for instance, to buy drinking water from him. This situation made many believe that they were losing control over their ancestral land and the wealth of their locality in favour of an allochthonous Bamileke who seemed to perpetuate the domination of his ethnic group.

In the end, the deportation of the former 'intimate stranger' from their quarter, as a result of the witchcraft charge that was instigated against him, enabled the locals to restore the social order that was undermined by the presence of this treacherous allochthon in their neighbourhood. It allowed them, moreover, to recover the wealth of their territory that had been monopolized by an allochthonous Bamileke.

References

Anderson, B. 1991, *Imagined Communities: Reflections on the Origin and Spread of Nationalism*, London: Verso.
Appadurai, A. 1998, 'Dead Certainty: Ethnic Violence in the Area of Globalisation', *Development and Change* (29): 905-26.
Awasom, F.N. 2001, 'Autochthony and Citizenship in Postcolonial Africa: A Critical Perspective on Cameroon', African Studies Centre seminar, University of Leiden.
Bataille, G. 1967, *La Part Maudite. Précédé de la Notion de Dépense*, Paris: Minuit.
Bongmba Kifon, E. 2001, *African Witchcraft and Otherness: A Philosophical and Theological Critique of Intersubjective Relations*, New York: State University of New York Press.
Courade, G. (ed.) 2000, *Le Désarroi Camerounais: L'Epreuve de l'Economie-Monde*, Paris: Karthala.
Dongmo, L. 1981, *Le Dynamisme Bamileke (Cameroon)*, vol. 2, Yaounde: CEPER.
Foko, E. 2000, 'Gestion du Risque et Accumulation Communautaire Chez les Bamileke', in: G. Courade (ed.), *Le Désarroi Camerounais: L'Epreuve de l'Economie-Monde*, Paris: Karthala, pp. 177-90.
Foucault, M. 1970, *The Order of Things: An Archaeology of Human Knowledge*, London: Tavistock.
Geschiere, P. & F. Nyamnjoh 2000, 'Capitalism and Autochthony: The Seesaw of Mobility and Belonging', *Public Culture* 12 (2): 423-52.
Kristeva, J. 1991, *Strangers to Ourselves*, New York: Columbia University Press.

Malaquais, D. 2001, *Anatomie d'une Arnaque: Feymen and Feymania au Cameroun*, CERI, 77.

Malkki, L.H. 1995, *Purity and Exile: Violence, Memory, and National Cosmology among Hutus Refugees in Tanzania*, Chicago: University of Chicago Press.

Mauss, M. 1985/1950, 'Essai sur le Don. Forme et Raison de l'Echange dans les Sociétés Archaïques', *Sociologie et Anthropologie*, Paris: Quadrige/Presses Universitaires de France, pp. 145-279.

Mbunwe-Samba, P. 1996, *Witchcraft, Magic and Divination: A Personal Testimony*, Bamenda/Leiden: Phyllis Kaberry Centre/African Studies Centre.

Roitman, J. 2005, *Fiscal Disobedience. Anthropology of Economic Regulation in Central Africa*, Princeton/Oxford: Princeton University Press.

Séraphin, G. 2000, *Vivre à Douala: L'Imaginaire et l'Action dans une Ville Africaine en Crise*, Paris: Karthala.

Tabapssi, T. 1999, *Le Modèle Migratoire Bamileke (Cameroun) et sa Crise Actuelle. Perspectives Economique et Culturelle*, Leiden: CNWS.

Taguieff, P.-A. 1985, 'L'Identité Française et ses Ennemis: Le Traitement de l'Immigration dans le National-Racisme Français Contemporain', *L'Homme et la Société* 77 (8): 169-200.

Trani, J.-F. 2000, 'Les Jeunes et le Travail à Douala: La Galère de la Deuxième Génération après l'Indépendance', in: G. Courade (ed.), *Le Désarroi Camerounais: L'Epreuve de l'Economie-Monde*, Paris: Karthala, pp. 153-76.

Warnier, J.-P. 1993, *L'Esprit d'Entreprise au Cameroon*, Paris: Karthala.

5

Neighbourhood formation process: Access to housing land in Kamwokya, Kampala, Uganda

Emmanuel Nkurunziza

> *It is almost a truism that much of urban development and many of the neighbourhood-formation processes in cities in the developing world are informal in nature. However there is also compelling evidence that these developments are not anarchic but are regulated and structured by social institutions largely formed through a pragmatic process of borrowing from different normative orders or rule systems, or 'bricolage' in Cleaver's (2003) terminology. Based on recently concluded research on informal land delivery processes in Kampala, this chapter examines the process of formation of Kamwokya, one such informally developed urban neighbourhood. The formation and consolidation process of Kamwokya neighbourhood is examined through an analysis of mechanisms by which land for housing development is accessed and subdivided, highlighting the key events and actors in the process. These key actors, including micro-level state agents, are shown to be constantly crossing the formal-informal divide by performing duties that sometimes violate their legal mandate. The chapter also demonstrates the importance of social networks in informal land access, particularly those formed on the basis of primary social groupings. They not only offer immediate benefits to those transacting in land through reduced transaction costs but also enforce non-state rules within the neighbourhood.*

Introduction

In the introductory chapter to this book (Chapter 1), two approaches to the study of the neighbourhood are distinguished. In the geographical approach, the emphasis is on the functional use of the neighbourhood, focusing on the activities in which the residents of a physically bound urban territory are engaged. The anthropological approach stresses the existence of non-geographically bound social networks and interactions, a distinction that coincides with Webber's (1964) concepts of 'community of space' and 'community of interest' respectively. The two approaches do not exclude one another and this chapter utilizes both approaches. The first part of the chapter focuses on the nature of Kampala's Kamwokya neighbourhood with respect to its spatial characteristics and the socio-political and economic activities of its inhabitants. The position of the neighbourhood within the city space is examined by looking at its place within the local government structure and its general population characteristics. The following part of the chapter then uses the lens of land access processes to understand the manner in which the neighbourhood of Kamwokya has evolved from being a rural village to one of the city's most densely populated settlements. An attempt is made to examine sequentially the process of acquiring rights to land for housing development, the actors involved and the procedures followed. What is demonstrated is the fact that neighbourhood development, even in so-called unplanned informal settlements, is not entirely organic or unstructured but follows procedures that are well-known to the inhabitants of the settlement in question.

This chapter is based on a study undertaken as part of a comparative research project aimed at understanding the institutions that underpin and regulate informal land delivery processes in six African cities, including Kampala. The fieldwork for the study in Kampala was conducted between September 2002 and January 2003 and covered three neighbourhoods, including Kamwokya. Understanding that a phenomenon as complex as informal land delivery processes needs the complementarity afforded by utilizing both quantitative and qualitative data, a multi-method data collection approach was adopted.

Data were collected using a combination of document review, questionnaire survey, interviews and focus-group discussions. Documentary review, involving the gathering of both published and grey secondary material, served two important purposes. First, secondary sources were helpful in providing the important background information necessary to facilitate the collection of primary data by guiding the construction of primary data collection instruments such as interview schedules. Secondly, secondary data aided the construction of a clear picture of the economic and social-political milieu within which the management of land in Kampala, and Uganda in general, has evolved from pre-colonial times to the present. A household survey to map the key activities and actors involved in the process of accessing land for housing development was conducted. The survey, conducted using structured interviews, not only assisted in collecting primary data on the prevalence of informal processes but also provided pointers to issues that needed in-depth investigation using qualitative approaches. The subjects of the survey were landholding heads of household who were randomly selected from the three case-study settlements. Semi-structured interviews were utilized in this study to elicit important information from key informants at different administrative levels. At the national, city and division levels, semi-structured interviews were conducted with key policy-makers and administrators, particularly those concerned with land policy, tenure and registration, land use and planning. These respondents were very valuable in providing insights into land policy issues otherwise not available in the public domain. To ascertain the history and politics of settlement development, general socio-economic characteristics of the study settlements and the roles played by various actors, semi-structured interviews were conducted with key informants at the settlement level, including Local Council chairpersons, community elders, knowledgeable residents and land brokers. Interviews at this level were less structured and more informally conducted than those with officials at the national and city levels. Semi-structured interviews were also conducted at the settlement level with selected heads of households with a view to triangulating and probing further data obtained from focus-group discussions and the household survey. Focus-group discussions were also used as one of the principle data collection methods. The discussions were aimed at eliciting information on the different ways in which households of different socio-economic categories access land for housing and the relative importance of these land access mechanisms. In an attempt to understand the social milieu within which informal land delivery processes operated, focus-group discussions were used for collecting data on settlement dynamics such as growth patterns, subdivision processes, local politics and the social regulation of land transactions.

Neighbourhood profile

Location
Kamwokya II is a parish in Kampala Central Division (see Map 5.1). It is one of the two parishes (the other being Kamwokya I) that cover an area called Kamwokya. The name 'Kamwokya' is said to have come from the word

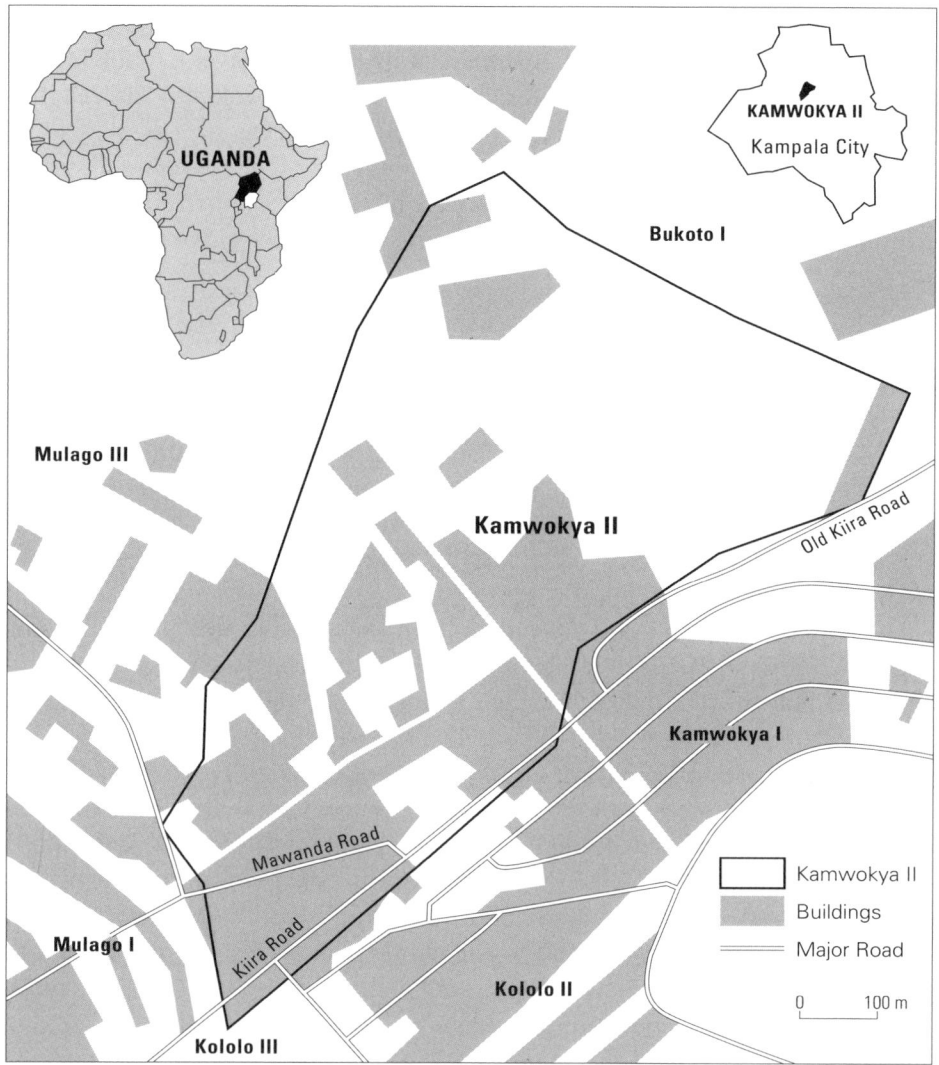

Map 5.1 Kamwokya neighbourhood

Kanjokya literally translated as 'It [the sun] is burning me', referring to the sunscorching experience of walking through the area (Wallman 1996). The parishes of Kamwokya I and Kamwokya II are physically separated by Old Kiira Road, a main road that in fact divides them into different neighbourhoods. While Kamwokya I is a formally developed area that was originally set up for Asian civil servants working for the colonial administration and is currently predominantly occupied by relatively wealthy households living in high-cost housing,

Kamwokya II is a typical informal settlement largely inhabited by low-income households and characterized by poor-quality housing and rudimentary infrastructure services. Kamwokya II is the focus of this chapter and hereafter any reference to 'Kamwokya' should be taken to refer to Kamwokya II. Indeed, this is consistent with the way in which the inhabitants of the two areas identify themselves. While residents of Kamwokya II identify themselves as living in Kamwokya, the inhabitants of Kamwokya I often identify their area as Kisementi, named after one of the popular pubs or social centres in the area.

Housing characteristics

Kamwokya's general spatial structure is typical of most of the unplanned saturated settlements in the city. With the exception of a few houses located along Kiira and Mawanda roads, most dwelling units are arranged in a haphazard manner, rarely in conformity with any of the city's formal planning and building regulations. Most access routes in the neighbourhood are not accessible by car and very often accommodate multiple uses including food vending and other petty business activities. They also act as play areas for youths and serve as a dumping ground for domestic waste.

As far as the dwellings are concerned, Kamwokya has a mixture of housing types ranging from rudimentary temporary shacks to high-cost block-walled-tile-roofed houses. The latter are mainly located along Kiira and Mawanda roads which form the southern and southeastern boundaries of the neighbourhood. Indeed, these small belts of high-quality housing signify a transition from the predominantly low-income informal developments that characterize Kamwokya to the more affluent formally planned neighbourhoods of Kololo II and Kololo III. The majority of the dwellings in Kamwokya are of a semi-permanent or temporary nature, made of mud walls and rusty tin/iron roofs. About 60% of the houses are of mud and wattle, while over 70% have cement-screed floors. The majority of the houses in the neighbourhood are of the *muzigo*[1] type.

While the study on which this chapter is based did not deal with house-rental issues, it was evident that the majority of the residents in Kamwokya rented their dwellings. Indeed, most of the landholders surveyed had rental premises on their plots accommodating an average of about 3 households. The prevalence of rental tenure in Kamwokya is consistent with the general pattern of Kampala as a city where about 70% of households rent their homes (Uganda Government 1992). Kamwokya is a particularly attractive neighbourhood because of the availability of affordable rental accommodation in close proximity to the city centre, albeit with limited or no services. Monthly room rentals (without

---

[1] These are single-room tenements built in rows with as single building having a number of such rooms, each accommodating at least one household (plural: *mzigo*).

electricity) range from about Ushs 10,000[2] to Ushs 25,000. For rooms with electricity, rents start from about Ushs 30,000 upwards, depending on the level of extra-servicing in terms of water supply and accessibility. Business rentals for activities such as salons, phone-card/accessories vending, retail shops or tailoring/shoe repair businesses were higher, some charging about Ushs 100,000 per month or more depending on factors such as the social relationship between the transacting parties. While in the more formal areas of the city a tenant is often required to pay about 3-6 months in advance, there is greater flexibility in Kamwokya where rent is invariably paid on a monthly basis and in some cases can even be paid in two or three instalments over the course of a month.

Generally, the level of infrastructure service provision in the neighbourhood is rudimentary. Hardly any of the typical rental tenements have on-site water sources although a number of the houses owned by the few affluent households have piped water and reticulated sewerage facilities. Indeed, most Kamwokya residents, especially if they are tenants of the same landlord, share toilet facilities, which are invariably ordinary pit latrines. It is also not unusual for people from different homes to agree on modalities of sharing toilet facilities. For instance, there are households that rent latrines at about Ushs 5,000 per month if they have no space to dig their own. This is normally an agreement between landlords for the benefit of their tenants. The lack of space for erecting pit latrines is exacerbated by the fact that most homesteads are not easily accessible, making it difficult to use emptying trucks.

Economic activities

The main economic activities undertaken by Kamwokya residents within and outside the neighbourhood include small-scale businesses (petty trade) such as shops selling groceries, vegetables, fruit and charcoal; food vending and the sale of *Waragi*;[3] tailoring; hair salons; butcheries; shoe-repair stalls and carpentry. Most of these enterprises are located along the main access roads that traverse the neighbourhood. Although the neighbourhood's dwellings are intended to be primarily residential, they tend to have a multi-purpose role: the front rooms or verandas (in the case of single-room dwellings) are very often used for petty-trade activities while the back rooms are the living quarters. In some cases extensions to the dwellings have been built along footpaths and access routes for this purpose.

---

[2] US$ 1 = Ushs 1,800 at the time of the survey.
[3] Local gin widely brewed in the countryside and sold in most low-income neighbourhoods.

Evening markets[4] are found along the main access routes into the neighbourhood targeting residents returning from work in the city centre who often buy snacks, foodstuffs or ready meals on their way home. These markets are locally called *toninyira mukange*, literally translated as 'do not step on mine'. The name of the markets symbolizes the overcrowded nature in which the items on sale are arranged and the fact that they are spread out virtually in the middle of access routes. The situation is made more precarious by the fact that there is often limited lighting as vendors depend on the use of small tin paraffin candles locally known as *tadooba*. In such conditions it is possible for the goods on sale to be stepped on and the market's name is a signal to both vendors and clients to walk carefully lest they destroy someone's source of livelihood.

Political process at neighbourhood level
This section provides an understanding of the basis of political activity and social organization at neighbourhood level, highlighting both the *de jure* and *de facto* decision-making mechanisms. It describes the *de jure* local government system as provided for by existing local government statutes but also outlines what happens in practice.

In the local government arrangement, Kampala has a district status, which is the highest level of local government. Being the only city in the country, it has a unique system of Local Council (LC) structure, which is unlike any other municipality or district. Local government law has established the following hierarchy for Kampala:

Zone	Local Councils (LC I)
Parish	Local Councils (LC II)
Division	Local Councils (LC III)
District	Local Councils (LC V)

Kampala does not have an LC IV Council because it is both a municipality and a district. The city of Kampala comprises five major divisions (Rubaga, Central, Nakawa, Makindye and Kawempe) and the two newly formed divisions of Makerere University and Kyambogo, which are home to the universities of Makerere and Kyambogo respectively. Kamwokya neighbourhood is on the second rung of the local government administrative hierarchy (described below), referred to as Local Council II (LC II) or Parish. Within the neighbourhood there are 10 zones (LC Is), which form the lowest tier of local government, namely: Central, Kifumbira I, Kifumbira II, Mawanda Road, Market Area, Contafrica, Kisenyi I, Kisenyi II, Green Valley and Church Area.

---

[4] Part of the reason for selling stuffs in the evening is to avoid city-council law enforcement forcers who would confiscate the traded merchandise because of both the illegality of street vending and the demand for taxes.

The highest political organ in a local government unit is a council comprised of elected members representing constituent electoral areas and special interest groups, such as the youth, the elderly, people with disabilities, and women. With the exception of representatives of the youth and people with disabilities, who are elected through electoral colleges, all other representatives are directly elected through a secret ballot system. It is a requirement that women form at least one third of the members of these councils. The manner in which the council is elected and its composition is meant to ensure ample representation of all sections of the population. A chairperson who is directly elected by universal adult suffrage heads the council and is answerable to it. At the LC I level, the council consists of persons of 18 years of age or above residing in the zone. It is the members of the constituent village/zone executive committees that make up the council at LC II (parish) level. The election of the LC I executive is such that the chairperson is elected by secret ballot by all the members of the council. It is the elected chairperson who nominates candidates for the various positions on the executive. The council is then asked to make a choice from the nominees, often by a show of hands or by lining up behind their preferred candidates. Invariably the chairperson nominates individuals who are close to him, often those who assisted him/her in getting elected. This often results in the chairperson assuming a domineering role *vis-à-vis* the other members of the executive.

The functions of an administrative unit council are, *inter alia,* to resolve problems identified in the area, monitor the delivery of services within its area of jurisdiction, assist in the maintenance of law, order and security, and to carry out functions assigned by a higher local government council. From interviews with LC I chairpersons in Kamwokya, it was clear that most of them view their role in the zone as being unlimited in scope and indeed they intervene in, and are consulted on, all sorts of activities in their areas of jurisdiction. Besides being part of the local-government hierarchy, they see themselves as the legitimate successors of traditional institutions in an area with a highly heterogeneous population. They thus constantly cross the formal-informal divide by performing duties that are outside their legal mandate. They do this in a number of ways: by re-interpreting the law to suit the circumstances in their areas of jurisdiction; by exercising discretion in the execution of their legal roles and often straying into illegality; by inadvertently violating the law because of a lack of adequate knowledge of the relevant legislation; by confusing their official roles and their presumed customary functions; and through personal benefits in the form of bribes and other incentives that accrue from participating in illegal activities.

Because of the incongruence between a Local Council's *de jure* and *de facto* roles, there are often conflicts with other authorities – such as chiefs and deconcentrated civil servants – operating at this level. The position of a chief at the Division and Parish levels, appointed by the District Service Commission, is provided for by the LGA. The Chief is the administrative head and accounting officer of the respective local administrative unit. S/he is also charged with the responsibility of ensuring implementation of district and government policies and programmes in their areas of jurisdiction. Because of the involvement in oppressive politics in the past, the position of chiefs in the current local government structure remains controversial. Indeed, the system of LCs, originally called RCs (Resistance Councils), was introduced by the current National Resistance Movement (NRM) government to replace chieftainships as one of the ways of promoting grassroots democracy and reverse citizen disengagement with the state resulting from past oppressive regimes (Mamdani 1995). Chieftainship in Uganda was promoted by the British during the colonial era and inherited, with minor modifications, by successive post-colonial governments. The chiefs, who were political appointees, held executive, judicial and legislative powers over the areas under their control. By introducing RCs, the NRM government sought to trim these powers and leave the chief as a civil-servant administrator. Chiefs, therefore, play a marginal role in the management of local affairs and often play second fiddle to LCs, who enjoy significant levels of legitimacy amongst their constituents.

The local council system in Uganda was designed to create opportunities for participatory decision-making at all levels and has been quite successful in achieving this (Devas & Grant 2003). There are multiple opportunities for citizens, including the poor, to participate in public meetings and elections, from the village level to the district. Gender and minority interests are protected by law through reserved seats for women, youth and the disabled at each level. Other provisions to enhance citizen participation at the local level include the legal requirement that LCs meet at least once every two months. Such meetings are chaired by a speaker or his/her deputy elected by the councillors from their ranks. These meetings are supposed to be open to the public and require the attendance of at least half the councillors to constitute a quorum. To enhance transparency and accountability, even an ordinary citizen living within the jurisdiction of the local government in question is entitled to a copy of the minutes of a council meeting, as long as s/he pays the fee prescribed by the council. However as Steffensen *et al.* (2004) point out, there have been few instances of ordinary citizens applying for a copy of council minutes. Some councillors have also made an effort to summarize the proceedings of meetings and the key decisions taken, and have communicated them to their constituents.

There are also a number of provisions in the LGA and other decentralization guidelines that provide links between local government and civil society. The planning guidelines for local government provide for the participation of civil-society organizations in the planning process as well as the incorporation of civil-society plans into those adopted by the local governments under whose jurisdiction they operate. NGOs are playing an increasingly significant role in the monitoring and evaluation of service delivery by local governments. Furthermore, procedures for the preparation of local-government budgets require the conducting of annual open budget conferences, which has promoted interaction between local government and citizens on local priorities.

Despite the above-noted provisions for citizen participation in local politics and the involvement of all sections of the population in the management of the affairs of their locality, and notwithstanding the reasonable success that has been attained in that respect over the past decade or so, there remain significant problems with the way the system operates in practice. These include:

- The requirement for elected councillors to report back to their constituents has been criticized for not being systematic and effective (Francis & James 2003). Often constituents are not aware of the decisions made by their councils. Moreover, although there is the opportunity for the public to purchase council minutes, this provision is rarely utilized. Participation by ordinary citizens is also constrained by high levels of illiteracy.
- The requirement to hold LC 1 public meetings every two months is often disregarded and even when these meetings take place there are limitations on the effective participation of certain groups, such as women, youth and the poor.
- Conflicts and antagonism have been reported between chiefs and other technical staff and elected leaders, often as a result of inefficient communication mechanisms (Francis & James 2003).
- There is a marked dominance of chairpersons, particularly at LC I level, over executives and councils because of their much stronger political mandate and the fact that they nominate the executive.
- It has also been noted that councillors, even at LC 1 level, are almost exclusively drawn from households in the highest income tercile. Francis & James (2003: 329) claim that this is because 'poorer individuals cannot afford the "goodwill gestures", such as beer, soap, or salt, handed out as an inducement to potential voters in elections at all levels of local government'. As a result, the poor tend to be sidelined in terms of positions of responsibility within their areas and their voices are often drowned out by those of their better-off neighbours.
- The principle of reserving seats on councils for women and other disadvantaged groups has also had limited impact on the effectiveness of the participation of such groups in the affairs of their areas. Councillors elected by such a process tend to have limited legitimacy compared to

counterparts elected by universal adult suffrage. Women councillors are reported to be generally inadequately equipped with the skills required for public office (Ahikire 2003).

Neighbourhood development process

Despite the old and rusty physical nature that currently characterizes Kamwokya settlement, its urban history is relatively short. This section traces and illuminates Kamwokya's urbanization process and the rapid transformation of the settlement's land uses from those of a predominantly non-urban nature to a high-density urban neighbourhood. The origins and growth of Kamwokya can only be understood within the overall city development context. A brief account of the historical origins of Kampala and its growth, particularly the urban structure/administrative duality introduced by colonialism, are presented below. Against this background, the formation and consolidation of Kamwokya is examined in the subsequent sections.

Historical context
To understand the nature of contemporary land access processes, it is important that the social context and history within which they have evolved and operate is clear. As pointed out by Berry (1994), the urbanization trajectory in several developing countries has been significantly influenced by historical contingencies, particularly colonial rule. Uganda is no exception and the evolution and growth of Kampala has been, to a considerable extent, influenced by colonial rule and its legacy. This section therefore presents, albeit briefly, the historical context within which the emergence and development of Kamwokya neighbourhood occurred. Of particular importance are the effects of colonial rule on the nature of landholding, and the duality of urban development in present-day Kampala that was occasioned by colonial policies.

Unlike most other urban areas in Eastern Africa, Kampala grew out of an indigenous town, Kibuga (located on Mengo Hill), which had been the royal capital of the Kingdom of Buganda since the 1700s. Foreigners including traders, colonizers and missionaries who entered the kingdom had to first get clearance from the *Kabaka*[5]*,* and Kibuga, therefore, became their first port of call. When Lugard (British colonial agent) arrived in Kibuga in 1890, he set up a fort on the site of today's Old Kampala, a hill adjacent to Mengo but not commanded by it, choosing it and not the more vulnerable site that the *Kabaka* had suggested (Southall & Gutkind 1957) (see Map 5.2). While the *Kabaka*

---

[5] Title for the king of Buganda.

initially exercised discretion as to who to admit to the kingdom and allocated them different hills in Kibuga for settlement purposes, this changed once the colonial machinery was in place. Arguably, the most significant changes in the levers of power in the kingdom were brought forth by the 1900 Buganda Agreement. These were to have important implications for the way Kampala developed as an urban area.

The 1900 Buganda Agreement, which constituted the political settlement between the colonizing power and the indigenous Ganda state, had a significant influence on the way the development of Kampala proceeded in at least two ways. Firstly, the land settlement clause in the agreement effectively divided the area on which the current city is built into two zones of differing tenurial regimes. It removed the existing forms of landholding and introduced two systems of tenure namely Crown landholding and *mailo* land tenure, with the former being vested in the imperial power while the latter was divided between the *Kabaka* and his officials. The term *mailo* came from the English word *mile* because the allotments were measured in square miles pronounced as *mailo* in the local dialect. The nature of holding shows that *mailo* land is owned on the same principles as English freehold, although the former is often encumbered by occupants who lived on the land under various forms of pre-colonial tenure (Mukwaya 1953). The introduction of the two forms of land tenure added another dimension to an urban area that was divided into a 'native' and 'European' city. On the one hand, there was the *mailo* portion of the city, referred to as Mengo, where land was in the hands of a few big landowners but occupied and used by households under traditional rules. The relationship between the landowners and occupants of *mailo* land was mainly regulated by a socio-political relationship that drew on pre-colonial practices (Nkurunziza 2004a). Kamwokya is located in the *mailo* part of the city. The eastern part of the city was, on the other hand, made Crown land by the 1900 Buganda Agreement. This meant that it was under the control of the colonial administration and all customary occupants of the land were tenants at sufferance. Consequently, all government urban developments were sited on this land, which was readily available for public purposes. The growth of the formal city therefore proceeded eastwards in alignment with the tenurial divisions that had been placed on the city.

The second influential point of the 1900 Buganda Agreement came by way of the political and administrative arrangements negotiated between the native

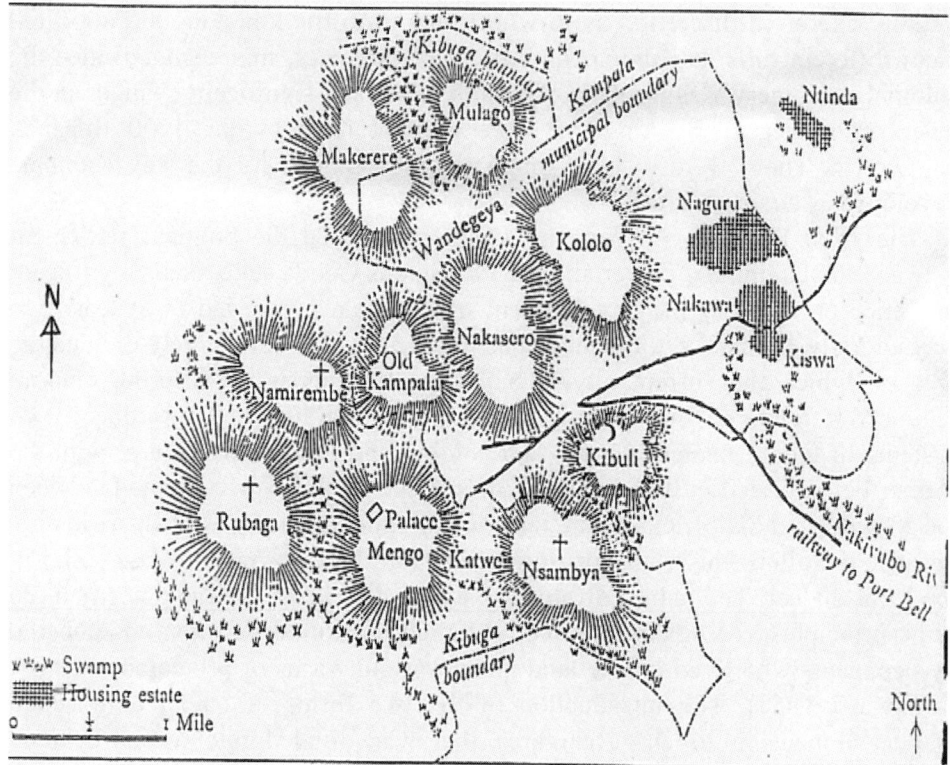

Map 5.2 The hills that made up Kibuga/Mengo and Kampala
(From: *Kampala Urban Study, Part II: Structure Plan Final Report*, p. 102)

Buganda government and the colonial administration. The agreement left the administration of most native affairs in Buganda to the *Kabaka*'s government.

This meant that the part of present-day Kampala then called Mengo municipality was fully controlled by the native government. Citing the 1900 Agreement, the native government always protested against interference in the management of affairs involving the native population, including the administration of land in the *mailo* part of the city. As a result, all the urban development plans and layouts were limited to the then Crown land areas of present-day Kampala. Indeed, two municipalities – Mengo[6] (Kibuga*)* and Kampala – developed under different land management and administrative regimes, with Kampala being formally planned while Mengo evolved organically and was devoid of any formal physical planning arrangement. The end of colonial rule was expected to mark the disappearance of the duality that had pervaded the

---

[6] Kamwokya was in this part of the city.

city but because of the constitutional arrangement that maintained the powers held by the *Kabaka*'s government, no such change occurred immediately. It was only after the 1966/7 political crises between the central government and the Buganda government (Nkurunziza 2004b) that all the urbanized areas around Kampala, including Mengo Municipality, were brought under a single administration (Kampala City Council) and became subject to similar legislative controls, at least in theory.

Restrictions preventing native populations from living in the formal part of the city resulted in a number of neighbourhoods emerging in Kibuga, particularly along the border separating the two entities. Kamwokya is one such neighbourhood that developed, accommodating natives who often commuted to the 'European' city for manual and other unskilled work.

The nascent nature of Kamwokya's urbanization process is illustrated by how recently most of the landholders (house owners) in the settlement acquired the plots on which they settled. As can be seen from Figure 5.1, most landholders in the neighbourhood acquired their plots after 1980, primarily in the 1990s. The data depicted are corroborated by interviews with long-standing residents in the neighbourhood who indicated that in the 1960s and 1970s there were only a handful of scattered homesteads in the area. According to these same neighbourhood elders, land in Kamwokya belonged to a few chiefs in the native Buganda government, who were largely absentee landlords. In their absence, these chiefs appointed stewards, locally referred as *Basigire*, to look

Figure 5.1 Date of plot acquisition

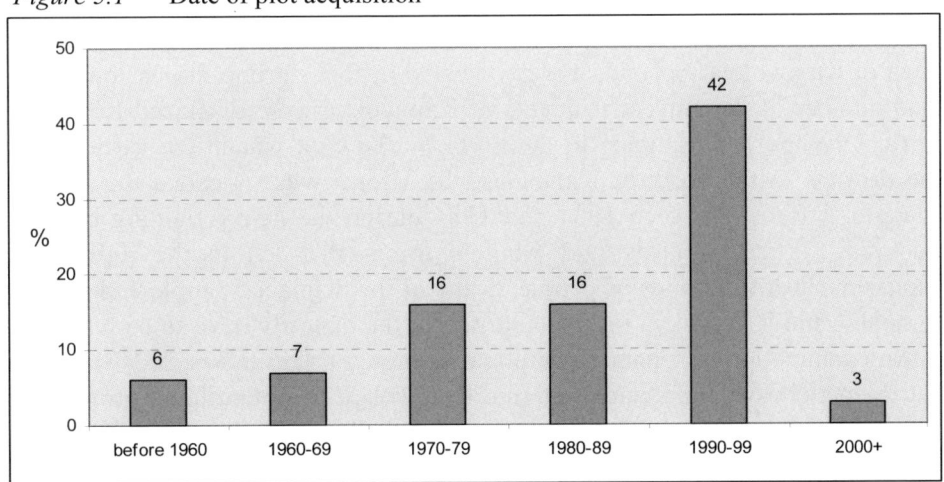

Source: Author's own survey, 2002

after their estates. The *Basigire*, in turn, rented out often large parcels of the land (*Bibanja*) under their care for cultivation, initially to Ganda commoners and later to immigrants from other parts of the country, and collected tributes for their masters (chiefs/landlords). It was often the *Bibanja* holders who invited their friends and relatives to share their holdings in what constituted some form of sub-letting. In line with traditional Ganda culture, those who were given plots of land expressed their appreciation by presenting a *Kanzu* (traditional Ganda dress for men), although this evolved into different forms and 'sizes', including cash of varying amounts. With the growth of Kampala and Kamwokya's proximity to the city centre, land values in the area increased and the form of *Kanzu* became cash and its size – in terms of the amount of money paid – also increased.

A number of explanations for the tremendous surge in land market activities in the 1990s were proffered by interviewees and participants in focus-group discussions held in the neighbourhood, most of which are closely linked to the country's political economy dynamics. First, like the rest of Kampala, the return of peace and security, which was absent in the 1970s and early 1980s, encouraged many people to acquire land, since they saw an opportunity for uninterrupted stable settlement. The assumption of power by the NRM government not only brought relative peace and stability but also a new set of political, military and business elites. Most of them were eager to acquire land and establish expensive structures, often using loans generously extended to them by the now-defunct Uganda Commercial Bank. The new elite took advantage of existing land tenure laws and their financial/political power to displace households from areas that were in public ownership, thereby pushing poor households onto swampy areas and other less attractive locations, such as much of Kamwokya. Second, it was revealed in focus-group discussions that a good number of the current residents of Kamwokya were displaced from rural districts that border Kampala to the north by the civil war in the early 1980s. The districts to the north of Kampala, which form what is called the Luwero Triangle, suffered between 1981 and 1984 during the heavy fighting between Museveni's guerrilla army and Obote's forces that led to the deaths and displacement of thousands of people. Some of the displaced people ended up in Kampala , and Kamwokya in particular where the majority have since settled.

An examination of Uganda's political economy (Nkurunziza 2004b) reveals that the pattern of land acquisition and Kamwokya neighbourhood growth and consolidation have mirrored the country's political and legal history. One of the characteristic features of Uganda's post-colonial history is the vacillating fortunes of urban and rural populations. In the 1970s, individuals and households escaped from insecure urban centres to the relatively peaceful rural areas, but in the early 1980s the hitherto relatively secure countryside was invaded by violence and war, driving people back into the cities. The comparative peace and security experienced in Kampala since 1986 has provided individuals/households with the confidence to invest in long-term assets such as land, whereas in the 1970s any signs of wealth, including land ownership, would attract the attention of and often violent attacks by Amin's soldiers (Sathyamurthy 1986). Recent policies aimed at women's emancipation and gender equality

---

Box 1: *Acquiring land through purchase from a private landowner*

Once the seller and the prospective buyer have been brought together and the buyer is interested in the plot in question, what follows is a process of bargaining with each party trying to secure the best deal possible. In a minority of cases, landowners – particularly absentee-landowners – give land brokers the authority to undertake bargaining on their behalf as long as they can deliver a reserve minimum sum of money at the end of the transaction. Similarly, prospective buyers, particularly those living and/or working outside the country, may use agents – relatives, friends or land brokers – to negotiate the transaction on their behalf. In most cases, however, the negotiations[7] are conducted between the landholders themselves and prospective buyers. Negotiations often centre on the price of the land and the mode of payment, and it is unusual for negotiations to be concluded during the first meeting, as often the parties need to go home to confer with their families before returning with a final commitment or a fresh offer. During the course of negotiations, as at every stage of land access, the parties employ various means, primarily recourse to social networks and other informal institutions, to minimize transaction costs. There are a number of issues that those transacting in land in Kamwokya take into consideration during the price negotiation process. These include the existence or absence of a registered certificate of title, the size of the plot, its physical location, its level of servicing and tenurial attributes. There are distinct sub-markets in titled and untitled land, with land transacted in the former being much more expensive than that in the latter. The difference in value between titled and untitled land is a reflection of both the cost of processing land titles and the extra security of tenure conferred by the possession of a land title. Indeed the first question most prospective land buyers in Kampala ask sellers is whether the land in question is titled. The buyer is then able not only to estimate the risks involved in buying the land but also the value bracket in which the land falls, subject to investigation of its other important attributes. The difference in value between titled and untitled land in the three settlements studied was estimated[8] to be about 65% to 75%, if other factors are constant.

---

[7] Such negotiations are often very discreet until the final agreement is reached and those intended as witnesses to the sale agreement are informed.

[8] In the absence of any published data on land prices, focus-group discussions involving land brokers were used to arrive at these estimates. This information was triangulated with estimates obtained from the Principal Valuer, Kampala City Council on 15 December 2002.

have provided opportunities for women, who can now acquire land in their own right, something that was almost unheard of in the past.

Modes of land access

Like most other informal settlements in Kampala, most households in Kamwokya currently access housing land through informal commercial channels. About 76% of the landholders surveyed in the neighbourhood accessed the plots on which they have settled by buying them from private individuals (see Box 1), while 83% of all the landholders in Kamwokya used informal channels to acquire land.

Given the nature of Kampala's terrain, which is dominated by hills and often swampy valleys, there is always a distinction between what has come to be referred to as 'wet' and 'dry' land. Because of the difficulties associated with developing 'wet' land and the environmental hazards that inhabitants of such land are exposed to, prices of plots in such areas are much lower compared to those in 'dry' areas. Besides titling and terrain, there are other factors that relate to the physical attributes of the plot, ownership details and neighbourhood characteristics. With regard to physical attributes, the obvious factor is the size of the plot. Most households in Kamwokya occupy plots smaller than the minimum standard set by Kampala City Council, primarily because they cannot afford larger plots of land. Generally, land prices are affected by the level and quality of the infrastructure and social services available on the plot or in the immediate neighbourhood. In the Kamwokya, while services were considered important – plot access in particular and water sources – their absence does not seem to have deterred households from seeking a place to live here. To those heads of household we talked to, concerns about services were less important than securing a piece of land where they could put up a shelter.

Table 5.1   Methods of land access in Kamwokya

Mode of acquisition	Frequency	Percentage	Valid percentage	Cumulative percentage
Bought	68	75.6	75.6	75.6
Allocated by traditional authority	1	1.1	1.1	76.7
Inherited	12	13.3	13.3	90
Gift from relative or friend	8	8.9	8.9	98.9
Other	1	1.1	1.1	100
Total	90	100	100	

Source: Author's own survey, November 2002

The only significant non-commercial channels of land acquisition are inheritance (see Box 2), mainly from parents and which had benefited 13% of the surveyed households, and gifts of plots from friends and relatives, which accounted for about 9% of the housing land supply in the neighbourhood (see Table 5.1).

Evidence from qualitative interviews, however, suggests that even within non-commercial channels some form of payment is made, as it is traditional for a grantee to offer a *Kanzu* to the grantor as a sign of appreciation. There were hardly any households in Kamwokya that reported having benefited from the administrative allocation of land. Before the enactment of the 1998 Land Act, much of the land in Kampala was held by Kampala City Council (KCC) under a statutory lease from the Uganda Land Commission. The City Council, therefore, had the responsibility of allocating land to eligible applicants but even before the changes ushered in by the new land law had taken effect, most City Council land had been allocated to the affluent, invariably in the formally planned areas of the city. Senior KCC officials, including the Chief Town Planner, have since declared that they no longer have any land to offer to applicants (*The New Vision*, 14 October 2002). Interestingly, in all the focus-group discussions held in Kamwokya, there was unanimous acceptance of, or resignation to, the fact that administrative land-allocation mechanisms were not meant for them (the poor). On the contrary, the focus-group participants viewed government agencies as 'land grabbers'. This land-grabbing tag derives from the occasional compulsory acquisition of land with little, delayed or no compensation. To them, the state is constraining rather than enabling in their quest for housing land and its subsequent development.

Attractions of the neighbourhood
As in most other residential neighbourhoods in Kampala, the primary motivation for households to acquire land in Kamwokya is to satisfy their shelter needs, while at the same time providing space to generate income by letting part of their premises or to conduct a home-based business activity. About 60% of landholders in Kamwokya use their land both for accommodating their own families and also for earning extra money by renting out rooms. The major factors influencing contemporary transactions in land are different from those that were obtained during the earlier years of land markets in Buganda (in the 1940s and 1950s). The overriding factor in the land market in the 1940s and 1950s was the socio-political benefits associated with private land ownership (Mukwaya 1953), while contemporary transactions, at least in Kamwokya, are primarily driven by the need to secure a basic livelihood.

Box 2: *Acquiring land through inheritance – custom and legal provisions*

After buying, the second commonest way of accessing land is through inheritance, which is largely guided by custom as opposed to legal statute. Under Ganda customary practice, issues of inheritance and disposal of property are decided by the family and clan members at the last funeral rites *(kwabya olumbe)*, which take place up to a year after the burial (Bikaako & Ssenkumba 2003). During the celebration of the last funeral rituals, the widowed spouse is socially elevated to a position of *namwandu* (widow) or *semwandu* (widower). It is also at this ceremony that clan provisions to cater for the welfare of the widowed and orphaned are announced (Kyewalyanga 1976). These include, *inter alia,* levirate marriage (rarely), settling inheritance issues, the adoption of orphans into the extended patrlineal family and, most importantly, the appointment of an heir to the deceased. As is custom, the heir is the eldest son or the eldest male relative in the patrilineal line. If the heir is a minor, the clan appoints a caretaker *(omukuza)* to look after his interests until he is mature enough to take over these responsibilities. The shares of the estate allocated to the male offspring of the deceased are determined by the clan in cases where there is no *bulamo* (will, which is sometimes orally communicated by the deceased to the clan head or another elder in the clan). The heir receives the largest share, including the family house although the widow is allowed to continue occupying the house until she remarries, dies or leaves voluntarily.

One of the reasons why inheritance claims continue to be settled through customary channels is the inadequacy of existing formal provisions. The law relating to marital property in Uganda is basically the common law of England as at its date of inception (1902). The Marriage Act and the customary Marriages (Registration) Decree 16 of 1973, which provide for the celebration of marriages are merely procedural. They have no provisions as to how marital property is to be held or distributed on the termination of a marriage. In common law, real property is presumed to belong to the person in whose name it is held, which is invariably the husband's. For this presumption to be rebutted, the divorced woman is required to provide evidence to the contrary. She has to provide documentary evidence of receipts to show her financial contribution to the property she is seeking a share in, or other cogent evidence. In discussions with a number of practising lawyers in Kampala it emerged that such cases are very hard to win and most women seeking a divorce are hesitant about making claims against property that is registered in their husband's name. The situation is worse for women who separate after years of cohabiting with their partners. According to legal experts in Kampala, there is no presumption of marriage or marriage by repute in Uganda and the Divorce Act, 1904, which is still in force, makes no provision for persons who chose not to marry under the recognized forms of marriage. Because of this, there are no legal provisions to determine what will happen to property they acquired jointly. Invariably women walk away from such relationships without receiving any share of the previously jointly held property.

Apart from the general motivations for buying land, households opt to acquire land in particular locations for reasons relating to the neighbourhood in general and the plot in particular. Attributes of plots of land are varied but Figure 5.2 provides a summary of the different reasons why households acquired land in Kamwokya.

Figure 5.2 Attraction to neighbourhood

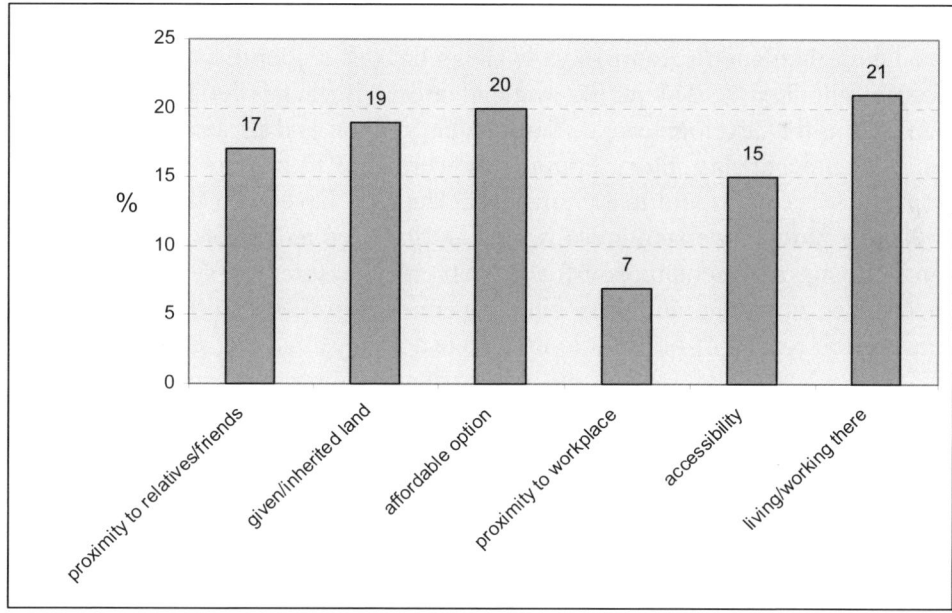

Source: Author's own survey, November 2002

The data presented in Figure 5.2 indicate the most important factors as perceived by the respective landholders, although follow-up qualitative interviews revealed that virtually all of them had more than one reason for their choice of location. Nevertheless the key factors can be determined as affordability, the place of habitation at the time of plot acquisition and proximity to relatives and friends. Of the landholders, 21% acquired their current plots because they happened to be living or working in the area. Indeed, further investigation revealed that the majority (67%) of those who acquired land in Kamwokya lived in the area, invariably as house renters (61%). As was pointed out with respect to other African urban areas (Epstein 1969), migrants from rural areas who come to Kampala often seek out their kin and kith relations who assist them in securing a foothold in their new environment. It is, therefore, often the case that these migrants begin their urban lives by sharing accommodation with their more established urban relations before gradually being able to rent their own *mizigo* from which they might eventually acquire land and put up their own dwelling. While some of these new urban residents may move to other areas of the city, depending on what opportunities are available, a large number of them establish their roots in the receiving areas which they are, invariably, most conversant with and in close proximity to the relatives and friends who invited them to the city in the first place.

A substantial number of landholders in the neighbourhood indicated that they had acquired their current plots because they could afford them. This is not to suggest that land in Kamwokya is cheap but this response came mainly from people who had settled in the wetland areas. Because wetlands are legally inalienable for development, difficult to build upon and present environmental hazards to occupants, many households were able to acquire plots of land at nominal fees, often paid to LC officials. The LCs have been implicated in the selling of plots in wetland areas, which are gazetted as inalienable government land. Being representatives of the state at the micro level, they present themselves as having authority over government property in their areas. They thus exploit formal institutions to undertake activities that are, strictly, illegal.

Although not cited as the most important factor by the majority of landholders, proximity to friends and relatives was a major consideration in the settlement decision process in virtually all households. This is reflected in the way families have settled in some form of family/tribal clusters within the Kamwokya neighbourhood. There are, for instance, two zones – Kifumbira I and Kifumbira II – in the northeastern quarter of the neighbourhood named after the *Bafumbira* tribe because most of the inhabitants are from that tribe. This is notwithstanding the fact that *Bafumbira* are a small tribe that originate from the most southerly part of Uganda (about 1000 km from Kampala) on the border with Rwanda. From interviews and focus-group discussions it emerged that most Bafumbira who come to work in Kampala, often on the invitation of kin already in the city, settle in Kamwokya and other neighbouring areas. The same pattern as that described for the *Bafumbira* is discernible in other tribes, creating tribal sub-neighbourhoods or enclaves within Kamwokya (Basham 1978). It has even been suggested by a number of scholars (Mitchell 1969, Basham 1978) that urban residence enhances tribal/ethnic identity among people who rely upon primary social networks for support, a phenomenon that Michell refers to as 'supertribalization' For Basham (1978), urban tribal identity cannot be reduced to a mere expression of primordial sentiment but it is instead an idiom for recognized continuity in social relationships and for the largely economic conditions that underlie such continuity. As far as Kamwokya is concerned, focus-group discussions revealed that the kin and kith affinity was most important in the earlier stages of neighbourhood evolution (1960s) when the area was still sparsely populated and unsafe to live in. The first inhabitants then often invited their kin to join them to enhance their security, not only against physical hazards but also as protection against possible eviction from the land they occupied.

Another geographically significant factor, which did not receive top ranking from many households, was accessibility to the city centre and other employment areas. However, during focus-group discussions, participants cited proximity to the city centre as being a major attraction for renters in Kamwokya. They thus argued that it made economic sense to acquire a plot of land in Kamwokya because it provided an opportunity to earn income by putting up rudimentary rental accommodation. There is such a high demand for rooms to rent in Kamwokya that most of the houses, including those built in the swampy and poorly accessible areas, are often booked out from when construction starts.

Housing land availability

To illuminate further the process of neighbourhood formation and consolidation, data on how different households obtained information on the availability of housing land in the area was collected. The predominant source of information about land availability is friends, neighbours or relatives, and was utilized by 92% of the landholders in Kamwokya. Forms of informal information exchange that are based on trust embedded in close familial bonds help minimize land transaction costs. Besides trust, strong systems of social control are more likely to be encountered in primary social groups (Wirth 1938). According to Wirth, 'identity' and 'continuity' are the two key ingredients of an effective system of social control. Rules would be meaningless unless they could be enforced, but to achieve this presumes the ability to locate the individuals concerned so as to apply the necessary sanctions. As Wirth correctly argues, identity and continuity are crucial factors in the 'locating' process because it is the combination of the two that implies knowledge of an individual's future whereabouts, which is essential for the implementation of sanctions for his past or present behaviour. Henslin (1968) reinforces and extends Wirth's arguments by introducing the concept of 'trackability', referring to the continuity achieved by knowledge of a person's network of family or friends. He argues that knowledge of an individual's social networks and his/her place in these networks provides an alternative route by which an expectation of continuity is generated, uncertainty is reduced, and social control is secured in urban situations. The importance of kin/kith networks as a source of information is thus critical in informal settlements where formal institutions and property rights are dysfunctional.

Land brokers, the informal version of estate agents, come a distant second to kin-kith networks, benefiting just over 3% of the households. In a focus-group discussion with land brokers operating in the neighbourhood, participants were adamant that their contribution was much more than that reflected by responses from the households in the survey. On further discussion, the land brokers presented a number of scenarios that might explain why very few households acknowledged them as their source of information on plot availability. First, they intimated that once they get information on the availability of a plot for sale, they spread the word by talking to a variety of people within and outside the neighbourhood, just in case they happen to know of a buyer. It is these people who eventually inform friends, relatives or neighbours who might be searching for housing land. Although land brokers are involved in the conclusion of the transaction, it is the friends/relatives/neighbours that are credited with availing the information to eventual buyers. To the land brokers, this partly explains why they receive little credit as a source of information on plot availability. Second, the land brokers argued that most of them are, first and foremost, part of the community in which they operate, only using brokerage as a secondary activity. They are thus viewed by friends/relatives/neighbours and by some of their clients not necessarily as 'estate agents'. This is reinforced by the fact that they do not charge buyers any fee, as the sellers invariably pay for their services. How much these particular scenarios could have affected the responses is hard to quantify, but what is undeniable is the overwhelming reliance on informal social networks for information on plot availability.

One mechanism of information exchange that was conspicuously not mentioned by any of the landholders in our sample was advertisements in the print or broadcast media. While newspapers and FM radio stations are becoming popular places for placing advertisement of plots for sale in the more affluent and high-cost housing neighbourhoods, their use by sellers in informal settlements is virtually absent. Besides the most obvious reasons of limited access to newspapers, high rates of illiteracy and the expense, there was a common perception amongst the landholders interviewed that plots of land advertised in newspapers are 'problematic'. Their argument was that advertising a plot in a newspaper implied that it had most likely been shunned by those with an intimate knowledge of it and was thus being marketed to those less likely to know the problems associated with it. For them, it is preferable to buy directly from someone you know (or is known to someone you know) as a form of guarantee of authenticity instead of buying, in their words, 'damaged goods' marketed through 'to whom it may concern' (in the public media).

Land use changes and land subdivision

To provide further understanding of Kamwokya neighbourhood's formation process, this section presents data on the nature of land uses when the current landholders acquired their plots (on average 10-15 years prior to the study). Much of the currently settled land in the neighbourhood was acquired fairly recently. Given that most plots in the neighbourhood were under non-urban uses (cultivation, bush and grazing) before they were acquired by their current holders (see Figure 5.3), it would seem that urban uses in the settlement are relatively recent. The progression from non-urban to urban uses is locally marked by ceasing to call the particular piece of land a *kibanja* and instead referring to it as a *poloti* (from the English word 'plot'). This nomenclature change, in essence, seeks to communicate the development density change that often accompanies the urbanization of land.

Figure 5.3 Plot use at acquisition

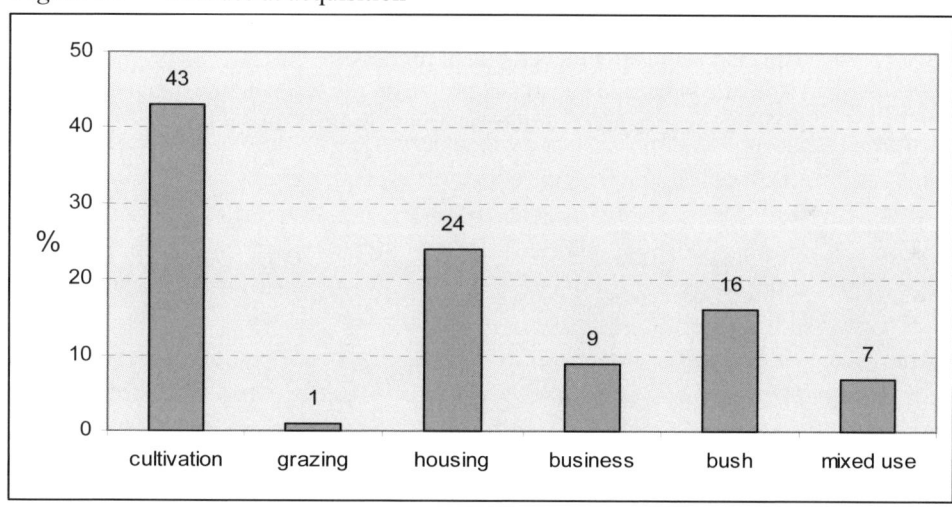

Source: Author's own survey, November 2002

One important fact to note about the land acquisition and neighbourhood consolidation process in Kamwokya is that they were never spontaneous in nature as often reported of informal settlements elsewhere, particularly in Latin America. For instance, in the wetland areas of the neighbourhood, actual settlement was preceded by some form of agriculture, particularly the growing of yams and sugar cane. This was aimed, first of all, at staking and consolidating a

Photo 5.1 The land acquisition/development process
(Note the yams and sugarcane grown on the land and the trenches dug to drain the area and provide materials for brick-making.)

Photo 5.2 Reclaimed and settled area in Kisenyi II zone, Kamwokya
(Photos: Emmanuel Nkurunziza)

claim to a piece of land and, secondly, at helping to drain it while at the same time harvesting any crops for consumption and/or sale. The cultivation was then followed by the erection of temporary structures, which would then be gradually improved *in situ* as the household consolidated its claim to the piece of land. It is this form of land access that we have chosen to call 'self-allocation' rather than squatting because invariably some form of payment would be made to LC I executives before any development could proceed. Once settled, the new landholders would then subdivide their hitherto agricultural plot (*bibanja*) to sell to other families seeking housing land.

Land subdivision
Because of the close proximity of Kamwokya to the city centre and, therefore, high land values, most households could not acquire plots larger than what they actually required for accommodation for themselves. According to data collected for this study, the average plot size in Kamwokya, at acquisition, was about a quarter of an acre, the median size was only 0.15 acres and the modal plot size was about 0.02 acres. Fewer than 22% of the households in the neighbourhood acquired a plot bigger than 0.25 acres, which is about the standard size of a residential plot in Kampala.

The generally small plot sizes in Kamwokya were cited as part of the reason why most households have not subdivided their plots. Over 80% of the landholders in the settlement had not subdivided their plots since acquiring them. However, even those landholders with relatively large plots argued that they would rather erect rental accommodation on the extra space than part with any section of their land through subdivision for sale. Kamwokya is a popular area where low-income earners like to rent, mainly because of its proximity to the city centre and employment and the availability of accommodation at affordable prices.

Not surprisingly, the majority of the households that have subdivided their plots did not seek permission to do so. Most of the household heads interviewed did not seem to understand[9] what 'seeking permission' actually meant and that is why about 17% of them did not respond to the question. Even most of the 39% who said that they had asked for permission suggested that the best way to put it is that they 'informed the authorities' rather than 'sought permission' because they felt that they were entitled to do whatever they liked with their land. The sentiment that there was hardly anything like 'asking for permission' to subdivide land became even more apparent when those who had not sought permission were asked why they had not done so. The majority – 71% of them

---

[9] The issue was not a lack of comprehension of the question posed to them but rather unfamiliarity with the requirement to seek subdivision permission.

– felt it was not necessary to ask for permission since they owned the land in question. This is both a reflection of the ubiquitous ignorance that there is of regulations and laws relating to land and the autonomy exercised by certain social fields from formal institutions. The other 29%, who seemed to be aware of subdivision controls and the necessity to seek permission, did not do so before subdividing their plots because they thought the process was cumbersome, lengthy and expensive. They thus chose the option that minimized transactions costs.

Among the few that 'sought subdivision permission' or rather 'notified the authorities', more than half (55%) consulted LCs or Chiefs.[10] It also emerged that notifying the authorities about plot subdivision mainly occurs when the purpose of the subdivision is immediate sale, in which case it is often the buyers who insist on involving the local authorities (LCs). This is one of many examples that demonstrate the astuteness of actors in informal settlements in determining when to use formal institutions to their advantage but to circumvent them when prohibitive costs are involved. Only in rare circumstances is permission sought from Kampala City Council (KCC), as required by law, although this is the only route through which land titles for the subdivisions can be obtained.

The 1964 Town and Country Planning Act and the 1964 Public Health Act authorize KCC to control development and enforce land development standards in the city. This includes the provision and enforcement of subdivision guidelines. In the absence of detailed planning schemes for most parts of the city, KCC requires any landowner intending to undertake a subdivision to seek permission from the Chief Town Planner (CTP). Once such an application has been submitted to the CTP, s/he, at the cost of the applicant, orders a location survey, which is used as the basis for the piecemeal planning of the location of the land in question. Very often private land surveyors[11] undertake the preparation of the subdivision layouts and only seek endorsement by the CTP. This practice is, however, only likely to be encountered in the city's more affluent suburbs. Despite the explicit and elaborate powers conferred upon KCC by existing legislation, the planners interviewed – both at divisional and city levels – confessed to being powerless when it came to controlling development

---

[10] Before the introduction of LCs in 1986, their current roles were held by local administration Chiefs. Thus, those who subdivided after 1986 consulted LCs, while those who did so earlier are likely to have consulted Chiefs.

[11] From interviews with KCC staff at division level it emerged that planners and surveyors employed by KCC undertake such work on a private basis and are paid by landowners, even though this is what they are employed to do. Because they are insiders, they find it much easier to have their layouts approved and are thus preferred, by clients, to freelance operators.

and the use of private land, particularly *mailo*. To the CTP, this powerlessness is partly borne out of the limited capacity in terms of material and human resources available to his department and, to a greater extent, a result of lack of political muscle to confront the vested interests of different urban actors.

The effect of political pressure on the performance of KCC's land management technical officers has been voiced by several other senior KCC personnel in various fora. For instance, in *The New Vision*, the Chairman of Nakawa Division was reported to have told the parliamentary sessional committee on public services and local government that political interference was the cause of the failure to plan the city. He is reported to have said that any attempts to destroy illegal structures or stop people from building on reserves and swamps were thwarted by politicians who interfered in the process. In the same presentation, he was quoted as saying that 'we have very many powerful people and I don't want to risk the lives of my officers. ... big people are building in road reserves, in swamps, but we just look on' (*The New Vision*, 25 March 2002). State actors and agencies are thus subjected to varying forms of pressure as they engage with other social actors, which consequently results in the ubiquitous incongruence between what state laws and regulations prescribe and what is actually implemented. During the study on which this chapter is based, there were several reported cases of informal urban land subdividers using patronage networks to accentuate their autonomy from formal institutions through the protection provided by their political godfathers from being punished for violating city planning regulations. This is a clear case of what Migdal (2001) calls an incoherent the state, exemplified here by some of elements of the state (political leaders) forming alliances with non-state actors (informal land subdividers) to undermine state institutions.

Conclusion

This chapter has attempted to increase understanding of African urban neighbourhoods by examining the process of formation of Kamwokya II settlement in Kampala and the salient day-to-day activities of its inhabitants. The chapter took a 'neighbourhood' to be a spatially bound unit within an urban area in which the residents are actively involved in various activities to enhance their well-being, and examined some of the economic and socio-political activities that characterize Kamwokya neighbourhood. Also of interest was the manner in which such a unit comes into being and this was explored by looking at how an area that was originally sparsely populated has, over time, been transformed into a high-density urban neighbourhood. The land access and subdivision process has provided an appropriate channel through which Kamwokya's formation and consolidation process can be examined. Land access processes, even in an informal settlement like Kamwokya, are not necessarily haphazard or spontaneous but instead proceed through mechanisms which, despite not being as predictable as formal processes, are often well known and adhered to by the actors involved. The key actors in the process, including those acquiring land and those disposing of it, have been shown to draw, in a largely pragmatic manner, from social rules of varying provenance, including the state and traditional custom. Cleaver's (2003) concept of 'bricolage' fits this process of pragmatic borrowing from different normative orders or rule systems quite well. The discussion has also demonstrated the importance of social networks in informal land access, particularly those formed on the basis of primary social groupings. They not only offer immediate benefits to those transacting in land through reduced transaction costs but also form the basis of enforcing non-state rules within the neighbourhood.

The critical influence that social context can have on the manner in which the formation and development process of a neighbourhood proceeds is important. In the case of Kamwokya, the settlement emerged as one of those enclaves on the edge of the exclusive 'European' Kampala municipality, primarily to accommodate native Ugandans who were only allowed to enter the formal city to work. Furthermore, the administrative and land management duality that existed between Kampala and Mengo meant that Kamwokya and the rest of Mengo developed outside the purview of the formal planning regime enforced in the European-settled Kampala municipality. In essence, the informal nature of Kamwokya has its roots in this period. The influence of context is not limited to the colonial period but has extended into the postcolonial era. The pattern of Kamwokya's development has followed the political and economic fortunes of the country, as exemplified by the general stagnation in the chaotic 1970s and the rapid densification during the relatively peaceful 1990s.

References

Ahikire, J. 2003, 'Gender Equity and Local Democracy in Uganda: Addressing the Challenge of Women's Political Effectiveness in Local Government', in: A.M. Goetz & S. Hassim (eds), *No Shortcuts to Power: African Women in Politics and Policy-Making*, London: Zed Books, pp. 213-39.
Alonso, W. 1964, *Location and Land Use: Toward a General Theory of Land Rent*, Cambridge, MA: Harvard University Press.
Basham, R. 1978, *Urban Anthropology: The Cross-Cultural Study of Complex Societies*, Palo Alto: Mayfield Publishing Company.

Berry, B.J.L. 1994, 'Africa's Urban Future: From Nation-States to a System of Regions', in: J.D. Tarver (ed.), *Urbanisation in Africa: A Handbook*, Westport, Co: Greenwood Press, pp. 439-61.
Bikaako, W. & J. Ssenkumba 2003, 'Gender, Land and Rights: Contemporary Contestations in Law, Policy and Practice in Uganda', in: L.M. Wanyeki (ed.), *Women and Land in Africa: Culture, Religion and Realizing Women's Rights*, London: Zed Books, pp. 232-78.
Buchanan, J. 1965, 'An Economic Theory of Clubs', *Economica* 32: 1-14.
Christaller, W. 1966, *Central Places in Southern Germany*, translated by C.W. Baskin, Englewood Cliff, NJ: Prentice Hall.
Cleaver, F. 2003, 'Bricolage and Natural Resource Management', in: T.A. Benjaminsen & C. Lund (eds), *Securing Land Rights in Africa*, London: Frank Cass, pp. 11-30.
Devas, N. & U. Grant 2003, 'Local Government Decision-making – Citizen Participation and Local Accountability: Some Evidence from Kenya and Uganda', *Public Administration and Development* 23: 307-16.
Epstein, A. 1969, 'The Network and Urban Social Organisation', in: J.C Mitchell (ed.), *Social Networks in Urban Situations*, New York: Humanities Press, pp. 77-116.
Francis, P. & R. James 2003, 'Balancing Rural Poverty Reduction and Citizen Participation: The Contradictions of Uganda's Decentralization Program', *World Development* 31 (2): 325-37.
Gharai, F. 1998, 'The Value of Neighbourhoods: A Cultural Approach to Urban Design', University of Sheffield, Department of Architecture.
Henslin, J. 1968, 'Trust and the Cab Driver', in: M. Truzzi (ed.), *Sociology and Everyday Life*, Englewood Cliff, NJ: Prentice Hall, pp. 138-58.
Kyewalyanga, F.X. 1976, *Traditional Religion, Custom and Christianity in East Africa*, Hosheschaftlarn: Klaus Renner Verlag.
Losch, A. 1954, *The Economics of Location*, New Haven: Yale University Press.
Mamdani, M. 1995, 'The Politics of Democratic Reform in Uganda', in: P. Langseth, J. Katorobo, F. Brett & J. Munene (eds), *Uganda: Landmarks in Rebuilding a Nation*, Kampala: Fountain Publishers, pp. 229-40.
Migdal, J.S. 2001, *State and Society: Studying How States and Societies Transform and Constitute One Another*, Cambridge: Cambridge University Press.
Mitchell, J.C. 1969, 'The Concept and Use of Social Networks', in: J.C Mitchell (ed.), *Social Networks in Urban Situations*, New York: Humanities Press, pp. 1-50.
Mukwaya, A.B. 1953, *Land Tenure in Buganda: Present Day Tendencies*, Kampala: The Eagle Press.
Nkurunziza, E. 2004a, 'Informal Land Delivery Processes and Access to Land for the Poor in Kampala, Uganda', International Department, University of Birmingham Working Paper No. 6.
Nkurunziza, E. 2004b, 'Informal Land Access Processes in Kampala, Uganda: A Legal Pluralist Perspective', Unpublished PhD thesis, School of Public Policy, University of Birmingham.
Rosen, S. 1974, 'Hedonic Prices and Implicit Markets: Product Differentiation in Pure Competition', *Journal of Political Economy* 82: 34-55.
Sathyamurthy, V.K. 1986, *The Political Development of Uganda: 1900-1986*, Aldershot: Gower Publishers.

Sennet, R. & R. Cobb 1972, *The Hidden Injuries of Class*, New York: Vintage.
Southall, A.W. & P.C.W. Gutkind 1957, *Townsmen in the Making: Kampala and its Suburbs*, Kampala: East African Institute of Social Research.
Steffensen, J., P. Tidemand & E. Ssewankambo 2004, *A Comparative Analysis of Decentralization in Kenya, Tanzania and Uganda: Country Study – Uganda*, Copenhagen: Nordic Consulting Group.
Uganda Government 1991, *National Population and Housing Census*, Entebbe: UPPC.
Uganda Government 1992, *A National Shelter Strategy for Uganda, Volume I*, Kampala: Ministry of Lands, Housing and Urban Development.
Van Nostrand, J. 1994, *Kampala Urban Study, Part II: Structure Plan Final Report*, Kampala: Town and Country Planning Board.
Wallman, S. 1996, *Kampala Women Getting By: Wellbeing in the Time of AIDS*, Athens: Ohio State University Press.
Warren, D. 1981, *Helping Networks*, South Bend: Notre Dame University Press.
Webber, M. 1964, 'Urban Place and Nonplace Urban Realm', in: M. Webber *et al.* (eds), *Exploration into Urban Structure*, Philadelphia: University of Pennsylvania Press,
Wirth, L. 1938, 'Urbanism as a Way of Life', *American Journal of Sociology* (44): 1-24.

6

Urban space, gender and identity: A neighbourhood of Muslim women in Kano, Nigeria

Katja Werthmann

> *Much anthropological research in African cities has focused on the formation of migrant communities and is frequently connected with the assertion, defence or invention of collective identities. This chapter explores women's contributions to shaping theses processes. A study of a neighbourhood of Muslim women in Kano, northern Nigeria, has shown that urban women develop a sense of community and identity that relates very specifically to the physical and social space they inhabit. Their identification with one particular neighbourhood is based on the physical properties of the neighbourhood and on the women's shared social status as wives of civil servants. The formation of friendships among women neighbours is based on and reinforces their sense of belonging.*

As noted in the introduction to this volume (Chapter 1), neighbourhoods have often been the focus of sociologists, geographers and anthropologists working in cities. For the sociologists of the Chicago School, city quarters constituted 'natural areas' that were further subdivided into 'community areas' and 'neighbourhoods'. For anthropologists, urban neighbourhoods were social and spatial units equivalent to the culturally homogeneous face-to-face communities they ideally studied in more rural areas. Individual identification with a neighbourhood is likely to be more pronounced if extensive social relationships are maintained within the socio-spatial unit. Whether a 'neighbourhood' as a community of significant others in an urban environment consists of a street, a block or a quarter depends both on the physical features and the symbolic boundaries drawn by its inhabitants (Hunter 1974).

Many studies in African cities have focused on the formation of migrant communities,[1] which are frequently connected with the assertion, defence or invention of ethnic identities. Beyond the domain of marriage strategies, the role of women in shaping these processes of collective identity formation in cities has received little attention. While African urban women traders and businesswomen, for instance, have been described as powerful economic and political actors (see, for instance, Clark 1994, Horn 1994, Robertson 1984, Sheldon 1996), their social relations seem to centre on kin and marriage. Women in urban Africa, however, do not only interact with family but also with neighbours, friends, customers and strangers, and move and interact in specific physical and social spaces.

Based on fieldwork carried out in a neighbourhood of Muslim women in Kano in northern Nigeria, this chapter shows how urban women develop a sense of belonging that relates very specifically to the physical and social space they inhabit. These women's identification with one particular neighbourhood is centred on their shared social status as wives of civil servants, on the physical properties of the neighbourhood, and on the formation of friendship among neighbours.

The police barracks in Kano

Kano is nowadays the largest city in northern Nigeria, a poly-ethnic urban centre with an estimated three million inhabitants (see Map 6.1). The centuries-old town wall, of which only parts remain today, still represents not only a physical but also a cultural barrier between the ancient Muslim quarters and the more recently built areas of the city. Many inhabitants of the Old Town (*birni*) rarely venture into the residential areas where non-Muslims and non-Nigerians settle, and many other inhabitants such as southern Nigerians, Lebanese or Europeans have never set foot in the Old Town. In terms of typology, Kano represents a typical 'dual' or 'hybrid' city where the ancient city is spatially separated from city quarters built since the colonial period, and where different communities or 'life worlds' coexist without necessarily overlapping.

In the Old Town of Kano, a local police force was established in 1925 under the colonial Native Authority. Its members were recruited from among former soldiers and members of the Emir's palace guards, and this local authority force patrolled the streets of the Old Town at night. The first barracks of the Native Police Force in the Old Town were built in 1925 but the police barracks referred to in this chapter consist of 48 houses that were built in the southeastern part of

---

[1] For an overview of classic urban research in Africa, see Hannerz (1980).

the Old Town in 1952/53.[2] These barracks are situated at an intersection between the Old Town and modern Kano and unlike other police or army barracks they are not surrounded by walls and gates. At its inception these police barracks – a terraced housing estate – resembled neither older quarters nor a *zongo* (strangers' quarter) as in many West African cities.

Originally I did not plan to carry out fieldwork in these police barracks but instead on Muslim Hausa women and Western education. This project did not materialize for various reasons, the most important being the closure of schools

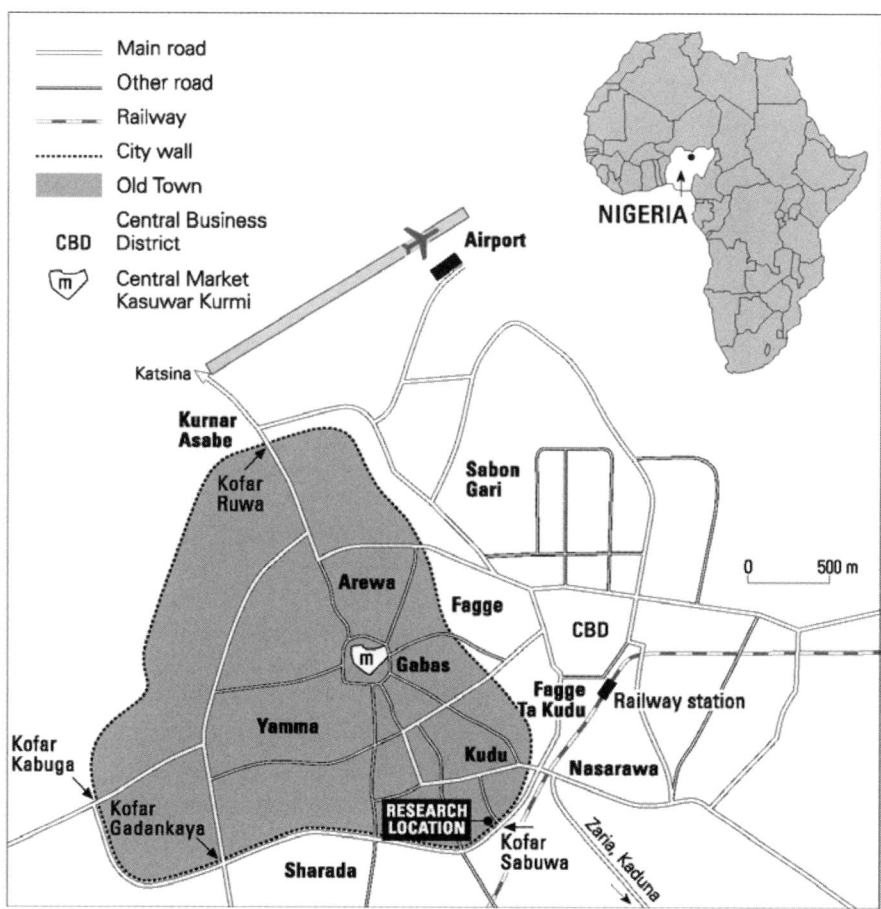

Map 6.1   Metropolitan Kano showing the Old Town

---

[2] Between 1992 and 1994 I conducted 18 months of fieldwork in Kano, visiting it for the last time in 1998. The house where I stayed was situated right next to the longest row in the police barracks (see Figure 6.1).

and universities in 1992 due to political disturbances (see Werthmann 2000). I was staying in a house right next to the barracks that had been used by foreign students and researchers for a long time (Werthmann 2004), so I turned to exploring the everyday lives of women in my neighbourhood in the Old Town of Kano, some of whom I had already come to know through brief conversations and visits.

Photo 6.1 Aerial view of the police barracks
(Source: Geonex 19/11/91, Kano Town, 157 91 C27, 1:6,000)

Unlike traditional quarters in the Old Town of Kano or *zongo* in other cities where neighbourhoods are often formed on the basis of common regional or ethnic origins, the *bariki* were characterized by the absence of relationships based on kinship or ethnicity. Many of the barrack's inhabitants at the time I worked there did not originate from Kano but were northern Nigerian Muslims who spoke Hausa as their first or second language. Most of the policemen held lower ranks and while many of the men had received secondary education, the majority of the married women had not gone to school, although they did have some Koranic education and some of the women attended adult literacy classes. Many of their daughters attended school up to secondary level, which was unusual in the context of the Old Town. Due to early marriage, many girls in the older quarters of Kano still only reach primary level.

There was a fairly high turnover of people – especially women – moving in or out of the barracks, although some families had been living there for more than twenty or even thirty years. Men normally move out of the neighbourhood if they are transferred or when they leave the police service. Women usually have to leave the barracks after a divorce or the death of their husband. Between March 1992 and October 1994, 11 women from 10 households (out of a total of 22 households that I studied more closely) moved out. Six women left after being divorced or ran away in order to get divorced, two co-wives moved away with their husbands, one woman was widowed, and two divorced women who had been staying with their mothers remarried. In addition, eight girls got married for the first time and went to new homes. With the exception of one man who moved to a new home and one man who died, no other men in those 22 households left the barracks within that same period of time.

Space and gender

The architectural layout of the barracks differed from that of houses and compounds in the Old Town of Kano. This was particularly evident in the division and allocation of space to men and women. In larger traditional houses and compounds there is a gradual passage from the outer to the interior rooms. A female visitor moves successively to the more exclusive spaces where access is restricted for most outsiders. This passage leads through the entrance room (*zaure*) to more rooms and passageways (such as *bfar gida* and *shigifa*) to finally the interior courtyard – the women's quarters (*cikin gida*). Even in smaller houses, the entrance room zaure serves as a threshold or a kind of filter between the outside and the inside. Whereas female relatives and visitors as well as children or servants (sometimes including male servants or clients who are classified as 'sons' of the household head) are allowed to pass through the entrance rooms and to proceed into the *cikin gida*, male visitors without specific kinship ties to household members are not allowed access beyond this point. The male members of the household receive male visitors in the *zaure*, and young unmarried sons spend the night there.

In contrast to more traditional houses, the houses in the barracks had only one small entrance room called a *zaure*, which was too small to receive guests. It had lost its function as a room for social gatherings and merely served to protect the interior from being seen from the outside. Moreover, the houses in the barracks lacked sufficient space and shade in front of the entrance door to put a bench or to spread mats. Consequently, men did not gather in or near their houses as they might do in a more traditional setting. Instead, they retreated to a place opposite the local mosque, or they did not spend their leisure time in the neighbourhood at all. Thus, during the day the houses and the entire housing area became an almost exclusively female domain.

Each house in the barracks had two rooms and a kitchen. If a man had two wives, each wife inhabited one room, the husband taking turns in visiting them at night. Even if there was only one wife, the other room was often used for older children who no longer slept in their mother's room. Whereas in large traditional compounds the household head's room (*turaka*) is often the most exclusive (and most interior) room, which may not be entered by male visitors or even by wives without permission, most men in the barracks did not have a room of their own. In the barracks, the *cikin gida* began right behind the *zaure* and was used almost exclusively by women and children, men being absent for most of the day. Thus, the seclusion of women inside the houses corresponded with the exclusion of men from the domestic realm.

The layout of the barracks also had an impact on the composition of the families. Both family and age structures in the *bariki* were different from those in older quarters: the households mainly consisted of nuclear families and, as the policemen tended to move away upon retirement, there were hardly any elderly people in the settlement. In contrast to compounds that are inhabited by extended families encompassing three or four generations, families in the barracks consisted of only two generations – parents and children. Houses in the barracks were rented so most men tried to buy or build their own houses before retirement. Moreover, due to a lack of space, it was impossible to accommodate other relatives for long periods of time or to expand the houses because alterations were not permitted. Unlike quarters in Kano's Old Town where local networks were based on kinship and ethnic origin, the *bariki* were distinguished by an absence of kinship ties. Many women in the *bariki* had no or only a few relatives in Kano and some went to see their families of origin once a year at most, sometimes even less frequently.

Although the women in the barracks complained about the absence of relatives, they nevertheless preferred the layout of the barracks to other urban settlements. In contrast with houses in the Old Town as well as buildings in the modern residential areas, they described the barracks as clean and functional. The cement walls and corrugated iron roofs indicated a clear difference with the more rural-looking buildings made of mud bricks. The houses were not situated too close to each other but were not so far apart as to prevent contact with neighbours in times of need, for instance when a woman gave birth and needed help. If there were two wives – and thus the potential for jealousy – their rooms were, at least, of equal size.[3] However, many women would have preferred

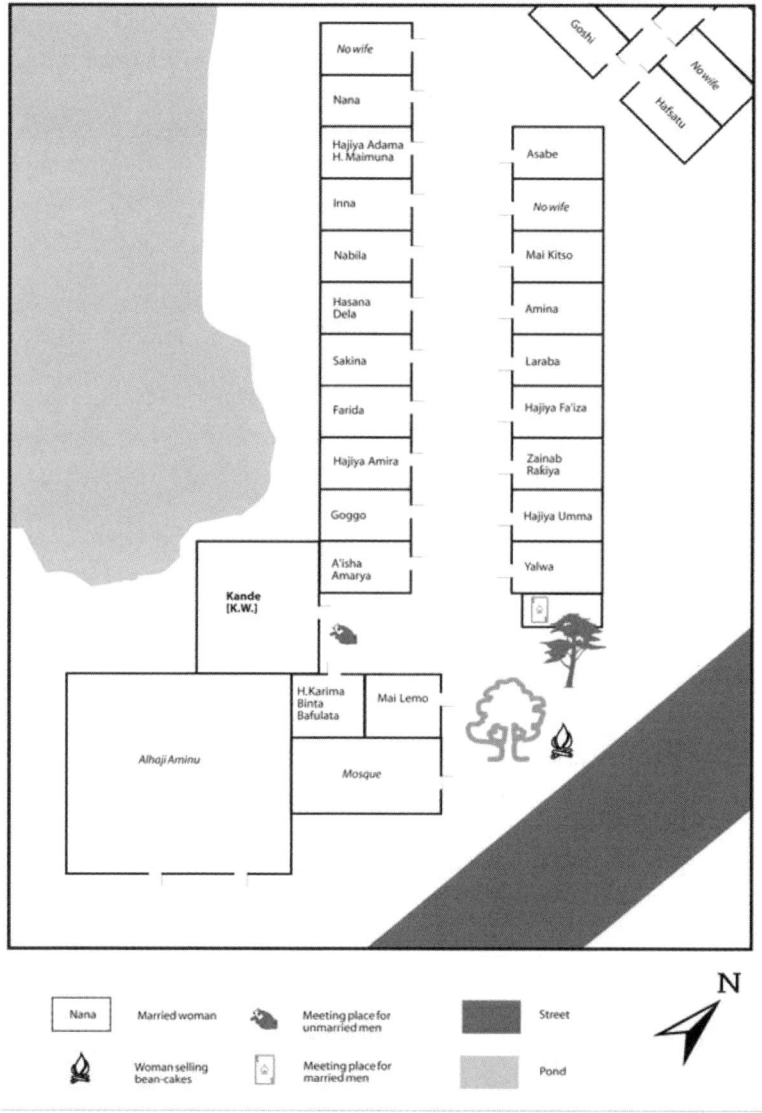

Figure 6.1   The longest row of houses in the barracks

---

[3] Ideally husbands should treat all their wives equally but this was obviously not always the case.

ciki da falo, a room with an ante-room or parlour. Their husbands, on the other hand, valued the fact that they did not have to share their houses with people not related to them, and that there was no landlord interfering in their affairs (cf. Pellow 1988).

Photo 6.2 A street in the barracks
(Photo: Katja Werthmann)

The married women with whom I worked defined themselves as secluded (*kulle*).[4] In Kano in the 1990s, according to the most common variation of seclusion, women could go out during the day or at night for specific reasons like visits, celebrations or for taking children to the doctor.[5] However, going out required the explicit permission of their husbands. Although most *bariki* women left their houses only with their husband's consent, they routinely manipulated their itineraries to include other houses along the way, allowing them the chance to greet relatives or friends without asking their husband's permission.[6] Often women were vague when asked about their specific destination and just said: '*Zan tafi unguwa*' ('I'm going to town'). However, direct neighbours were

---

[4] I have discussed seclusion in more detail elsewhere (see Werthmann 1997: 191-215, Werthmann 2002).
[5] I have not been to Kano since the introduction of Shari'a in the year 2000. The definition and practice of wife seclusion might have changed.
[6] This strategy was not limited to *bariki* women (cf. Pittin 1996: 184).

informed about each other's movements because they looked after their neighbour's children or kept their house keys in their absence.

The compounds had no windows looking out into the street but there were two vents in the kitchen. Although not at eye level, these vents could be used for peering out by climbing onto something. The women could also look out through the chink of the entrance door. Such peering (le_bwa) was considered typical and *bariki* women mentioned it explicitly as something which distinguished them from women living in stricter forms of seclusion in compounds where the women's rooms would not even be near the street. The difference between local variations of seclusion, due to different social backgrounds, was brought home to me when a neighbourhood girl married a teacher who lived on the college campus just across the main street. As a now-married woman, she was allowed to accompany guests to the gate of the courtyard (where she could be seen) to see them off.

In contrast with the varied economic activities of women in other quarters of Kano, only a few women in the barracks had occupations that generated more than a little pocket money. The everyday lives of these women were characterized by the prevalence of household activities although, in spite of seclusion, this is not necessarily a predominant feature of Muslim women's lives in northern Nigeria. Husbands are responsible for providing food, shelter and clothing, and many women – assisted by their children – earn money by producing food for sale, retailing manufactured items or doing handicrafts (see, for instance, Coles 1991, Hill 1969, Pittin 2002, Schildkrout 1982). Whereas women in large family compounds or in polygynous households can rotate household chores, most of the women in the barracks had to do all their own domestic work. Furthermore, they had little help from their children because not only the boys but also most of the girls attended school up to secondary level. Another factor that reduced the possibility of independent work for women was the lack of markets in this area.

Neighbours and friends

The absence of relatives meant that the women's daily social contacts were mainly with other *bariki* women. In everyday life there was much less interaction between spouses than between neighbours, and apart from the evening meal, husbands spent little time at home. Although the women were not allowed to visit each other daily due to seclusion, direct neighbours communicated over the walls that separated their courtyards. These walls were about two metres high so if a woman wanted to talk to her neighbour, she climbed

Photo 6.3   The kitchen vents are used for peeping out
(Photo: Katja Werthmann)

onto an upside-down mortar, onto a piece of furniture or any other object leaning against the wall in order to be able to look over. Kitchen utensils, matches, food, cola nuts and other items were passed over the walls.

When *bariki* women went out, they tried to avoid certain places at certain times of the day. In the late afternoon for instance, their husbands were back from work and gathered opposite the small neighbourhood mosque. Thus the men were able to observe everybody who came from or went into the main street. In order not be seen by the men, women preferred to take a detour using the settlement's back exit. They did not like visiting my house because some young unmarried men used to spend the day in front of it. Although these young men were their own sons or sons of neighbours, the women did not like to be seen by them.[7] In 1994 when a new male neighbour took to sitting in front of his house selling cigarettes and matches from a small table, the women tried to sneak out of the house when he went elsewhere.

In the longest row of the *bariki* there were two neighbourhood clusters of between four or five adjoining houses. Women in such neighbourhood clusters had the most frequent interactions, they lent things or money to one another, they left their keys with one of their neighbours when they went out, they took turns in looking after the children in each other's absence, and they sent food to their neighbours on special occasions such as religious holidays. Women also lent the use of their courtyards to direct neighbours when more space was needed for drying linen or for receiving guests for a large celebration. When a woman gave birth, her immediate neighbours would relieve her of her household chores and did the cooking and cleaning for her during the first week until the baby's naming day.

Good neighbourly relationships were characterized by terms like *mutunci* (respect), *zumunci* (solidarity) or *tarayya* (partnership) and were vital for daily interaction and exchange. Women lent each other kitchen utensils, spices and cash, or asked a neighbour's child to run an errand for them. Two kinds of loan are distinguished lexically: *aro* signifies borrowing a thing which will be returned the same or the next day, for example a bowl or a cooking pot; and *rance* means borrowing something that does not have to be returned immediately but later on, especially cash. Small things such as sweets or cola nuts are frequently given as presents (*kyauta*).

In addition, neighbours formed rotating savings groups (*adashi*) which comprised a specific number of participants and a fixed date for receiving one's share. One group, for instance, consisted of eight neighbourhood women plus the husband of two of the women and a female relative of another woman. They agreed to pay Naira 10 every five days. Many women secretly set aside part of their housekeeping money in order to participate in such savings groups. With the sum generated the women bought articles that their husbands did not provide, such as a small bath tub for babies or linoleum for the floor.

News and gossip spread rapidly among *bariki* women. When someone was ill, when a child was born, when someone died, when a couple was fighting or a woman was pregnant: all the neighbours were quickly informed of the news, although it was often impossible to reconstruct who first started the gossip. One day, for instance, a woman told me that a neighbour had had a miscarriage. I asked her: 'How do you know? Did she tell you?' She said: 'You don't tell

---

[7] For male neighbours who spied on women's movements, compare Pittin (1996: 185, n. 8).

people such a thing because of the shame (*kunya*)! Others talk about it. You go to a wedding, you go to a naming ceremony, of course you hear talk (*zance*).'

Smaller children were sent (*aiko*) to transmit greetings and messages. Through their children the women also learnt whether their neighbours were at home or had gone out. More delicate information and observations, for instance the details of arguments between couples or co-wives, were passed on by older girls. Unmarried girls often spent their time with older women like the widow Goggo. For her entire mourning period of four months and ten days, her house became a meeting place for several women and girls and served as a 'turntable' for news and gossip. After the mourning period was over, she had to move out.

Types of friendship

When a woman moved into the *bariki*, her first contacts were those with her immediate neighbours (*maƙwabciya*, pl. *maƙwabta*). Immediate neighbours greeted each other and passed news over the walls on a daily basis. Women who did not live directly next door sometimes saw each other when peering out of the house. If there was a celebration in the neighbourhood, the newcomer was also invited. Gradually her circle of acquaintances widened and, with time, some women formed bond friendships that continued to exist even after one of them had moved away.

The *bariki* women distinguished three kinds of relationships among women. First, there were the neighbours or 'friends of fortune' (*abokan arziki*) who greeted each other and invited one another to celebrations. These relationships were characterized by the stereotypical phrase: 'You greet, you joke, you laugh' (*ana gaisuwa, ana wasa, ana dariya*). Second, there were (bond) friends (*ƙawa*, pl. *ƙawaye*) who were obliged to exchange gifts with each other. Bond-friendships only exist between girls or women of the same age group. A *ƙawa* relationship starts when a girl gives a small present to another, thus initiating a ceremonial exchange. Later on, the *ƙawaye*, in particular the best friend (*babbar ƙawa*), will play an important ritual part during the wedding of her friend. These bond friendships often last a lifetime. Between adult women, too, they start with the exchange of gifts. Bond friends are always invited to naming ceremonies and weddings, and are supposed to give a present to the hostess that exceeds the obligatory cash gift. For instance, a *ƙawa* gives children's clothing on a naming day or dishes on a wedding day. When a woman's daughter gets married, the bride's mother's *ƙawaye* often completes the trousseau (*kayan ɗaki*) with more household articles or kitchen utensils.

Katja: How does one become a ƙawa?
Yalwa: With gifts. When a woman gets something, then she sends it to you and when you get something, you give it to her. Or when she gives birth to a baby, you give something to her.
Katja: When there is a naming ceremony, do you give money to the woman straight away?
Yalwa: Yes, if you have some. If you don't have any money, that's it. But if she has given birth and you are close friends, you go to her place and you do the work: you distribute cola nuts (to invite guests), you make *kunu* (gruel), you cook *tuwo* (the staple food) and so on. That's the way it is. You are there and you conquer someone's heart. This person's affection for you becomes very strong.
(Interview, 11 August 1993)

Third, there is the most trusted friend or confidante (aminiya) with whom a woman may share a secret (*asiri*). Among all friends only one is a woman's *babbar ƙawa* or *aminiya*, the best friend. While a woman cannot tell everything that is on her mind to a *ƙawa*, she may feel trust (*aminici*), affection (*ƙauna*), and love (*soyayya*) for her aminiya. Normally a woman is not supposed to talk about her marriage. The *aminiya*, however, becomes like a close relative (*shaƙiƙi*). Even marital conflicts that are not touched upon in casual conversation between neighbours or friends can be discussed with an aminiya. The relationship with an aminiya is the most exclusive of all. A woman may have several *ƙawaye*, but only one *aminiya*. Once Hajiya Umma explained the different kinds of friendship between women:

Katja: Is Yalwa your friend (*ƙawa*)?
Hajiya Umma: Yes, in those days (when I moved here) I was her guest (*baƙuwata*), it was a kind of neighbourly obligation (*hakkin maƙwabtaka*). Moreover, she was like my sister (*'yar'uwata*). You see, she is older than me. Therefore, I treat her with respect, I consider her as my mother, do you understand?
Katja: Yes, there is a difference between –
Hajiya Umma: – friend (*ƙawa*) and confidante (*aminiya*) and sister (*'yar'uwa*). I treat her as if we were relatives, you see?
Katja: What's the difference between *ƙawa* and *aminiya*?
Hajiya Umma: Well, with a friend you meet and you laugh, then she leaves again. But to a confidante you tell her everything that is on your mind and you can tell her about it. She won't tell others.
Katja: Like a secret.

Hajiya Umma: It's a secret. Now, this is a confidante, but not a friend. With a friend you meet, you joke, you laugh, and then you go on your way. A confidante by comparison – her affairs are with you, your affairs are with her. Nobody knows about them besides Allah and both of you, she won't tell them to anybody. It is as if you have come out of the same belly. You can't hide anything from a sister; if there's something on your mind, you tell her. That's the way it is with Yalwa and me: if something worries her, she tells me, if I am worried, I tell her. I give her advice, she gives me advice, you see? (Interview, 13 December 1992)

> Hajiya Umma compared the close relationship with her direct neighbour Yalwa to a relationship with close relatives like a sister or a mother from whom one cannot or does not have to hide anything. But although Hajiya Umma first described her relationship with Yalwa as a relationship between equals, she later qualified it: 'If Yalwa offends me, I am patient'. The relationship to a 'mother' is a confidential one in which both women exchange their ideas, but the exchange is unequal. The older woman does not tell everything to the younger one and the younger woman has to treat the older one with respect and is not supposed to criticize her. With a friend of the same age she can be more open.

Although many women interacted most frequently with their immediate neighbours, this did not necessarily lead to friendship. Bond friendship is only formed between equals in terms of age, never between an older and a younger woman. Hajiya Umma distinguished between three relative age groups in the *bariki*:

- mature women who have been married several times and who have grown-up children;
- younger women whose oldest children are not yet adults; and
- young women who have only recently got married and who do not have any children yet or only one very young child.

In addition, there were the unmarried girls. Childless women where classified according to their foster children. While the affiliation to an age group determined the type of friendship, it was irrelevant as to whether a woman was married or not (although married women would not normally discuss matters of sexuality and childbirth with unmarried girls). As a consequence of the high turnover, the few older women who had lived there for a long time had fewer friends than before.

> Yalwa: In the past our solidarity was much stronger. It was stronger than today.
> Katja: Why is it no longer strong today?
> Yalwa: This is what I told you: because some of them are still children. They are not loyal. In the past everyone could go to her neighbour and maintain friendly relations, but not today. When you go into a house today and tomorrow again, they will say: why is she coming, does she want to spread gossip? Nowadays three months can go by and I haven't seen anybody. (Interview, 10 September 1993)

The older women said that in the old days – in the 1960s – before there were buses and taxis, all *bariki* women used to gather after dusk, or even during the day, to walk to celebrations in the Old Town. Even without a special reason, neighbours used to meet in the evenings in one woman's house to chat. At that time (that is before the Biafran War) not only Muslims but also Christians lived in the *bariki*, and seclusion was less strict. Today, these women said, everybody only cares for himself (*kowa yana harkar gabansa*).

As I used to visit all the houses of the neighbourhood, my reputation was: 'Kande [my Hausa name] who has many friends' (*Kande mai ḳawaye*), implying a certain lack of seriousness, since a woman should not have too many friends. Even women who had been living in the *bariki* for years had not necessarily visited all the houses. Thus, over the course of time I became an informant for the women of 'our' row or *layi* (line) because I knew all the neighbours and even kept in touch with some who had moved away during my stay. Like other friends and visitors I became part of a network in which information about neighbours and friends was constantly exchanged and discussed.

Although they most frequently interacted with neighbours, the women also had friends and acquaintances outside the *bariki*. Many women knew at least two or three women in other quarters of Kano whom they visited on certain occasions or to whose celebrations they were invited and vice versa. A woman like Yalwa, who was born in the Old Town and had been living in the *bariki* for about 30 years, had relatives and friends all over town. But even women who had been living in Kano only for a short time got to know other women beyond their immediate neighbourhood, for instance when they were taken along to naming ceremonies or weddings. Some friendships among neighbours also developed on the basis of common regional origin or through relatives; for instance between two Tera women from Bauchi State whose husbands were related. Another basis for establishing friendships was similar experiences of life, as in the case of two women who had lived in other Nigerian cities before coming to Kano.

Sometimes friendships that were formed in the *bariki* lasted longer than these women's marriages. Even after having moved away from the *bariki*, many women kept in touch with their former neighbours and friends and came to visit, as did divorced women who came to see their children who were living with their fathers.

Barira had lived in the *bariki* from 1971 to 1977 and had maintained relationships there. In 1971, after a short first marriage in her home town, she moved to Kano to join an older brother who was a policeman and lived in the old *bariki*.[8] Later they moved to the new *bariki*. Through him she got to know her second husband, a colleague of her brother's, who also lived in the *bariki*. When they had been married for seven years, her husband took a second wife. About six months later Barira left him and went back to her father's family.[9] In 1980 she came to live in Kano again. When I got to know her in the 1990s, she was married but not living with her husband. She worked for the university's security service and was sharing a small compound in a suburb with another elderly woman. Some years ago Barira's older brother had retired but a nephew of hers had become a policeman too. He was now living in the same house in the barracks and had married a neighbour's sister. Whenever Barira found the time, she came to see Yalwa and Inna, her former neighbours and oldest friends in Kano, and to visit her nephew and his wife.

> Barira: I know the *bariki* women very well because we did everything together. When I still lived with my brother and not yet in my husband's house, we already did everything together. They already knew me and I knew them. We got along well together. If there was a celebration or somebody fell ill, they sent for me, and when I was ill, they came to see me. We helped one another. You know how it is – sometimes a woman has some money, sometimes she has none. Then you go to a 'sister' to borrow some; she'll give you some. If you have money again, you return it. We were all secluded but when there was a celebration we gathered at night and went there. If a neighbour was going to have a baby, we came to her house and did the domestic work for her. We did all these things.

Although Barira had moved out of the *bariki* many years before, she still felt at home in this neighbourhood where she had spent some important years of her life.

> Katja: If you could choose, where would you like to live?
> Barira: In the bariki!
> Katja: In the bariki? Why?
> Barira: Because I grew up here! This is the place I know best! (Interview, 19 September 1993)

As Raynaut (1972) pointed out, non-kin relationships or *relations électives* – such as neighbourhood and friendship – are important social factors not only in towns but also in villages. Neighbourhood and friendship constitute networks of

---

[8] The old *bariki* are situated in a neighbouring quarter. This is also a housing estate for policemen that was built in the 1930s. Some women had lived there before moving to the new *bariki*.
[9] The arrival of a co-wife is a frequent reason for divorce.

Photo 6.4 Three old friends: Inna, Barira and Yalwa
(Photo: Katja Werthmann)

mutual reciprocity, which are often no less binding than obligations in kinship relations. Solidarity and friendship among women neighbours in the police barracks were neither merely utilitarian nor a rudimentary remnant from the past.[10] The relationships among *bariki* women resemble types of institutionalized friendship as described by 'Baba of Karo' who lived in a northern Nigerian rural area in the first half of the twentieth century (Smith 1955), but there are differences that point to the peculiarity of this urban setting. There were no female patron-client relationships between bariki women. While *jawa* relationships existed in the days of Baba as well as in the *bariki* between girls or women of the same age, the patron-client relationship between an older woman (*yayar rana*, 'older sister of the day') and a younger woman (*kanwar rana*, 'younger sister of the day') did not. This patron-client relationship was

---

[10] For a recent survey of anthropological approaches to friendship, see Grätz, Meier & Pelican (2004). For friendship among migrant women in urban Kenya, see Schultz (1996).

normally initiated by the older woman and obliged the younger woman to do little jobs for her, while the older woman was obliged to give presents to the younger one and to support her. As in many patron-client relationships the patroness's prestige was enhanced by this relationship. Such a client relationship could also exist between an older woman and a younger man (*anen rana*).

There were no patron-client relationships between women neighbours in the *bariki*. One reason for this was that the *bariki* women were a relatively homogenous status group, whereas patron-client relationships are normally characterized by a clear social difference between a patroness and her client. Another reason was the fact that the division between the relative status and prosperity was unequally distributed in the *bariki*, where the older women were often the least wealthy residents and therefore not able to initiate patron-client relationships. It was however, not only a lack of material resources that prevented older women from initiating patron-client relationships but also a lack of interest on the part of the younger women to accept such a relationship. In the eyes of younger women, there was no obvious material or ideal value that would make establishing bonds with an older woman worthwhile. In Baba's days, a patroness was a classificatory 'mother' who could offer her 'daughter' advice, help and material support, who assumed ritual roles and therefore expected some degree of respect. Nowadays, younger and older women's views of life are too different. When Yalwa spoke about the younger women in the neighbourhood as 'children' (*yara*), she articulated a perceived rupture that is considered as a generation gap by the older women. In the eyes of Yalwa and Inna, who were not only amongst the oldest women but who had lived in the *bariki* longer than anyone, most of the younger women who were currently living there were children who did not know anything about life. Yalwa, Inna and their mutual friend Barira, who had lived in the *bariki* for several years and kept in touch with both of them, agreed that, in the old days, relationships between *bariki* women were closer and better than at present.

> Yalwa: In the past, people had more team spirit (*ri_bn zumunci*), they cared about others. They [the younger women] are inferior to us, we are superior to them. Today there are only children in the *bariki*. The adults all went away; their husbands retired, some of them died, some were transferred. Then new people move into the house; they come and stay. Therefore they are inferior to us because we know things they don't know. (Interview, 11 August 1993)

The neighbourhood as a stage

Open conflicts between neighbours were rare but I witnessed some occasions when disputes were 'acted out' at a gathering of women.

The day Zainab was to get a co-wife, some of her neighbours and former neighbours from the old *bariki* gathered in her courtyard in the afternoon. Zainab was sitting under the tree and had her direct neighbour, Hajiya Umma, plaiting her hair. From time to time, Zainab got up to check the boiling rice in a large cooking pot. Hajiya Umma's little daughter Sadiya was playing with some of the other girls but they started to quarrel and cry. Hajiya Umma called Sadiya and told her to sit down and be quiet. Several times she repeated: 'Calm down, calm down', but Sadiya continued to cry. Finally Hajiya Umma said: 'Well, then get up!' but Sadiya remained seated. Hajiya Umma became furious and started to beat Sadiya, first with her hand, then with a rubber sandal. All the women present were shocked and shouted at her to stop. Zainab put her arm around Sadiya to protect her. Then she took the child away from Hajiya Umma and put her down in front of herself. Hajiya Umma who was still angry called her other daughter Momi and asked her to take Sadiya away. The girls left with Sadiya still in tears. The women were silent and Hajiya Umma kept on complaining for a while. Finally the women continued their conversation and one of them started to distribute the meal. As the women began to eat, Hajiya Umma started to tell them about a conflict between her and another member of a savings group in the neighbourhood, Laraba, who was also present. The other women looked confused. Both of the women concerned – Hajiya Umma and Laraba – had now got up and were facing each other, with Zainab, who had also stood up, between them. The other women remained seated and continued eating, asking the three women again and again to sit down and to eat, too, which they refused to do. Both Hajiya Umma and Laraba told their respective versions of the story, never addressing their 'opponent' directly but talking to the other women. A heated argument developed and at some point everybody was shouting. Finally Laraba turned away and started to cry. There was no obvious solution. Hajiya Umma went away and the other women also prepared to leave while Laraba sulkily sat down on the doorstep, hiding her face. Finally one of the women made a joke that released the tension. Three women started ululating and everybody laughed. All the guests got up and said good-bye.

What was remarkable about this situation was the 'staging' of the conflict (Goffmann 1959). Hajiya Umma had chosen a women's gathering when mostly women from outside the *bariki* would be present. These women, who were not directly involved in the conflict, functioned as an 'audience' in front of whom Hajiya Umma could 'perform'. First, she showed her anger by beating her daughter and then she started telling the others about the dispute. She and her opponent Laraba got up and faced each other, with Zainab – the hostess – as the 'neutral' person between them. While the women in the audience commented on the scene and tried to calm down the opponents, I had the part of a non-person, belonging to the audience but not having any specific function. While all the other women were eating, Hajiya Umma and Laraba refused to participate in the communal meal. Zainab, the hostess, did not eat either. Instead, she acted as a buffer between the two opponents. Although the conflict was not settled, both parties had at least presented their respective versions publicly and had been heard (and, of course, the scene was soon reported to the other neighbourhood women).

The 'opening of a secret' (*tona asiri*), which is speaking publicly about or acting out a conflict (including a breach of social norms because women are supposed to be patient), leads to a crisis. To re-establish balance, redressive mechanisms such as personal advice or informal arbitration are employed (Turner 1957: 91-93). If there was an argument between a husband and wife, between co-wives or between two friends, often a third person – co-wife, friend or neighbour – would act as an 'audience' or mediator. Thus he or she prevented the escalation of the argument and 'gave patience' (*ba da ha_␣uri*) to both parties. Like other social relationships, friendship between women was not only an affair between the two individuals concerned. When it came to a conflict, the community was represented by auditors or mediators who helped settle the conflict and rebalance the relationship.

Matan bariki: A collective urban identity

In contrast with ancient quarters in Kano's Old Town where neighbourhoods are often based on common origin and kinship and have developed over a long period of time, the *bariki* were set apart by their peculiar layout and the absence of extended families. The houses were inhabited by two generations of families, and although some neighbours may have had previous ties through professional contact, regional origin or kinship, this was not the norm. The lives of women in these barracks differed from those in the Old Town because of their reduced possibilities of generating their own income and therefore their greater economic dependence on their husbands. This was partly due to wife seclusion which is mandatory inside the Old Town (in contrast with mixed quarters outside the city walls where seclusion may not be required for all Muslim women). On the other hand, access to schooling for their children, especially girls, was greater. In their daily lives, the female inhabitants of the barracks interacted most frequently with women neighbours, some of whom became close friends.

The women of this particular urban neighbourhood called themselves *matan bariki* ('women of the barracks'), thus stressing their own sense of community and their difference *vis-à-vis* other groups and milieus of women in Kano. However, *bariki* is a highly ambivalent term, indicating 'modernity' and 'westernization' but mostly in a derogatory way. For many Hausa speakers the term *matan bariki* is synonymous with 'prostitutes'. Why then did these wives and mothers call themselves *matan bariki*?

The word *bariki* was introduced during colonial rule, designating colonial buildings such as rest stations, military and police barracks or any European-style building. Soon, *bariki* came to be associated with everything untraditional, which in the northern Nigerian context implies non-Islamic. *Bariki* is both a spatial unit and a metaphor of deviation. *Bariki* is a place set apart from the ancient sections of northern Nigerian cities, such as Sabon Gari, the New Town of Kano, a quarter outside the city walls where Christian immigrants from southern Nigeria have settled since the start of colonial rule. *Bariki* provides the space for activities and relationships that are considered indecent, if not outright illegal, by more orthodox northern Nigerian Muslims. Contacts between Muslims and Christians that lead to the rejection of the true faith include the consumption of alcohol and drugs, gambling, *bori* spirit-possession cult, prostitution, homosexuality and the transgression of gender boundaries – activities that normally take place outside the town walls (cf. Gaudio 1996: 44). The abstract noun *barikanci* covers all these activities and belongs to a semantic field together with *iskanci* (profligacy, loose living) and *karuwanci* (prostitution, courtesanship).

Although they were well aware of these connotations of *bariki*, the Muslim housewives in this neighbourhood used the term *matan bariki* as a sometimes ironical self-designation. In their local modification of the term, *bariki* identified three aspects of urban lifestyle: first, living in a clearly demarcated modern housing estate, second, middle-class membership, and third, the establishment of relationships that were not determined by ethnic ties or kinship, but by friendship and solidarity among neighbours. By redefining the term *matan bariki*, the women of the barracks managed to locate themselves cognitively within a complex social structure and a heterogeneous urban space. Thus, they created a specifically urban identity that was not based on ethnic or regional origins. This was not merely a temporary identification but in fact helped to reproduce a social class: many girls who grew up in the barracks or women who left the barracks after divorce would (re)marry policemen or other civil servants who lived in similar housing estates.

However, this concept of identity remained as ambiguous as the urban space to which it related. Although *bariki* signified being 'sophisticated', 'educated' and 'modern' according to local standards, the women rarely used it outside their immediate neighbourhood. When they visited other parts of the town, they did not use the word *bariki* to indicate their place of residence but rather referred to the name of the quarter that enclosed the barracks or to the name of the nearby city gate. The only places where the term *bariki* could be used on the basis of a shared meaning were in other barracks or civil servants' quarters. When a neighbourhood girl married a member of the Kano State Government, for instance, she moved to a newly constructed terraced housing estate just outside Kano. Together with some of her friends, I visited her in her new home. Her friends jokingly commented her new status: *ta bar bariki, ta koma bariki* – 'she has left the barracks and come to the barracks again'.

As elsewhere, the neighbourhood in this case study was both spatially grounded and imagined. The *bariki* as a neighbourhood was a clearly delineated spatial unit *and* a 'symbolic community'.[11] The physical features of this housing estate, the cohabitation of strangers, the absence of kin ties and the formation of friendships among women neighbours are factors that all contributed to the emergence of the collective identity of *matan bariki*. In contrast with other collective identities or categories (such as 'Hausa', 'Fulani', Kanawa 'Kano people' or *matan aure* 'married women'), these women explicitly referred to the distinct physical and social setting in which they found themselves. Relationships with neighbours, some of whom became close friends, were not merely a substitute for kinship but created a sense of belonging. The daily interaction and mutual support among women provided not only material but also emotional stability in lives that were frequently troubled by financial problems, illness and marital conflict.

References

Clark, G. 1994, *Onions Are My Husband. Survival and Accumulation by West-African Market Women*, Chicago: University of Chicago Press.
Coles, C. 1991, 'Hausa Women's Work in a Declining Urban Economy: Kaduna, Nigeria, 1980-1985', in: C. Coles & B. Mack (eds), *Hausa Women in the Twentieth Century*, Madison: University of Wisconsin Press, pp. 163-91.
Gaudio, R.P. 1996, *Men Who Talk like Women: Language, Gender and Sexuality in Hausa Muslim Society*, Stanford University, Dissertation, Ann Arbor, MI: UMI (2000).
Goffman, E. 1959, *The Presentation of Self in Everyday Life*, London: Penguin Press.
Grätz, T., B. Meier & M. Pelican 2004, 'Freundschaftsprozesse in Afrika aus sozialanthropologischer Perspektive', *Afrika Spectrum* 39: 9-39.

---

[11] For neighbourhood women as a 'moral community' in Kampala, see Ogden (1996).

Hannerz, U. 1980, *Exploring the City. Inquiries toward an Urban Anthropology*, New York: Columbia University Press.
Hill, P. 1969, 'Hidden Trade in Hausaland', *Man* 4 (3): 392-409.
Horn, N.E. 1994, *Cultivating Customers. Market Women in Harare, Zimbabwe*, Boulder/London: Lynne Rienner Publishers.
Hunter, A. 1974, *Symbolic Communities. The Persistence and Change of Chicago's Local Communities*, Chicago: Chicago University Press.
Ogden, J. 1996, 'Producing Respect: The "Proper Woman" in Postcolonial Kampala', in: R. Werbner & T. Ranger (eds), *Postcolonial Identities in Africa*, London/New Jersey: Zed Books, pp. 165-92.
Pellow, D. 1988, 'What Housing Does: Changes in an Accra Community', *Architectural Behavior* 4 (3): 213-27.
Pittin, R. 1996, 'Negotiating Boundaries. A Perspective from Nigeria', in: D. Pellow (ed.), Setting Boundaries. *The Anthropology of Spatial and Social Organization*, Westport: Bergin & Garvey, pp. 179-93.
Pittin, R. 2002, *Women and Work in Northern Nigeria: Transcending Boundaries*, New York: Palgrave Macmillan.
Raynaut, C. 1972, *Structures Normatives et Relations Electives: Etudes d'une Communauté Villageoise Haoussa*, Paris: Mouton.
Robertson, C. 1984, *Sharing the Same Bowl. A Socioeconomic History of Women and Class in Accra*, Ghana, Bloomington: Indiana University Press.
Schildkrout, E. 1982, 'Dependence and Autonomy: The Economic Activities of Secluded Hausa Women in Kano, Nigeria', in: E. Bay (ed.), *Women and Work in Africa*, Boulder: Westview, pp. 55-83.
Schultz, U. 1996, *Nomadenfrauen in der Stadt. Die Überlebensökonomie der Turkanafrauen in Lodwar/Nordkenia*, Berlin: Reimer.
Sheldon, K. (ed.) 1996, *Courtyards, Markets, City Streets. Urban Women in Africa*, Boulder: Westview.
Smith, M.F. 1955, *Baba of Karo: A Woman of the Muslim Hausa*, New York: Philosophical Library.
Turner, V. 1957, *Schism and Continuity in an African Society: A Study of Ndembu Village Life*, Manchester: Manchester University Press.
Werthmann, K. 1997, *Nachbarinnen. Das Alltagsleben muslimischer Frauen in einer nigerianischen Großstadt*, Frankfurt/Main: Brandes & Apsel.
Werthmann, K. 2000, '"Seek for Knowledge, Even if it is in China!" Muslim Women and Secular Education in Northern Nigeria', in: Th. Salter & K. King (eds), Africa, *Islam and Development: Islam and Development in Africa – African Islam, African Development*, University of Edinburgh: Centre of African Studies, pp. 253-70.
Werthmann, K. 2002, 'Matan Bariki, "Women of the Barracks". Muslim Hausa Women in an Urban Neighbourhood in Northern Nigeria', *Africa* 72 (1): 112-30.
Werthmann, K. 2004, *A Field Full of Researchers. Fieldwork as a Collective Experience*, Arbeitspapiere des Instituts für Ethnologie und Afrikastudien der Johannes Gutenberg-Universität Mainz 33.
http://www.ifeas.uni-mainz.de/workingpapers/WerthmannFieldwork.pdf

Maps of what matters: Community colour

Deborah Pellow[1]

> *Sabon Zongo, a migrant community in Accra, was established about 100 years ago by Hausa from northern Nigeria and was, even then, a socially and spatially distinct community. Its population has since diversified considerably but the Hausa Muslim influence has remained. The neighbourhood continues to be home to 'outsiders' and does not fit the cosmopolitan profile and Western ethos of Accra, Ghana's capital, which functions as an administrative and commercial primate city. By using 'mental mapping', or 'cognitive mapping', research techniques – whereby the images of the community that residents carry in their heads are recorded – this chapter investigates how the residents of Sabon Zongo have spatialized their social relations and culturized their physical environment. It explores the places, the activities and the concerns residents have and interprets how these translate into spatial practices. What is missing from these mental maps, however, is the vitality of the neighbourhood's street life: the maps reduce the richness of the landscape.*

---

[1] I am particularly grateful to my assistant Muhsin Barko, without whom this project would have been very difficult, if not impossible, to carry out. My Syracuse University colleagues Anne Mosher in Geography and Anne Munley in Architecture, and Denise Lawrence-Zuniga, an anthropologist at Cal Poly Pomona, have been superb guides through the methodology of cognitive mapping and advised me on an earlier draft of this chapter. David Stea, a pioneer in the field, has guided me on cross-cultural issues. Would that I had had all of them with me in the field!

Introduction

Accra, the capital of Ghana, is an administrative and commercial primate city with an international airport, several four-star hotels and an outward-looking Western ethos. It is also home to diverse populations and neighbourhoods, many of which do not 'fit' Accra's cosmopolitan profile, with people who are insular and culturally inward-looking, and locales that have few modern facilities. This chapter looks at the core neighbourhood of one migrant community, Sabon Zongo, which was founded almost 100 years ago by Hausa from northern Nigeria. While its population has diversified considerably, a heavy Hausa Muslim influence endures, and the neighbourhood continues to be home to people who are strangers to Accra.

Initially, the goal of this chapter was to illustrate the spatialization of identity, as manifest in everyday social and cultural life. I was searching for places and practices that matter to explore how their layout and the residents' involvement in them help to produce neighbourhood identity. Sabon Zongo is socially produced, as is the residents' knowledge of the locale. As a social construct, Sabon Zongo has different meanings and different values to different people.

To delve into individual perspectives, I experimented with the field research method of mental mapping: asking a sample of men and women to sketch what they see as Sabon Zongo. Mental maps, also known as cognitive maps, are images we carry around in our minds about our environment and present social knowledge.. Everyone's mental map is unique depending upon what is salient to the person in the physical environment: each is a selective representation. I saw this methodology as an alternative means of eliciting information on which streets, businesses and landmarks are particularly meaningful to inhabitants. I had a variety of questions to pursue along these lines: whether people in Sabon Zongo saw their social ties, i.e. their community, in terms of people; how one inscribes people on maps; and how we create a map based upon social ties. Do people's maps present focal locales and, if so, might they be considered community spaces? Indeed, how does neighbourhood vitality as a social construct present itself? As I considered both the exercise and people's engagement in it, I had to ask whether the method of cognitive mapping was useful or appropriate to use with a non-Western and/or illiterate population. And if so, would it provide information different from regular ethnographic techniques?

Mapping Sabon Zongo

Accra was a colonial city and, like colonial cities throughout West Africa and indeed elsewhere in the world, its development had a particular impact on the local inhabitants' social and physical spaces, in part a manifestation of relations of power (King 1976). Since Accra is a large city, a local community such as Sabon Zongo has become 'an intermediate area between the dwelling and the whole city, which is better known, with which one has more identification …' (Rapoport 1980: 71).

Sabon Zongo was founded by a Hausa, Malam Mohammed Bako, who had migrated with his father from northern Nigeria to Accra in the late 1800s. In THE OLD CORE AREA OF downtown Accra, Malam Bako became a patron to members of the Hausa community who lived among other Muslim 'strangers' such as Yoruba, Nupe and Wangara in a *zongo* (stranger quarter). In 1908, the plague hit Accra, and Governor J.P. Rodger commissioned an urban renewal plan to deal with the congestion in the old downtown area that was hard hit by the disease. The Hausa community at Zongo Lane was growing and relations within the muslim community were fractious. So Malam Bako decided to create a new settlement for his Hausa followers, which served the British plan of vacating the old area while compartmentalizing different social (ethnic) groups in different spaces. They laid out Sabon Zongo ('New Zongo') on farmland a couple of miles northwest of Central Accra.

While Malam Bako remained in downtown Accra as Chief Imam until 1915 when inter-ethnic disturbances among the Muslims led the British to close the central mosque, by 1912 his followers had built about 165 compounds in Bako's 'New Zongo'. The streets were carefully laid out on a grid, and the original compounds were built within the block pattern. Fast forward now to 1969, when the Lands Department carried out an aerial survey of Accra and the original grid remained apparent, even though most of the streets were never completed. Only one interior street was completely paved (the north-south Malam Bako Street) and some compounds were extended into planned but not completed streets. In other words, in the early twentieth century, the British imposed their view of community space as a grid, and through this prism, compound and community life evolved. Some residents ignored it when building their houses, as is apparent in the southeastern quadrant, others in renovating and expanding theirs. The municipality's adherence to the colonial spatial pattern emerges when streets are to be paved (Malam Bako St.) or proper gutters to be laid (the eastern half of Korle Bu). On these infrequent occasions, structures that extend into the street are cut back. Thus, the Western grid continues to remain even today.

Sabon Zongo was incorporated into Accra in 1943 and for many who reside there, it is a point of orientation in the urban system. When first established, the

Maps of what matters in Accra 145

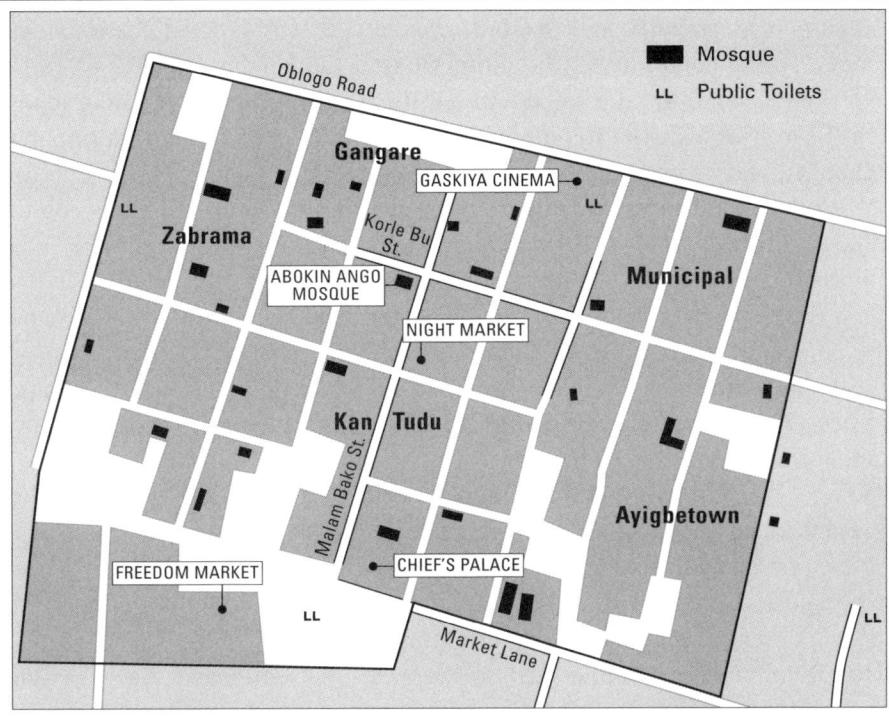

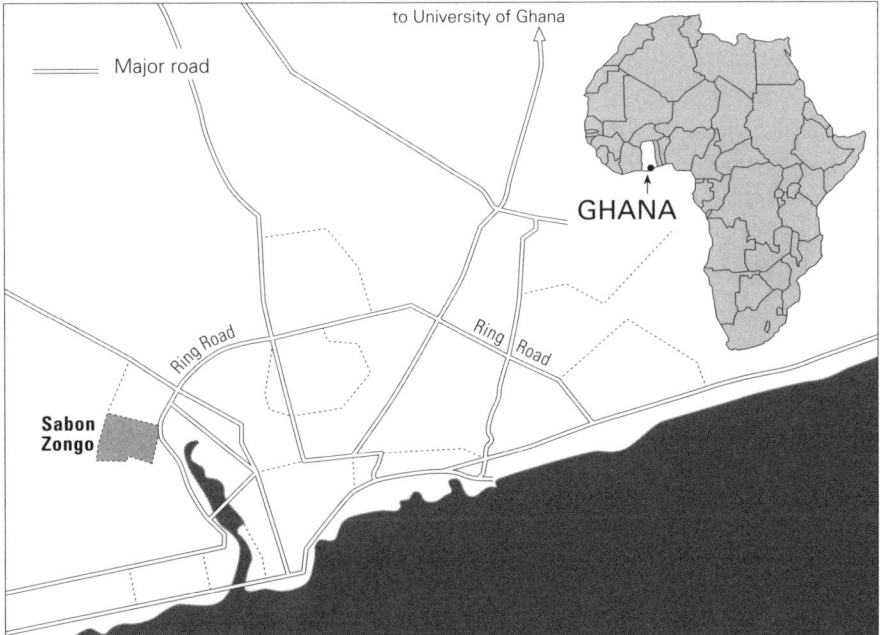

Map 7.1 Sabon Zongo and Accra, Ghana

community was socially and spatially distinct: it was created for outsiders – primarily Hausa migrants to the Gold Coast – and it lay outside of the city limits. (One needed to take a ferry to get there from downtown.) Like many in Accra, I see it as a distinct community even today, even though its population has changed and its physical boundaries are somewhat vague. This is evidenced in the clothing and behaviour of its residents, its physical structures, its commercial enterprises, and its sounds and smells. Ephemeral delineations include its infrastructural neglect with the absence of paved streets, properly dug gutters, flush toilets, schools, a post office and health facilities when compared to the adjacent communities of Larte Biokorshie, Abossey Okai and Kaneshie. While today there is a Christian presence in the neighbourhood, there are no churches. The community's strong Muslim atmosphere is expressed in an abundance of mosques – 30 in total.

Oblogo Road forms Sabon Zongo's northern boundary, and it is clearly delineated as an access road into Accra for commuters from suburban or outlying areas such as Dansoman, Awushie, Darkuman and Kaneshie. Commercial transportation, in the form of lorries and taxis, runs along Oblogo Road. 'Bus Stop' is a common picking-up and dropping-off point. Oblogo Road terminates at Ring Road, a semi-circular dual carriageway that delineates Accra's Central Business District. And Ring Road, which becomes Mortuary Road going south toward Jamestown and the old core, is the informal physical boundary of Sabon Zongo to the east. As one turns west on Oblogo off Ring Road, the profiles of two of the community's mosques are immediately visible: Municipal (aka Zana), built alongside Oblogo and Abokin Ango, a block in from Oblogo but taller than the neighbouring buildings.

Market Lane is seen by many as the southern boundary, although the community line in fact extends further south through Freedom Market, Sabon Zongo's local market. While most traders operate downtown at Accra's famous markets – Makola, Salaga and Timber – local neighbourhoods have their own local versions. Freedom Market sells provisions, fresh foods and cooking requirements, as well as notions of various sorts. To the west, the line of demarcation is less a street than two infrastructural elements: Ojo Primary School and one of the four sets of public toilets.

There are, therefore, spatial delineations to the community. But more than that, I would say that what holds it together is an overarching shared morality and the attachment that residents feel for the place. As I have written elsewhere (Pellow 2002), this is operationalized by exchange as social practice in everyday life and it defines the boundaries of Sabon Zongo.

Internally, the community is divided into neighbourhoods, although where one begins and another ends is vague. These neighbourhoods are known to all and have histories and qualities that distinguish one from another. For example,

Photo 7.1   A roof-top view of Sabon Zongo, with Abokin Ango Mosque in the background

Photo 7.2   One set of public toilets, on the west edge of Sabon Zongo
(Photos: Deborah Pellow)

Kan Tudu ('on the top') is at the top of an incline and Malam Bako's palace is located there. It is densely settled and has considerable street activity. *Gangare* ('down') is at the bottom of the incline and includes the sub-area of Kariki, the name of a prominent local family. *Unguwan Zabrama* (Zabrama quarter) is where Zabrama people settled, and *Ayigbetown* (Ewetown) is where the latecomer Ewe found housing.

People living in Sabon Zongo, and in Accra more generally, do not use maps or addresses, or base directions on street names other than the main streets. No one in Sabon Zongo uses his/her house number and many residents do not even know theirs. The numbers are inscribed by the municipality but for tax or census purposes only. Rather, it is communities, neighbourhoods, edges, margins, landmarks and problems that are salient to residents: they symbolize and embody relationships, social institutions and activities, and the social and physiccal concerns that people deal with on a daily basis in Sabon Zongo.

Indeed, in the mental mapping exercise, respondents commonly used landmarks to characterize the community. Taking the Lands Department's aerial survey, let us mark popular landmarks and places to create footprints on a basic map. There are the 30 mosques where the men congregate for prayer, for conversation and for relaxation. (Only Abokin Ango is specifically noted on Map 7.1). There is Malam Bako's palace: showing its age and rather dilapidated. It represents Sabon Zongo's founder and the chieftaincy but, to many residents, and along with the Night Market, it is the heart of the community (Pellow 2002).

And there are the public toilets. According to Accra Metropolitan Authority (AMA) ordinance, every home in Accra should have toilet facilities. A 1999 study reported that 77.5% do, but less than 20% have functioning indoor plumbing (Tipple 1999: 256). Twenty-five per cent of Accra dwellers make use of 127 public toilets (Obirih-Opareh 2001). Only with septic tanks can houses in Sabon Zongo have indoor plumbing, but the combination of cost and population density have made this impossible in most areas. Thus, public toilets are a necessity, not a convenience. The four sets (each with one for men and one for women) are very public, often blocks from one's home, inadequate for the number of people who use them, and not particularly clean. They are located on the western periphery, next to the Gaskiya Cinema, near Freedom Market, and just beyond the neighbourhood's southeastern boundary. If one consults the basic map, the public latrines bound Sabon Zongo. Every resident certainly knows where they are located and the structures are significant because they are needed and because they are not gathering places. (Due to the odour, they are nicknamed Lavender Hill.)

There are the markets – Freedom Market, patronized by women purchasing ingredients for cooking or household items. The Night Market, down the street from the Chief's Palace, is where prepared food is sold from late afternoon until about 11 pm. Here, men, women and children make their purchases and may sit and eat. The Night Market, however, is not just about food; it is sequentially multifunctional. Different populations engage in different activities: 'barefoot young boys play football, older shoed youths play football, Nigeriens hold wrestling matches during the dry season on Sundays, ritual dancing on Id il Fitr is held at the end of Ramadan, Arabic schools perform plays on the anniversary of the birth of the Prophet, political rallies are staged' (Pellow 2002: 88). There are also the grilled meat locales, for kebabs or slabs of lamb, where primarily men buy food and may stay to eat it. The Gaskiya Cinema, located on Oblogo Road, is known to Accra's taxi drivers. Here men and boys hang out on the stairs and verandah, talking and eating food that they have bought on the street.

Trading is the largest occupational category in Ghana and 32% of those employed in Accra are traders. The commerce that is responsible for Accra's growth and prosperity, and that may be its single most conspicuous social feature, is informal-sector trade (Dakubu 1997). Like the rest of Accra, and urban Ghana, Sabon Zongo has an active commercial life that is primarily based on informal trade. The three main businesses in this kiosk economy are provisions stores, communication centres, and barber-shops – all three of which are also gathering places. All provisions stores sell the same goods. On any one block there may be three or four; some are kiosks, some are storefronts. Prepared-food sellers are lined up along the sides of streets, and despite the fact that the number of cars has increased, the streets are still used for eating, selling and hanging out. Indeed, I have written elsewhere that prepared-food specialties and their spatial arrangement are core to Sabon Zongo and the practice of everyday life, and that they help to define and sustain this community (Pellow n.d.).

Mental maps

Human environments are socially produced and constructed. Human experience is spatialized, which is to say, social relations and social practice are located – both physically and conceptually – in social and physical space. Space is socially produced, which helps define the formation of urban space, and socially constructed, transforming that space into places and events that carry meaning (Low 1996: 861-62). Thus people construct their own realities and meaning in space, and they experience that space in their daily lives (de Certeau 1984). They engage in spatial practices.

The residents of Sabon Zongo have created a socially meaningful world through their social and spatial practices – through exchange in public and domestic spaces – spatializing their social relations while culturizing their physical environment (Pellow 2002). They have spatialized their identity in social and cultural life through various practices of consumption – engaging with one another by shopping, frequenting religious institutions, and participating in life-cycle rituals. These activities all help to produce community identity. Here, I have chosen to focus upon the public spaces in this urban community in Accra that make the place vibrant and meaningful to its residents. One might take an etic view, observing regularly and looking for patterns, or an emic view, through the eyes and thoughts of the people who live there. I will combine the two but the latter provides my entrée, and I enter through mental or cognitive mapping, which is fundamentally linked to people's decisions 'as to what to do where' (Downs & Stea 1977: 25).

> *Cognitive mapping* is an abstraction covering those cognitive or mental abilities that enable us to collect, organize, store, recall, and manipulate information about the spatial environment. ... A *cognitive map* is a product – a person's representation of some part of the spatial environment. (Ibid.: 6)

These mental representations are an expression of people's assessment of and reaction to the world they live in. Social scientists use mental mapping for a variety of reasons, one of which is to tell us what places or activities matter and where to locate them. According to urban planner Kevin Lynch (1960), people come to understand the layout of a city through the continual reformulation of not only what they think the city contains but also how those contents are laid out. This process is, on one hand, individual, but on the other hand also social. Thus the city and the mental representations or images of it are characterized by unique elements, some of which are important only to a few people due to their unique engagement with aspects of the city, while other elements are valued by many, if not all, its residents. According to Lynch, it is through the physical, perceptible elements of paths, edges, districts, nodes and landmarks that people make sense of the city. They are invested with memories and meanings, and it is through them that people locate themselves and others.

Paths are 'the channels along which the observer customarily, occasionally, or potentially moves. ... For many people, these are the predominant elements in their image' (Ibid.: 47). Edges are linear elements not considered as paths, but are important organizing features. 'They are the boundaries between two phases, linear breaks in continuity: shores, railroad cuts, edges of development, walls' (Ibid.: 47). Districts are identifiable from both inside and outside, the observer can mentally enter inside them, and they 'are recognizable as having some common, identifying character' (Ibid.: 47). 'Nodes are points, the strategic spots in a city into which an observer can enter, and which are the intensive foci to and from which he is traveling' (Ibid.: 47). Landmarks are a type of point reference, and 'they are usually a rather simply defined physical object: building, sign, store, or mountain. ... They are frequently used clues of identity ... and seem to be increasingly relied upon as a journey becomes more and more familiar' (Ibid.: 48). Lynch was able to illustrate his thesis of mental mapping and the significance of the five elements through interviews in Boston, Jersey City and Los Angeles, in which he asked informants to draw simple sketch maps.

In recent years, with the blossoming of interdisciplinary space and place studies, in which anthropology plays a significant role, cognitive mapping has re-emerged and is theoretically lodged in post-modernism. Moving on from Lynch's modernist project, Jameson (1991: 51) defines cognitive mapping as a process by which the individual situates himself within a 'vaster and properly unrepresentable totality which is the ensemble of society's structures as a whole'. He compares this ideological process of cognitive mapping to the physical process of locating oneself geographically. In his work, the mapping is intimately related to practice – to the individual's successful negotiation of urban spaces and places.

Contemporary anthropologist Marc Augé (1995: 57) writes of place as being 'mappable': in a geometric sense, he speaks of lines, intersections of lines, and points of intersection. In the dailiness of practice, these

> correspond to routes, axes or paths that lead from one place to another and have been traced by people; to crossroads and open spaces where people pass, meet and gather... and lastly, to centres of more or less monumental types, religious or political, constructed by certain men and therefore defining a spaces and frontiers beyond which other men are defined as others, in relation with other centres and other spaces.

My interest in mental mapping follows from the work of Lynch and Auge, as I explore ways in which to understand the community that Zongo people have constructed, the places there that are meaningful to them, and their attachment to it and them. Lynch's interest was in trying to operationalize imageability, to show how people would learn to navigate the city and, as a consequence, develop an attachment to it. I depart from Lynch, in that I look at both the common social perspective as well as the individual person, shifting between the two perspectives.

An additional incentive is to see if the sketches confirm what I have learned after years of doing research in Sabon Zongo. And finally, there is the simple question of whether the methodology is appropriate in this non-Western place. Can we assume that non-Westerners are familiar with maps and are comfortable sketching them? Would they view their world through the grid – the layout of Sabon Zongo as designed by British town planners – because it assumes a

Western, almost-Cartesian, view of space – something to be viewed from on high? Psychologists have long acknowledged the perceptual relationship that Lynch's work supported between real and represented space (Deregowski 1989). Research has shown how people's perception of pictures varies (Segall *et al.* 1963), such that members of some cultures may not see a picture as a representation at all. Does this mean that we cannot use such a method in non-Western locales? Descartes understood the physical world as being easily explainable in terms of geometry. His philosophy led analysis to move towards abstract linear spaces from spaces of concrete objects such as sequence spaces.[2] Is a method based on this perspective so biased that it is not useful as a source of information and cannot be used for comparative purposes? David Stea observed that people may have mental maps, that is that they do think in map terms and yet may find it difficult to externalize their maps for a variety of reasons.[3] But this does not mean that the mapping exercise is inappropriate for such a population. Stea himself applied it in Mexico (Stea & Wood 1971) and Rodwin (1969) used it as the basis for planning Ciudad Guayana in Venezuela. There is also a line of research involving development projects on the ground that incorporate rural rapid assessment and participatory action mapping (Chambers 1992), which uses insider knowledge in constructing projects.[4]

In June 2004, my research assistant had 11 Zongo residents draw mental maps of Sabon Zongo; and I asked one woman do the same. To elicit their responses, we asked the following questions in Hausa and English, depending upon linguistic need:

Wani iri abu ne mai muhimanci gare ka a cikin Zango?
What matters most to you in Zongo?

Wani irin abaaba ne ake gaane Zango da shi?
What are the visible structures that can be seen in Zongo? Or what are the things that Zongo is noted for?

Izan a ka ce ka 'draw' Zango kan takarda, yaya za ka yi shi?
If you were asked to put Zongo on paper, how would you represent it?

---

[2] See http://www-gap.dcs.st-and.ac.uk/~history/Mathematicians/Descartes.html
[3] In a personal communication, Stea put forward several reasons– unfamiliarity with pencils, viewing the interviewer as the 'expert' who would do this better than they could, seeing themselves as being of low status and thus not capable.
[4] This is a recognized methodology that is used in the developing world, as it tries to engage people on Western terms. For example, people may have trouble after a daily walk-through synthesizing what sequential behaviour is.

I was struck by the dominance of the grid in all of the responses that my assistant collected. To some extent it makes sense: Sabon Zongo was created by the British Colonial Administration as a town site around 1910. When first surveyed, the land at Sabon Zongo was sub-divided into thirty-two parcels and allocated by its headman Malam Idrissu Bako to his followers (Pellow 2002). This 75-acre landscape of farms lost its freedom 'from the constraints of a frame' (Ingraham 1991: 65).

> As an embodiment of the human effort to conquer space, surveying has enormous impact on the understanding of land use, the perception of landscape, and the ensuing land development; it shaped the outline and content of any piece of land available as a location for architecture. (Burns 1991: 151)

By the same token, we know from the building patterns within Sabon Zongo that even as the grid has infiltrated social consciousness, the 'people's architecture' has resisted the grid. Despite street layouts, individuals have built out into them in an aggregative or accretive manner, often on a different orthogonal. As Hubbard and Sanders (2003: 83-84) observed, areas are not just produced 'by the actions of the authorities ("from above"), but are produced "from below" … [and] by misusing spaces, escap[e] their constraints without necessarily disturbing their boundaries'. As I have related elsewhere (Pellow 2002), the formal physical attributes of Sabon Zongo's site plan in fact are not coincident with social practices: as residents of compounds have built into the courtyard space, activities such as wedding celebrations have relocated to the street. So why the near-omnipresence of the grid?

Most of the Zongolese sampled were completely intimidated by the task and could not draw a map, even one made up of simple lines. Several asked me or my assistant to draw it for them, after which they then indicated what to inscribe and where. In February 2005, I asked my assistant to collect several more maps and to insist that each interviewee do his/her own drawing. Of the six, two have framed the map with the street grid; the other four do not show streets as such but do inscribe relationships among features. The Zongolese maps include places both on and off the grid. There is also considerable overlap, which tells us something about what carries meaning, and the residents' perceptions of the community and its social and physical elements.

Landmarks, Lynch's external point references (1960), are frequently mentioned, with the most noted being Freedom Market (6x), the Night Market (10x), Abokin Ango Mosque (10x), the Chief's Palace (6x), the public toilets (6x) and Gaskiya Cinema (6x). Two people drew in the kebab sellers. All but

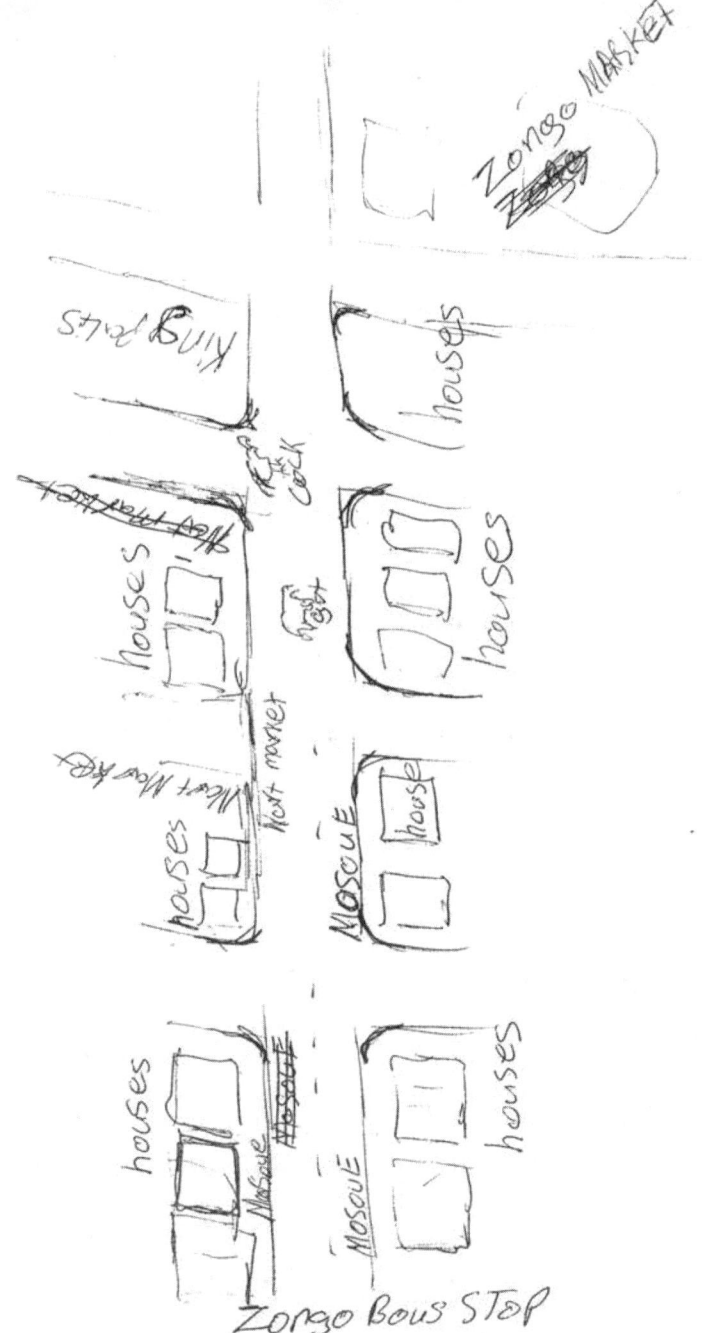

Figure 7.1 'Map' drawn by a 30-year-old Grunshie male carpenter who has primary-school education and lives in the family home in Siko Paa (Kan Tudu)

four of the mappers organized their sketches around paths and edges; they followed the grid pattern of streets (which they drew themselves or asked to have drawn), and most focused on one street (Malam Bako Street and/or Korle Bu Street) with cross streets ('nodes') and landmarks noted. A few note Market Lane and Oblogo Road, the two circumscribing main streets that in effect demarcate the community. Besides the Abokin Ango landmark, the tallest of the 30 mosques with an electrified muezzin, there are ten other mentions of mosques; usually helping to identify a neighbourhood (Lynch's 'district') as each is a local mosque. A couple of the drawings include the bus stop, an important node for travel. Only one person has drawn (and written out) several blocks of houses and only six have indicated their own houses. One man and one woman both indicated the corner barber, another hang-out for men. And then there are the personal locales – one's office, one's store, a hairdresser, a set of showers, the wee smokers.

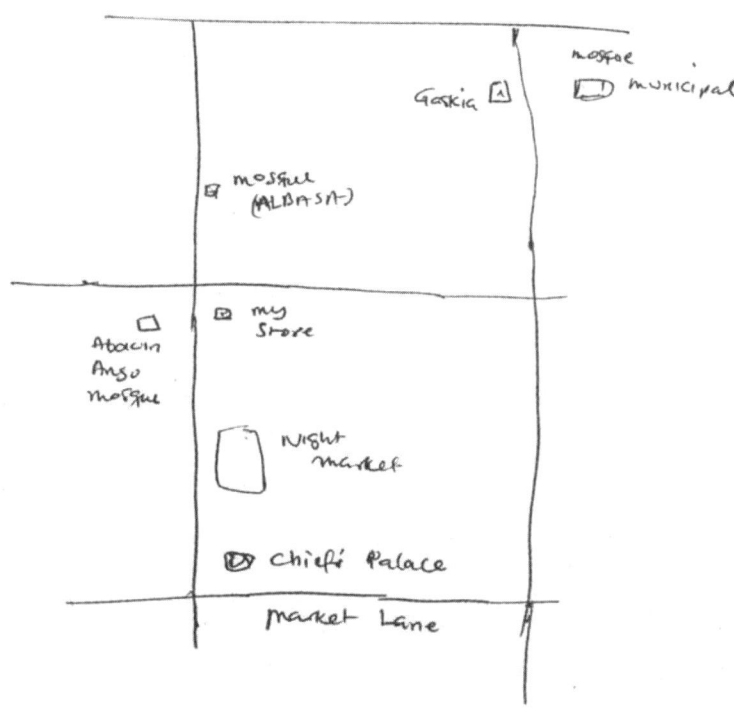

Figure 7.2 'Map' drawn by the author/her assistant on the instructions of a 60-year-old female Hausa trader

As they drew, or instructed me/my assistant to draw (as in Figure 7.2), they told (usually idiosyncratic) stories. One man complained that most of Zongo is dirty. 'When you come, you see animals, toilets, gutters not well done', and indeed he drew a goat and a rooster walking up Malam Bako Street. A woman who could not orient herself on paper at all was completely focused on the proximity of rubbish to the mosque (Abokin Ango) and to the food sellers from whom she often buys soup. But she was not the only one concerned with Sabon Zongo's condition and is cognizant of social practice. Three others translated 'what is important' into 'what is of concern'. One person believed the community needed a recreational centre for kids and adults. Another respondent (who drew the sketch in Figure 7.3), who lives in *Unguwan Makafai* (the blind quarter, also known as 'South Africa' because bad things happen there) was unhappy about the area, in part because of the wee (marijuana) smokers and also because of the neighbour's pan toilet that always smells. And another person focused on the negative environment where she lives, primarily the gutter in front of her house, also noting the mosque across the street and down the block.

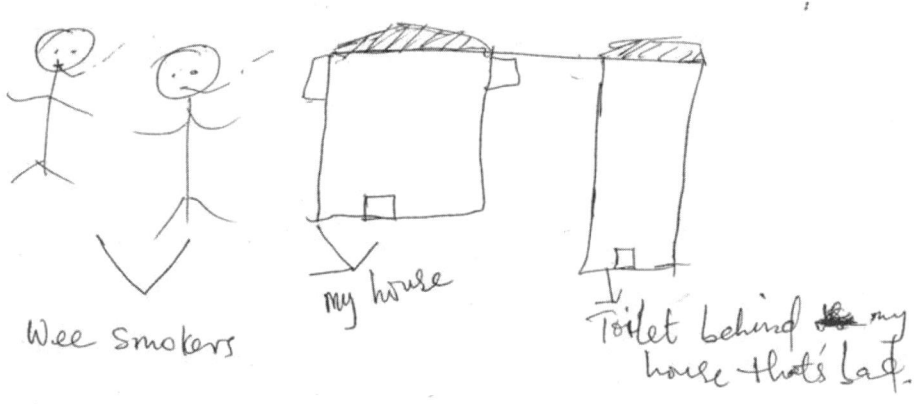

Figure 7.3   'Map' drawn by a 25-year-old female Fante store clerk with secondary-school education who rents a house in Makafai

The idiosyncratic nature of a person's local world is also evident on the maps. A man talking about the shortest way to get to his house did not show where his house was. A trader from a teacher's family noted the school her son attends across Oblogo Road and marked 'our house', which was actually her father's family house. A staunch National Democratic Congress (NDC) partisan marked the local NDC office. The man who drew showers (*shawa*) on his map in fact owns – and rents out – showers in front of his compound. And an 80-plus-year-old man who spends most of his waking hours sitting by a mosque while overseeing the care and training of race horses, when asked what was important in his community, quickly replied (and drew) a horse!

Food is extraordinarily important to the identity of this community and helps to sustain it (Pellow n.d.). Freedom Market makes it possible for women to feed their households without taking transport to one of the big markets in downtown Accra. The Night Market is located at the heart of the community and women trade in locally (Accra) prepared foods, as opposed to Hausa specialties that are sold along the side of the road. (The kebab sellers are not noted on the maps). I believe that the Hausa prepared-food specialties and their spatial arrangement are core to the community and everyday life. What is curious is that only one of those interviewed actually noted the food sellers, and this was to reinforce her concern about the omnipresence of garbage in the community and its propinquity to the food they were selling.

A composite sense of community

The maps were not necessarily a Hausa representation, although 12 of the 18 sampled were Hausa. Nine were men. Eleven lived in their own quarters, which would be in family housing, and six were renting rooms. A widow had moved to her mother's house following her husband's death. The women ranged in age from 25 to 60-plus, three (two 60-plus and one 30 year old) were uneducated, six had finished or were attending secondary school, and three primary school. Five were traders, one a teacher, one a housewife, four were students. Three women were not Hausa: two were Dagomba (from the north of Ghana) and one was Fante (from the coastal region of Ghana).

The men were primarily in their 30s – although one was in his 80s and one was 22 – and most had been to school: two to primary school, two to middle school and four to secondary school. The last four were a fashion designer, a computer teacher, a data entry clerk and an unemployed man. Of the other men, one was a trader, two were fitting mechanics, one trained race horses (having been a professional jockey when young) and one was a carpenter. The three non-Hausa were Grunshie, Gruma and Zabrama.

In creating a composite map, I want to first note what the individual mapmakers delineated as their world of Sabon Zongo, which is to say, what is salient or representative of the community to each of them. Virtually everyone included a landmark of some sort – a building like a mosque, an institution like a market, or his/her home. Following Lynch's system of elements, there are the maps organized through *paths*: One informant's map (Figure 7.1) demarcated the main north-south street, the only paved north-south street, noting the wandering animals, houses, mosques and the palace. Another informant, whose sketch is organized by *paths* and *edges* with landmarks, was a trader who lived at his family house in Kan Tudu, the original part of Sabon Zongo where the Chief's Palace is located. His local world, as he drew it, encompasses the far south end of Kan Tudu and beyond, Freedom Market and one of the schools. Yet another map employs *paths* and *edges* as it orients to the northern and southern borders – Danmalley Mosque at the north in Unguwan Zabrama, Freedom Market and Ojo School to the south. The informant also included her home and the toilet nearby and the Night Market. My assistant for the past nine years drew a perfectly proportioned street map, marking the northern edge, Oblogo Road, the southern edge, Market Lane, three landmarks – Gaskiya Cinema, Abokin Ango Mosque and the Night Market – and his former business. A mechanic organized his map around *edges* and *district*; he marked his family house but his map focused on the north and northeast area of Sabon Zongo. As it happens, most of the car mechanics work on the north side, along Oblogo Road, down the street from Gaskiya. The map by a male, who described himself as a mechanic, is clearly oriented to the immediate neighbourhood (*district*) where he had his side business, namely the showers he rents out. Interestingly, he did not mark his house, which is right behind the showers. Similarly, the fashion designer's map (*district* and *node with landmarks*), drawn by my assistant while the interviewee was working on his sewing machine, encapsulated the core north-south area, going from the bus stop on Oblogo Road, past Abokin Ango Mosque, the Chief's Palace and the Night Market. He also noted four local landmarks – Gaskiya Cinema, the blind people's mosque (*Makafai*), the kebab sellers and the corner barber.

Lynch's *node with landmarks* was the organizing principle for several of the women, all of whom had drawn what I would consider the core or focal area. For one, it was the intersection of Malam Bako Road (leading to the Night Market and the palace) and Korle Bu Street, the main east-west road. She marked Abokin Ango Mosque, the Night Market, and the palace – all institutional landmarks – her *family* house (she lives around the corner with her husband in his family house) and two local businesses (but not her own!). Another three were all framed by the grid but drawn by my assistant. The woman who was a housewife and lived in Unguwan Zabrama, drew a map that was similar to the fashion designer's but with a nodal centre: her map follows Malam Bako Street, the main paved north-south road, noting Abokin Ango, the Night Market, the Chief's Palace, but also the corner barber (a hang-out spot for middle-age men), and the blind people's mosque. The map by an elderly trader was also similar: Malam Bako Street, with Abokin Ango, the Night Market, and the Chief's Palace. She also included two other mosques – Albasa and Municipal/Zana – and her own business. Another female mapper delineated the core area: Malam Bako Street, Abokin Ango Mosque, the Night Market, Freedom Market; her store and the toilet near where she lived to give it a strong home focus. It was she who also marked the NDC's local headquarters.

Moving now to Lynch's *landmarks* alone: one interviewee included many community landmarks – four mosques, three schools, the Night Market and the cinema. The next drawing contained three elements, drawn in the following order – Iddrisu's Mosque, where the interviewee who was an elder of the Bako family spent most of his waking hours, a horse (his lifelong work had been with race horses) and his home: this was clearly what he regarded as his local daily world, even though, as a community elder he moved around a lot. And one interviewee had a very basic map indicating *landmarks* and *district*: the relative street location of her mother (*matan police*), her mother's shop, the nearby clinic and the road to the toilet.

The last of the maps were quite interesting and while they fitted into Lynch's scheme, they also included data that he did not deal with. All of them related tales of *problems*, and they did this in the local neighbourhood (*district*) by noting *landmarks*. The interviewee who could not draw a map, delineated the community as a very circumscribed area with particular landmarks – Abokin Ango Mosque, the food sellers a block from her house (where she often bought meals) and her family house *Gidan Makaranta*, which was also a Koranic school – and ticked off issues of cleanliness. She found the rubbish near the mosques and the food sellers problematic. Someone else suggested the need for a community centre, having noted the location of two of the 'bases', gathering places for young men where some believed unsavoury behaviour went on. His map included a variety of *landmarks* – the Night Market, an arrow to Gaskiya, the Abokin Ango and Makafai (blind people's) mosques, and the Chief's Palace. The last two indicated their unhappiness with the immediate neighbourhood (*district*) – for one it was the wee smokers near her house, as well as the toilet in the house behind hers (see Figure 7.3); for another her concerns, in order of salience, were her home (a very large family house), Danmalley Mosque across the street, the condition of the gutter and that of the street.

So if we put these maps together, we see a couple of different things. For those who used the grid, Sabon Zongo was delineated along a north-south axis, from Oblogo to Market Lane, with a primary focus radiating from the Malam Bako/Korle Bu Street intersection. For those who did not, drawings primarily depicted local sights and issues of concern, such as garbage in the streets. All of them, as exemplified by the 'map' with the mosque, horse and house, indicated what was important to them in their community. Yet the results were ambiguous: the mapping exercise did not elicit certain kinds of knowledge (for example, what was vibrant in the community or more local neighbourhood). On the other hand, it is good because it works as a mnemonic to tell stories and to elicit people's concerns. As geographer Anne Mosher found in the project she and architect Anne Munly carried out in Rome NY,[5] participants cannot engage in mental mapping without complaining about what is wrong. On the one hand, they express nostalgia – they value the streets and buildings – but they are also irritated about how the area is becoming polluted because of what the government has or has not done.

Discussion

As an outsider who has spent a lot of time in this community, I see much of the community as I know it in the maps that this group have drawn: the landmarks such as mosques and the Night Market, the animals in the streets, the dirt and decay. Apparently, in thinking about or telling others about their community, however, this group of map-makers do not consider the prepared-food sellers a landmark or salient. This really is a disconnect with the outside because the prepared Hausa specialties, sold at specific times in specific places, are central to the community's vitality, to its street traffic and to those who congregate to eat. This particular trade is also a draw for outsiders. Perhaps those we talked to assumed one could get this food anywhere. Or perhaps it is because buying food on the street is so normalized that it does not stand out.

There are three primary foci to the Sabon Zongo maps. The first is institutional. Everyone drew in one or more of the following: mosques (religion), markets (family and economy), the chieftaincy (governance), schools (education) and the Night Market space (ceremony and ritual). The second is the local neighbourhood. Even though only two map-makers noted his/her own home (a few others included the family house), the maps revealed a very strong home bias. This is to say that many think of the community and express community attachment in terms of their own neighbourhood area. And third, there is a real sense of the core or heart of the community.

Does the instrument of mental mapping work here? The core focus of the resident map-makers does reinforce the concurrence of Sabon Zongo opinion on the community's socio-physical centre, as I reported earlier after years of study there (Pellow 2002: 88): centripetal socio-spatial structures, including the chieftaincy and its palace, the Abokin Ango Mosque, and the Night Market. As observed early on, streets are incomplete – they may remain unpaved, or they are discontinuous, and they can be used as extensions of the compound yard –

---

[5] Entitled 'Urban Mapping Research Initiative: Cognitive Mapping as Weak Cartography'.

for children to play, for selling food, for keeping animals and for life-cycle celebrations, such as weddings and birth outdoorings. Indeed, the streets are for eating, selling and hanging out, even though there is more car traffic than even just five years ago.

Perhaps what is important is what people leave out – what they take for granted, such as the street food. Under pressure, they said what they thought of first. Imageability, as Lynch made clear, is really important – but it is imageability-plus. How do people feel? Is their community or neighbourhood space embraceable space? The maps that I collected reduce the richness of the landscape. What is absent is the vitality of street life, the scene of traders and regular provision stores, with the foot traffic, noises, smells, nodes for gathering, and the music that envelopes public spaces when families privatize them for celebrations. These pedestrian practices of consumption, which are salient to residents because they nourish their families physically, spiritually and culturally, have been omitted from the maps. I believe that these informal spaces matter because they provide meaning and content to the individual neighbourhoods and the community as a whole. I believe they were omitted from the maps because they were taken for granted. The map-makers were more focused on formal properties (à la Lynch) and also on local problems. Both are important and, with accompanying stories, they help encapsulate the spirit and practices that are representative of Sabon Zongo.

References

Augé, M. 1995, *Non-Places: Introduction to an Anthropology of Supermodernity*, (transl. John Howe), London: Verso.
Burns, C. 1991, 'On Site: Architectural Preoccupations', in: A. Kahn (ed.), *Drawing Building Text*, New York: Princeton Architectural Press, pp. 146-67.
de Certeau, M. 1984, *The Practice of Everyday Life*, Berkeley: University of California Press.
Chambers, R. 1992, 'Rapid but Relaxed and Participatory Rural Appraisal: Towards Applications in Health and Nutrition', in: N.S. Scrimshaw & G.R. Gleason (eds), *Rapid Assessment Procedures: Qualitative Methodologies for Planning and Evaluation of Health-Related Programmes*, Boston: International Nutrition Foundation for Developing Countries, pp. 295-305.
Dakubu, M.E. Kropp 1997, *Korle Meets the Sea: A Sociolinguistic History of Accra*, New York: Oxford.
Deregowski, J.B. 1989, 'Real Space and Represented Space: Cross-Cultural Perspectives', *Behavioral and Brain Sciences* (12): 51-119.
Downs, R.M. & D. Stea 1977, *Maps in Minds: Reflections on Cognitive Mapping*, New York: Harper & Row.

Hubbard, P. & T. Sanders 2003, 'Making Space for Sex Work: Female Street Prostitution and the Production of Urban Space', *International Journal of Urban and Regional Research* 27 (1): 75-89.

Ingraham, C. 1991, 'Lines and Linearity: Problems in Architectural Theory', in: A. Kahn (ed.), *Drawing Building Text*, New York: Princeton Architectural Press, pp. 63-84.

Jameson, F. 1991, *Postmodernism, or the Cultural Logic of Late Capitalism*, Durham: Duke University Press.

King, A. 1976, *Colonial Urban Development: Culture, Social Power, and Environment*, London: Routledge and Kegan Paul.

Low, S.M. 1996, 'Spatializing Culture: The Social Production and Social Construction of Public Space in Costa Rica', *American Ethnologist* 23 (4): 861-79.

Lynch, K. 1960, *The Image of the City*, Cambridge: MIT Press and Harvard University Press.

Obirih-Opareh, N. 2001, 'Public or Private? A Policy Dilemma of Liquid Waste Management in Accra', in: S. van der Geest & N. Obirih-Opareh (eds), *Toilets and Sanitation in Ghana: An Urgent Matter*, Amsterdam: Council for Scientific and Industrial Research, pp. 13-23.

Pellow, D. 2002, *Landlords and Lodgers: Socio-Spatial Organization in an Accra Community*, Westport: Praeger.

Pellow, D. n.d., 'Attachment Sustains: The Glue of Prepared Food', in: C.A. Maida (ed.), *Sustainability and Communities of Place*, New York: Berghahn Books.

Rapoport, A. 1980, 'Neighbourhood Heterogeneity or Homogeneity: The Field of Man-Environment Studies', *Architecture and Behavior* (1): 65-77.

Rodwin, L. 1969, *Planning Urban Growth and Regional Development: The Experience of the Guayana Program in Venezuela*, Cambridge: MIT Press.

Segall, M.H., D.T. Campbell & J.M. Herskovits 1963, 'Differences in Perception of Geometric Illusions', *Science* (139): 769-71.

Stea, D. & D. Wood 1971, *A Cognitive Atlas: Explorations into the Psychological Geography of Four Mexican Cities*, Chicago: Environmental Research Group.

Tipple, A.G. 1999, 'Housing Supply in Ghana', *Progress in Planning* 51 (4): 255-324.

8

Not quite the comforts of home: Searching for locality among street youth in Dar es Salaam

Eileen Moyer

> *Working among street youth in Dar es Salaam demands a recognition of the transient and uncertain nature of their everyday lives. Despite this, or perhaps because of it, they expend a great deal of time and economic resources trying to establish networks of locality and feelings of belonging. Uprooted from their childhood homes and often isolated from rural support networks, they work to develop networks that provide safety and security from the threats of street life, protection from police harassment and, importantly, friendship and love. This chapter examines two 'locations' that formed important loci among those with whom I worked in Dar es Salaam – the first was tied to work and the second to leisure and relaxation. It examines how these locales factor into the imaginaries of the young people who inhabit them, as well as into the imaginaries of more established residents of the city, focusing on contestation and social unease.*

While doing research among young men and women living and working in the streets of Dar es Salaam, it was often difficult to maintain long-term continuous contact with many of the participants in this study.[1] Efforts to establish meaningful ties with individuals frequently ended in failure when they disappeared. People were always coming and going between city and village, work and home, and between freedom and imprisonment. A few even made the epic

---

[1] Fieldwork for this chapter was carried out over a one-year period in 1999-2000 and 2 months in 2002. Research was made possible by the Fulbright-Hays Foundation, the University of Iowa Graduate School and the Amsterdam School for Social Science Research, University of Amsterdam.

journey from life to death. It would be possible to argue that they were among the most transient and marginal people in the city. Yet, the more I examined my data with a theoretical lens focused on understanding transience, the clearer it became that many of these marginalized people were continually struggling to carve out niches of semi-permanence where they could fashion a dream of belonging and locality, and the possibility of staying put. It seemed as if living on the edge, sleeping on the streets, and hustling from meal to meal led to a desire for the security that one gains from being part of localized social networks. It makes sense that people living in highly transient circumstances would strive for a sense of locality and belonging. Research that focuses too closely on the transience of street life risks failing to recognize how desperate most of those living on the streets are to develop networks of human and spatial relations to ease anxieties about being alone in the world.

The people with whom I worked most closely all knew one another to varying degrees and most of them could be traced through a particular street corner in the downtown business district of Dar es Salaam, not far from the Sheraton Hotel. The street corner, which I refer to as Maskani in this chapter, is like many other loci of activity in the city where young men gather for work and pleasure, where female food vendors serve hot meals, and where numerous people pass through to hang out for a while, eat lunch, read the newspaper, and hear the news that may not be fit to print.[2] While this street corner is not the specific focus of this chapter, I open with a brief discussion about it to situate the reader in the world of Maskani and the people who lived and worked there, hereafter referred to as Wamaskani (see Footnote 2), as well as to introduce some theoretical ideas about space to frame the remainder of the chapter.

The primary focus of this chapter is another place in the city, a place where some Wamaskani lived and where others visited when searching for some of the things that street life could not provide them. Not all of those who participated in this research slept at Maskani but among those who did, it was not uncommon for them to have attempted to establish some sort of domestic permanency in the past. The area of the city is known as Uwanja wa Fisi, or the Field of Hyenas, and is a place where many Wamaskani have lived at one time or another. I deliberately focus on one particular household in Uwanja wa Fisi where the majority of in-depth interviews for this research were carried out to

---

[2] In Dar es Salaam, these corners are known as either *maskani* or *kijiweni* depending on whether an individual recognizes them as a place of leisure or work. To reduce confusion for the reader, whenever referring to the Sheraton Maskani I capitalize it and refrain from italicizing the term. All references to other *maskani* are not capitalized and remain in italics. At times I also employ the neologism wamaskani, or the people of *maskani* to refer specifically to 'the many different people with whom I worked who make their living in and around the Sheraton Maskani'.

emphasize the importance of domesticity and familial ties. Spencer, the young man who was the head of this household, worked hard to provide suitable shelter for his own family and, at various times, a place of refuge for young men trying to make it in the city, including several from Maskani.

The last sections of the chapter consider some introductory thoughts on leisure and play, pleasure and desire. For, if Maskani (and *maskanis* in general) served as a locus of labour and work activities, Uwanja wa Fisi served as a locus of play and pleasure, of *sterehe*. Most significant to this discussion are the sections that take a closer look at the relationship between transactional sex and AIDS. The link between pleasure and death is explored in the final sections through a story about the death of a young woman named Rehema who lived and worked in Uwanja wa Fisi.

Maskani as space, place and non-place

Dar es Salaam's downtown business centre is many things, but a neighbourhood it is not. In fact, this part of the city feels like a ghost town by seven in the evening on weekdays and all day on Sundays. The streets are virtually empty, the shops are closed, and traffic is minimal. Yet people live here, sleeping in the shadows of various buildings and businesses. Given the topic of this collection, I gave considerable thought as to whether Maskani could be considered a neighbourhood. Wamaskani have no houses, not even makeshift ones; they sleep on pieces of cardboard placed on the top of food vendors' benches and tables. Aside from occasional fun with a prostitute, they never sleep with their girlfriends at Maskani. They never cook for themselves and they keep their clothes in bags and suitcases that are placed inside a nearby kiosk in exchange for a small fee. Yet, Maskani remains central to their social and work lives. Friends and relatives trying to find Wamaskani always visit the street corner first, and there is a fairly strong sense of community among those who work and sleep there. Despite this, there is no sense of permanence about Maskani. Though it has been in existence since the mid-1990s, everyone who has earned a living there is acutely aware of how quickly circumstances could change, how fast the police could close them down, or new formal businesses could be erected that might challenge their informal use of space.[3] Everyone who slept at Maskani claimed they were only doing so until they could start a business, find an apartment and settle down with a nice girl. None planned on being there for very long. While there were plenty of social rules, Wamaskani have never

---

[3] In fact, this is exactly what happened. A bank was erected on the empty lot behind Maskani, and most of the kiosks were destroyed by the police. To all intents and purposes, Maskani has ceased to exist.

thought of themselves as living in a neighbourhood. Maskani is a *maskani*, a place where young people gather to look for work and engage with one another socially.

From this perspective and following the work of Marc Augé (1995), Maskani might be considered a non-place, produced by processes of what he refers to as supermodernity or, to be more specific in the case of Maskani, global processes in the form of economic and political liberalization. For Augé, non-spaces are marked by their transitory nature. They are 'spaces which cannot be defined as relational, or historical, or concerned with identity' in juxtaposition with a place, which is 'relational, or historical, or concerned with identity' (Augé 1995: 77-78). 'Places and non-place are rather like opposed polarities: the first is never completely erased, the second never totally completed' (Ibid.: 79). He lists sites of transport, transit, commerce and leisure as producers of simplified, relatively anonymous, temporary identities and, thus, as non-places. Augé makes several interesting and cogent points about the proliferation of non-spaces in the West and offers insights into understanding them. He is less careful, however, when he extends his definition to include sites like shanty towns and refugee camps, which I am inclined to imagine have much more in common with Maskani than an airport lounge, for example. The idea of being 'never totally completed' is certainly at work at Maskani, but the idea that as a non-space it should not be considered relational, historical or concerned with identity would lead to a false understanding of life there. Of course Augé does not refer to Maskani as a non-place, but I have a good idea that he would, and the problem with such an understanding is that it denies the creativity of the individuals who live and work there. By denying them access to history and identity, one denies them their humanity.

It is useful to combine Augé's perspective on non-places with de Certeau's (1984) ideas about geographical poetics that also unfold in spaces devoid of particular meanings and histories. Of particular interest to him are the transitory spaces at the edges of, and in-between, formal places – spaces like Maskani. For him, their liminality allows them to 'become liberated spaces that can be occupied. A rich indetermination gives them, by means of semantic rarefaction, the function of articulating a second, poetic geography on top of the geography of the literal, forbidden or permitted meaning' (Ibid.: 105). Despite efforts by individuals to occupy such spaces, according to de Certeau, they still remain spaces rather than places. I would contend that the very occupation of spaces emplaces them in history, even if only momentarily, at least for the occupiers. They become entwined with their identities and, if the occupation lasts long enough, perhaps with the identity of the city as well. While for Augé such sites are produced by supermodernity, for de Certeau they serve to rupture the master narratives of modernity. Fusing the views, I would contend that it is possible, at least in the case of Maskani, for a site to be both produced by supermodernity and a challenge to modernity's claims. So while Maskani may be a non-neighbourhood, it is not a non-place. Perhaps this suggests that neighbourhood and place are not necessarily tied to one another.

At the other end of this spectrum is Uwanja wa Fisi, located in the heart of Dar es Salaam's popular areas. Though similar to what Augé and others would call a 'shanty town' – and thus a non-place – one must seriously question such a categorization. First, neighbourhoods like Uwanja wa Fisi are home to a large majority of Dar es Salaam's residents, as is the case in most of urban Africa. Second, they are places teaming with activity: there are schools, police stations, football fields, churches, mosques, businesses, markets and innumerable homes. Though such spaces are considered primarily informal in the context of city planning and though they are in many respects 'off the grid' in terms of official power and water supplies, there is no doubt that they are true neighbourhoods. If we rhetorically erase these neighbourhoods by calling them non-places, informal settlements etc., we essentially erase what citizens of Dar es Salaam consider to be the African city. Though this does indeed seem at times to be the aim of many urban planners, it is not the aim of this chapter. Rather, I want to draw attention to such sites and to highlight their importance in shaping urban residents' sense of self and belonging, their sense of rootedness and community, even if it is only fleeting.

Uswahilini: Home of the masses

I use the term *Uswahilini* here to refer to these informal neighbourhoods, as it is the term used in Dar es Salaam. Uswahilini or Uswazi,[4] as it is also known, refers to the densely populated areas of Dar es Salaam where the majority of the city's residents live. Most of Dar es Salaam is at or below sea level and the lowest lying areas of the city – those that are most prone to flash flooding – have become the domain of the poor and working classes. Those with enough money opt for more expensive real estate above the flood plains. The areas of the city marked by a slightly higher elevation or far enough away from the city's waterways are sometimes colloquially referred to as Uzunguni, or the place of the Europeans, though the majority of the people living in such areas are African .

Historically, the wealthier areas of the city have been located along the coast north of the city. Oyster Bay, on the Msasani Peninsula, is reserved for those

---

[4] Several people told me that *Uswazi*, literally meaning the place of the Swazi peoples, alludes to the densely populated areas found in South African townships.

with the most money and the most power. During colonialism it was an enclave reserved for Europeans but shortly after independence much of the area was taken over by Tanzania's new political and economic leaders. It is difficult to know who owns the beautiful seafront properties today but most are rented by wealthy expatriates or foreigners. Oyster Bay and the Msasani Peninsula together are known as Uzunguni. The slow northern expansion of the wealthy suburbs and the inland spread of Uswahilini are spatial manifestations of the changes that have come about in conjunction with liberalization.[5] Mikocheni, Kawe and Mbezi Beach, which benefit from the cooling sea breezes, are currently sites of large-scale construction with beautiful new, gated houses seemingly going up everyday.[6] There is a lot of disagreement as to whether there is in fact more money in Tanzania since the introduction of liberalization policies, or whether it is just that people are no longer afraid of spending it conspicuously. Many say that Tanzanians were afraid to build ostentatious houses while Nyerere was alive, that they were afraid he would show up at their houses personally and demand to know how they had accessed the necessary resources in a poor country like Tanzania. It seems that any lingering restraint that might have existed following the collapse of socialism has completely disappeared since his death.

Though houses have been mushrooming up all over the city since the mid-1980s, the greatest growth has taken place in Uswahilini, where every piece of land, regardless of how precariously it is situated, is considered prime real estate among those with minimal resources and maximum desire for a place to call home. Perched on the edge of rivers and on the sides of steep hills with the ground sometimes visibly eroding away from under them, the houses in Uswahilini are an engineering wonder. Most are simple Swahili-style houses with six rooms – three on each side of a central passageway running front to back – and a small courtyard behind. Individual families rent one or more rooms from the owner of the house. Everyone living on the premises shares the passage and the courtyard, which is primarily reserved for domestic tasks like cooking and laundry. Close living quarters, combined with the fact that one rarely chooses

---

[5] I suggest here that the expansion is slow to indicate that it is occurring gradually, but relatively speaking, the expansion is taking place at quite a rapid pace in comparison with past rates of growth. This is true of housing in the city, just as it is true of the city's population, which has an annual growth rate of 8-10% making it one of the fastest urbanizing cities in Africa.

[6] Much has been made in the social-sciences literature in recent years of the proliferation of gated communities and the privatization of public space, both of which seem to be an unfortunate side-effect of increasing economic liberalization and democratization. See, for example, Caldeira (1996; 2000), Davis (1992 [1990]), Harvey (2000), Kuppinger (2002), Low (2001), Sassen (2003) and Waldrop (2002).

one's neighbours, often leads to tense social situations. Gossip and rumour prevail, and one constantly feels that one is being watched. The women who live in Uswahilini spend much of their time there, taking care of their children, cooking food for their families and keeping their households in order. Many are also engaged in some sort of income-generating activity from their homes, while most of the men in Uswahilini attempt to find ways to earn money outside.

In general, there are very few jobs in Uswahilini. Many of the young I interviewed who lived in Uswahilini and worked in other parts of the city found it difficult to spend more than a couple of days at a time in Uswahilini. They reported feeling oppressed by the endless arguing among neighbours and the need to escape the confines to search for a degree of privacy. Although there were more than enough ways to express a desire for privacy in Kiswahili, the demands for it were such that in 2000 at least two English expressions were incorporated into popular speech. 'Don't spy my life' was a phrase that was heard in response to unwelcome advice or was painted on the back of local buses. In addition, the English verb 'mind' was appropriated into Kiswahili in the phrase, *usimindi*, 'you should not mind', or more appropriately, 'mind your own business'.

It is possible to drive to Uswahilini but not if one really wants to go into it. Uswahilini begins at the edge of the tarmac road where people step off the bus and are forced to enter a world the car has yet to conquer. To get in (*ndanindani*), one has to go on foot along the hundreds of winding paths that criss-cross between the thousands of houses scattered throughout the valleys of the city, each one apparently constructed according to its owner's whims. De Certeau's trope of walking and poetics is useful here. When I walked in Uswahilini I was almost always escorted. The verb *kusindikiza*, usually used to describe the act of escorting a departing guest part of the way home, was often used by those who guided me through their neighbourhoods. Some would go out of their way to direct me along the straightest and cleanest paths, while others would draw my attention to crumbling foundations and open sewers, sheepishly apologizing, laughing or inviting me to comment.

Observing various escorts I noted how different the city looked depending on whose footsteps I was following. I began to see how the act of moving from home to work and back again was like composing a poem. People move quickly but carefully, weaving along footpaths, past market stands, along riverbeds and sidestepping the ubiquitous children all intent on running about and having fun, seemingly indifferent to their surroundings. One is assaulted by sights, sounds and smells on all sides, resulting in a multi-sensorial experience difficult to put into words – hearing the sizzle of potatoes as they hit the hot grease of a fryer, and not smelling the countless open sewers one is forced to cross over every day, while keeping one's eyes on the rolling hips of a young woman as she walks, effortlessly carrying a bucket of water on her head and composing a cartographic poem of her own.

Photo 8.1 'Don't Spy My Life' minibus in Dar es Salaam (2000) (Photo: Eileen Moyer)

In 'Orientalism and the Exhibitionary Other', Timothy Mitchell (1995: 305) writes of the frustration encountered by European writers and photographers visiting the Middle East in the nineteenth century. Longing to understand the labyrinth of streets characteristic of so many Middle Eastern cities, they were constantly at work seeking out a 'point of view', which would allow them to look down on and order the city spaces they came across. They almost uniformly commented on the seeming disorder and chaos they saw as they gazed at Middle Eastern cities with the same totalizing intentions as the voyeurs critiqued by de Certeau (1984: 93). It is only by walking that one is able to begin to comprehend the labyrinths of streets and paths in Uswahilini. Efforts to find a vantage point, whether literally or figuratively, will necessarily prove fruitless for it is impossible to fathom the consciously contestatory order of things from above.

Photo 8.2 'Don't Mind' minibus in Dar es Salaam (2000)
(Photo: Eileen Moyer)

A certain air of amusement and incredulity always marked conversations about Uswahilini. Uswahilini is imagined as a place where ordinary rules of order and discipline do not apply, where the world is turned on its head. Life becomes carnivalesque and seemingly anything can happen. Humour, laughter and irony are the most powerful weapons for coming to grips with what Bakhtin (1984) calls 'the eternal incomplete unfinished nature of being'. Uswahilini is this way, but only because people celebrate and embrace the resistances that such spaces embody. Through their appreciation and imagination they actively contribute to the creation and continuation of alternative readings (and writings) of space.

Photo 8.3   Karibu Uswazi by Hassani Mwanyiro (2002)

In 2002 I had the opportunity to commission a series of paintings from Hassani 'Mwanyiro' Mwanga, a 21-year-old Tingatinga[7] artist who came to Dar es Salaam in 1995 from Kilosa in Morogoro. The first painting I bought from him illustrated a panoramic view of daily life in Dar es Salaam transposed onto a map of Africa. Intrigued and wanting to hear more about his views of space and mapping, I struck up a conversation with him. I told him about my research interests and we agreed that he would paint three more pictures for me, including one representing 'Uswahilini'. I was more than pleased with the results. Mwanyiro's 'view' of the city is exceptionally broad and, looking at his paintings, it is difficult to find a focus. The eye is forced to wander across the canvas, delightfully discovering amusing representations of the minutia of

---

[7] Tingatinga is a form of popular painting produced primarily, though not exclusively, for tourist consumption. Artist Edward Tingatinga, after whom the style is named, first developed the style in 1972. Out of his small workshop grew a thriving cooperative that is still operational today (Mwansanga 1998, Mwidadi & Chilamboni 1998). Hassani Mwanyiro is one of approximately 150 artists who sell their work from stalls lining the road that leads to the entrance of the cooperative.

everyday life. This style, markedly present in his other paintings, is intensified in 'Uswahilini', a subject that he said he had never painted before. When commissioning the paintings, I had encouraged him to 'map' the city as he saw fit. He delivered 'Uswahilini' with particular pride, pointing out all the details – such as the women braiding each other's hair and the rocks holding down the tin roofs – to ensure I would not miss them. Mwanyiro's painting illustrates the joy in their lives rather than focusing on poverty and suffering. His representation is by far the best I have encountered. The painting illustrates the way life flows in Uswahilini, encouraging the eye to walk across the canvas in the same way a pedestrian might make his way through the labyrinths he has so expertly configured. Schoolgirls skipping, one of them revealing her panties, while a group of men gather to drink Kibuku (a thick millet beer) and talk. People wash their clothes, prepare dinner and go about their business, all in public, while the houses remain shuttered, illustrating a desire for privacy in the domestic sphere.

Caldeira (2000: 310) discusses the way that *favelas*, a Brazilian equivalent to Uswahilini, become private enclaves where 'only residents and acquaintances venture'. Although she criticizes the increasing privatization of space in general, it is possible to see from her point of view that there are also advantages to be gained by encouraging spatial relations that are exclusionary. As threatening as Uswahilini may feel to outsiders, those who live there gain a certain degree of security from knowing that outsiders will rarely venture in. Hiding from the police, or from anyone else for that matter, is relatively easy in Uswahilini. Most pursuers would not only not know *where* to search, more importantly, they would not know *how*. Yet negotiating the spaces of Uswahilini can also pose problems for its residents. As Harvey (1990: 5-6) argues, despite there being unbridled freedom in certain urban spaces, too many people also lose their way in the labyrinth of the city. He cautions that it is 'when we lose our grasp on the grammar of urban life that violence takes over'. The poetics of Uswahilini can change rapidly and are often complex, making it that much easier to lose one's 'grasp on the grammar' of the city. Despite my general optimism regarding the possibilities and potential for contestatory social spaces like those found in places such as Uswahilini and Maskani, the story about the death of a young woman presented below might best be read as a cautionary tale serving to warn against the dangers of 'misreading' the city. It illustrates the importance of social relations and locality for those living in Uswahilini. First however, I would like to introduce the Field of Hyenas, a part of Uswahilini central to the lives of many of the young men from Maskani.

Finding Uwanja wa Fisi

If one follows the low-lying river valleys, or *mabondeni*,[8] away from the centre of Dar es Salaam to the surrounding suburbs of Uswahilini, you will eventually end up in the Tandale section of the city; and where Tandale meets Manzese, there is perhaps the most notorious piece of real estate in all of Tanzania: Uwanja wa Fisi, or the Field of Hyenas.[9] According to long-time residents of the area, the place received its name in an innocuous enough fashion. Before the city of Dar es Salaam began its slow expansion through the river valleys, the area was part of the surrounding bush and known as a place where hyenas gathered at night.[10] The hyena, however, is also a rich symbol: its unusual behaviour and appearance imbue it with a potential that encourages even the most unimaginative of minds to impose significance on the beast's very being (Roberts 1995: 75). Many in Tanzania believe that witches ride hyenas, holding tightly to their bellies as they fly through the night sky. Athumani, a car washer from Maskani, laughed uncomfortably as he described the way hyenas will follow a man in the bush for days waiting for the fingers to fall from his dangling hands. This story, highlighting the hyena's unusual combination of patience and voraciousness was told to me so that I might understand similar qualities said to be exhibited by residents of Uwanja wa Fisi. Though Athumani did not live in Uwanjani,[11] he, like many of the other young men from Maskani, did frequent its guest houses, gambling halls, drug dens and video parlours whenever he had extra money in his pocket and a yearning for fun and pleasure.

Visiting Uwanja wa Fisi, one is first struck by how small everything is for a place with such a big reputation. By coincidence, my first visit there was on the

---

[8] *Mabondeni* literally means 'in the valleys', and is used along with Uswahilini and Uswazi to designate the least desirable places to live in the city. Health and ecological and aesthetic reasons are routinely offered as justifications for not wanting to live there. Since the areas are low-lying there is often standing water to contend with and the increase in mosquitoes and malaria that comes with it.

[9] Tripp, who also conducted research in Manzese, reports that 'Manzese has a reputation throughout Dar es Salaam, especially among people who do not live there, as a place bustling with activity, especially illicit activities. ... Outsiders fear Manzese because it is said that most of the criminals in the city live there. Nonresidents also talk about "Radio Manzese" as the rumour mill of the city. Yet there is little to distinguish Manzese from Buguruni, Temeke, or any other part of the city. To its inhabitants, Manzese is an area of mostly hard-working and respectable citizens' (Tripp 1997: 39).

[10] Several sources supported the notion that Uwanja wa Fisi was a place favoured by hyenas in the past, though most agree that the name did not become popular until the mid-1990s as the area increasingly became associated with criminality.

[11] *Uwanjani* is the locative form of Uwanja, and was one of the words most commonly used to refer to Uwanja wa Fisi. I use the two interchangeably in this chapter.

last day of the month when many employees receive their wages. Tens of men were lined up outside the many guest houses where prostitutes rent rooms. It was the middle of the day and many of those awaiting their turn to be with the lady of their choice were night guards, young Maasai warriors dressed in their distinctive red clothes, beadwork and braids, a spectacle that could only be enjoyed on payday. Several guest houses along with bars and video parlours are located around the open field that gives Uwanjani its name and that serves as a sort of public square-cum-red-light district for those living in the area. In the centre, numerous vendors set up tables to sell raw meat, mostly leftover bits and organ meat that, I was told, would have 'fallen off the back of delivery trucks', or would have been reclaimed from condemned meat that had failed to meet health-code requirements. The air in and around the square is usually thick with flies, while the smell of blood mixed with that of home-brewed alcohol is truly unique. Those who escorted me to Uwanja wa Fisi the first time were tense, not really knowing what to expect. They need not have worried, however, for despite its reputation and the fact that this part of the city was probably the least likely to receive *wazungu* visitors, most people noted my presence with only mild curiosity and amusement, giving the impression that nothing would be considered too surprising for those living near Uwanjani.[12]

I was first taken to Uwanjani by Maatata, a young man from Arusha. I knew him first as a car washer from Maskani. When I met him, I assumed he was a street child sleeping and hustling to make a living on the streets of Dar es Salaam. As it turned out, Maatata and a couple of other young men from Arusha were among the first to begin doing business at Maskani in the mid-1990s. Although there were no formal leaders at Maskani, at the age of eighteen Maatata had become a street-corner elder. Even so, his behaviour was hardly above reproach.

He was nicknamed Mjela, or 'jailbird', in dubious honour of the years he had spent in the juvenile detention centre less than ten minutes' walk from Maskani. His crime of choice, it was said, was petty thievery and his illegal activities, no doubt, contributed to a personal history best described as that of a transient. Since the age of thirteen, Maatata had been constantly on the move between his home village in Kilimanjaro Region and the cities of Arusha and Dar es Salaam. When things got too hot in one place, he would move on to the next, giving both the local authorities and the victims of his crimes time to forget his

---

[12] The only problems we ever encountered were from men intoxicated to the point of belligerence, incidences that were more likely to occur later in the day. It was primarily for this reason that we rarely stayed in Uwanjani after nightfall. I did not want to be harassed, and even less did I want those who were with me to be placed in an uncomfortable situation.

transgressions. Since much of his thievery in Dar es Salaam targeted members of the expatriate communities and tourists in Arusha, it was often just a matter of waiting until the person attempting to press charges left Tanzania. Every once in a while though, he would steal from the wrong person or brag too loudly about his exploits. When he was sent to the juvenile detention centre he had just come to Dar es Salaam and had not yet established the social networks he had by the time I met him, networks that would most likely have served to warn and protect him when the police came looking, providing him with places to hide until they lost interest, and bail money when he was unfortunate enough to get caught.

Although I met Maatata at Maskani where he worked, the majority of his Dar es Salaam social ties included people who lived and worked in Uwanja wa Fisi. Maatata felt that it was important for my research that I know that he had on two separate occasions during his years in Dar es Salaam attempted to establish a permanent domestic base in Uwanjani with two different young women. Most of those I met were adamant about not being seen as street children and Maatata was no exception (see Moyer 2003a, Chapter 3, and 2003b for more discussion on this point). I believe that, apart from wanting me to know what a crazy place it was, this was why he wanted me to see his home. Uwanja wa Fisi's reputation fit neatly with his, and there was always a degree of bravado surrounding conversations pertaining to it. Of the young men at Maskani, he was the only one daring enough to suggest that I should go to Uwanja wa Fisi. Most of the others were incredulous when they heard I was considering it and several refused to be involved in helping to orchestrate it. Most of them, however, only visited Uwanja for purposes of pleasure, while Maatata had actually lived there. For him, Uwanja wa Fisi was more than its reputation: it was home.

Most of those at Maskani whom I asked to discuss Uwanja wa Fisi said that it was the place they went in search of *sterehe*, a word associated with pleasure and enjoyment. Mostly they spoke about the women there and their experiences with them, but stories about *bangi* (cannabis), *gongo* (locally brewed drink with a high alcohol content and low price) and violence also figured heavily. Though none of them spoke very respectfully about the women with whom they were involved at Uwanja, some were more interested in establishing longer-term relations with them than others. I never had the opportunity to interview Maatata about Uwanja wa Fisi but our informal discussions suggested that his views were similar to those expressed by Dixon, another young man from Maskani who had also made efforts to establish serious relationships with women there. Dixon offered his views during a group interview in which others from Maskani were bragging about their various adventures and conquests in

Uwanja. When I asked the car washers to talk about Uwanja wa Fisi, it was Athumani who began.

> People go to Uwanja wa Fisi for *sterehe*. Some people live there, while others just visit. They go for *gongo* and *bangi*, but mostly for women. Sometimes they go for 'short time', and sometimes they find a woman and settle down for a while.[13] For a long time I never went there. I heard stories about it all the time though. Mjela used to go every day to see his girlfriend. The first time I went there it was with him. We went to their place and she cooked for us, then we went to see a video. Afterwards I met a girl who I had sex with but I didn't spend the night with her. I returned to Maskani to sleep. Once I had a girl there named Hilda with whom I thought about setting up something more permanent. I paid for her guest house and spent two weeks with her. I realized I could never stay permanently there though, because there are too many thieves. One night when we were sleeping at the Nyota guest house we were awoken by the police. They pulled us out of bed and arrested us for loitering. I was released later and my girlfriend was already out of jail. She told me she was let go after promising to meet the chief of police later to have sex with him. She agreed on condition that he would let me go too. I didn't know about the arrangement and paid him a bribe as well. I was only 15 at the time and didn't know much about life but I had to wonder what kind of guest house allows the police to raid the rooms of customers who have already paid. I knew I hadn't done anything wrong but I was afraid of being sent to Segerea (prison), so I paid the bribe. I was released from jail around eleven in the morning and my girlfriend was supposed to meet the police chief at one. She didn't go though. I was angry so I went back to the guest house and demanded my money back. The manager would only give me the bus fare to the city so I came here to Maskani and borrowed enough money to rent another room. By the time I got back to Uwanjani there was a big fight going on. I ducked into a video parlour to wait until things calmed down. When I came out I rented a room and went to find my girlfriend. When I finally caught up with her she was with another man. That's when I realized she was really a prostitute (*malaya*) and that I could never trust her. She asked me what I expected her to do for food and a place to sleep when I was gone. Since then I've never gotten attached to a woman from Uwanja. All they want is money. You need to pay for food, beer, food the next day, and for a room if you want to keep a girlfriend. It costs at least Tsh 5000, which is what I can make at Maskani on a good day. Mostly I only go there now to visit friends and only once in a while for *sterehe*. It's too expensive and it's too easy to ruin your life there … drugs, thieves, etc. Women try to manipulate men into supporting them, but if you're smart you only go there when you want sex. You pay for your time and don't get caught up in a relationship where you have to pay for everything.

---

[13] 'Short time' is the expression used to describe transactional sex that entails sex only. Though I asked several times how long 'short time' would last, I was always rather prosaically told that 'every person has his own time'.

As Athumani finished to nods of agreement from the other young men gathered around, Dixon replied with his take on Uwanja.[14]

> Uwanja is a place where you can get girls to fuck easily, can get *gongo* or any other illegal brew. Some people do go there just to fuck but that isn't most people. Most have women there with whom they have set up house (*mchumba*).[15] They make an arrangement with a woman who agrees not to settle down with any other boyfriend. She may still sleep with other men for money though. It's not true that women are only interested in trying to take advantage of men. When I go home at night it's just like any other guy who goes home to his girlfriend at the end of the day. We spend the whole night together and we stay together whether or not I have money. Men like you (meaning Athumani) who pay a woman for sex are like someone who buys a watch from a *Machinga* (street vendor). You have no idea what you are getting. You pay her and of course she tries to take advantage of you but you should know that she might use that money to support her boyfriend. My girlfriend used the money she made off her customers to buy me new shoes when mine were stolen. I lived in Uwanja when things were really bad for me and I had no money. I don't always have to give money to my women. Sometimes it's based on love. The first night I was with Esther, a friend of mine came in while we were having sex and asked to borrow my new Adidas shoes. Later he was arrested while wearing them and they were stolen while he was in jail. When I woke up, I didn't have any shoes or money. Esther bought me a new pair and gave me money to get back into town. She told me that she really cared about me and asked me to stay with her. I told her I would only do it if she stuck by me in good times and bad. We were together for six months before I had to go back to Arusha for my father's funeral. She was very supportive while I was mourning and I missed her while I was gone. I came back early and surprised her. She had already made plans to sleep with a customer that evening but she made him take her to another room. She kept our room when I was away and we ended up staying together again after I got back. The only problems we ever have are because she likes to say bad things about me when we argue. When she gets angry she talks to everyone but me. She can't keep her mouth shut.

There was a certain beauty in the earnestness expressed by those like Maatata and Dixon who struggled to create what they imagined as lives of normalcy despite the daily hardships they faced. Domestic unions like those serially formed between Dixon and Esther and between Maatata and his girlfriends at Uwanjani would usually last a couple of months, but some would

---

[14] As the nodding heads of those who were listening to Athumani's story might indicate, most of the young men I interviewed agreed with the view that women were only interested in money and that without it, men were destined to remain alone. Similar observations have been reported by Tadele (2005) regarding Ethiopian street youth.

[15] In the past, *mchumba* was mainly used to refer to a fiancée. Today it is used to describe any semi-serious relationship with a woman, in the same way one might expect the word 'girlfriend' to be used.

stretch over several years, sometimes resulting in marriages, children and the building of homes. They usually entailed the joint rental of a room in a house, the purchase of a stove and utensils for cooking, and an agreement among partners that each would help the other to make ends meet. Although men are expected to provide most of the economic support in these situations and women are expected to cook, clean and provide a certain degree of what Luise White (1990) calls 'the comforts of home', women would routinely help out with the economic running of the household as well. Although their money was almost always earned through sex work, all of the women I spoke to were adamant that they would never allow their boyfriends to see them with a client. The young men would no doubt know where the money came from – most having been clients at one time or another – but they would never be confronted with it.

When I went to Uwanjani the first time in the company of Maatata he had, unbeknownst to me, agreed with Mbelwa, my research assistant, that I should extend my research activities to include working there. He had arranged for me to meet Esther, who at the time was his girlfriend (this was before she and Dixon moved in together), and a few of her fellow sex workers who were also based in Uwanjani. It takes a great deal of courage and honesty for someone to say, 'this is my girlfriend, she's a prostitute, you should interview her'. Esther proved to be a great help in assisting me to establish research networks in Uwanja wa Fisi. She told horrific stories beautifully, constantly reminding me of the aesthetics of communication. She first introduced me to some of her female friends, several of whom either had been or would soon be involved with men from Maskani. She encouraged them to be open and forthcoming with me but, while most of them made an effort, none were as eloquent as she was. In time, I began meeting Esther and Zamoyoni, one of her friends, regularly. Several of the other women to whom she introduced me were no longer to be found in Uwanjani, having either moved to another part of Dar es Salaam or returned to their family homes.

Esther was born in Butiama – the same village as Nyerere – but she had not lived there very long. Following her mother's death, her father, who lived in Dar es Salaam, took her to live with her grandmother near Dodoma but, after she was treated badly there, she decided to come to Dar es Salaam. Midway through my research period, however, Esther disappeared. The story I heard from Dixon, who was her boyfriend by then, was that her father, a former soldier, had heard what she was up to and had come to the guest house where she was staying to retrieve her. To prove his love for her, he humiliated her by publicly beating her before dragging her back to a home she had chosen to run away from. Dixon did not know how to reach her nor did anyone else I asked in Uwanja.

Like so many of the people I worked to establish ties with, Esther was gone. By this time, Maatata had left Dar es Salaam as well. He had returned to his *maskani* in Arusha when things became too hot for him in Dar es Salaam, but I occasionally received news of him from others who moved between the Dar es Salaam Maskani and a *maskani* to which several had ties in Arusha. Not long afterwards Dixon ended up in Segerea prison for theft, and his friends from Maskani were torturously letting him sit. In their minds, he had gone too far and even my offer to put up bail for him was rebuffed. His actions had brought too much unwanted police attention to Maskani of late and people seemed to feel he had forgotten the importance of friendship. Some argued that he would only learn his lesson by serving out his sentence in the harsh conditions of Segerea. It was rumoured that he had refused to give up his shoes (maybe the shoes that Esther had bought him), which was the price the police demanded for his freedom. All the other young men who were initially picked up with him were set free when their girlfriends paid bribes to the police on their behalf. But Esther, Dixon's girlfriend, was gone and the woman he was sleeping with refused to bail him out because he had gotten drunk the night before and beaten her.

Dixon's story is heartbreaking, as are the stories of those with whom his was entwined. I was witness to several serious arguments between Esther and Dixon but am still convinced they loved each other. They did their best to make meaningful lives for themselves and to comfort one another, but it was not enough. I suspect that their paths will cross again and perhaps love will finally win out. But I remain doubtful. It seems to me that there are too many forces conspiring against them. Their stories illustrate how difficult it is for even those with the best intentions to stay in touch. Dixon and Maatata were practically best friends but with Dixon in prison and Maatata on the run from the law, they were no longer in contact either.

My brothers' keeper

Although I had originally intended to base my research in Uwanja wa Fisi on the lives of young women who provided female companionship to men from Maskani, the task of maintaining long-term contact with any of these women proved too difficult. A young man named Spencer, who lived with his two brothers in a small house they had inherited from their parents was, however, kind enough to invite us to conduct our interviews with his friends in the courtyard of his home, which also served as a gathering point for those wishing to smoke and buy cannabis from Spencer. I had first met him through Maatata on the evening of our first visit. As our mutual friends at Maskani had refused to come with us to Uwanjani, Maatata sought out some of his close friends there to walk with us at night. Spencer, I eventually came to learn, had many ties and a great deal of power at Uwanja wa Fisi and was a natural choice for providing protection. When I left Uwanjani that first evening, Spencer was among those who escorted me to the bus stand on the main road. He was in his mid-twenties and had already been taking care of his younger brother for several years. When we first met he explained that his mother, father and stepmother had all died in rapid succession, but it was not until several months later that he felt comfortable enough to tell us that they had all died of AIDS. In addition to his younger brother, he also looked after his older brother, Abu, who, though not using drugs at the time of our research, had previously been addicted to heroin. It was largely through Spencer's efforts that he was able to quit. Spencer and Abu were part of the original discussion group we formed at Uwanjani. Also included were Haji, another young man living in Uwanja wa Fisi who helped Spencer in his various business endeavours, Esther and her friend Zamoyoni. Of the original five, only Spencer and Abu were able to work with us throughout the entire research period. Esther was taken away by her father and Zamoyoni disappeared without trace. Like Dixon, Haji, too, was in prison for theft.

At first I was frustrated by being unable to work closely with a group of young women at Uwanjani. I have now come to realize how fortunate I was to be able to work with a family like Spencer's that could boast some stability in an area of the city so defined by transience. As people living in a place that so many others visited in search of *sterehe* or lived only temporarily, they were witness to the eternal mobility of those central to my research and, more impressively, had managed to create a home in a place where most were afraid even to visit. It was through my visits to this home that I came to realize how important locality, belonging and relations were for those living on the margins of society in Dar es Salaam. I also came to see how difficult it was to achieve and maintain stability when economic circumstances were eternally uncertain. Spencer's case was classic in many ways. He had inherited his father's small plot of land, which certainly helped fulfil his desire to create a home for his brothers, but it was not enough to provide him with the income necessary to feed and clothe them, or to pay for his younger brother's school fees. Following his parents' deaths he gave up his job transporting merchandise with his three-wheeled cycle and cart and began selling oranges and cassava to save enough capital to open a small sidewalk eating establishment not far from his front door. These activities allowed him to be closer to home to look after his brothers but still did not meet his economic needs.

In an effort to provide for his brothers properly, to pay school fees, medical fees and run a proper household, Spencer began supplementing his income through the regular sale of cannabis.¹⁶ For several years now he has been buying it in bulk, several *puli* or handfuls at a time.¹⁷ He divides the *puli* into *kete*, cigarette-size packages that he sells along with rolling papers for Tsh 100 a piece. He also sells ready-made cannabis cigarettes and would sometimes rapidly roll thirty or so at the beginning of our interviews. He would tuck these under his *kofia* (an embroidered Muslim prayer cap) before stashing the remains of the cannabis in one of his several ingenious hiding places. By doing this, he would have enough ready to sell during our conversations and would not have to worry about being bothered by the impatient customers who would inevitably continue to flow through the door. Most would buy two packets and roll their own jumbo joints rather than buy the ready-made ones, sit down in the courtyard where we were talking, and begin smoking. Some would join in the conversations but most just listened and gawked in confusion, wondering I imagine – as I often did – how I had ended up in such a place.

The policing of thieves, the thieving of police

According to Spencer, Uwanja wa Fisi has only been called that since the mid-1990s when its notoriety began to grow. At that time the number of prostitutes, *nyama choma* (grilled meat) and *gongo* establishments in Uwanjani also grew. The reputation of the place has now spread throughout the country, and many young people who choose to move to the city in search of employment and a good time come first to Uwanjani. They often go through their money faster than they expected and when they ask their new acquaintances about the best way to make more, they are quickly introduced to the world of petty crime. Thieves abound in Uwanja and many people believe it is the safest place in the city to hide from the police. In recent years, the local Tandale police have responded to the rise in theft with a rise in corruption, by targeting innocent people. Most people say that though harassment has increased, the number of robberies has not gone down at all. The police routinely pick up young people hanging around *maskanis* and in guest houses and threaten to charge them with

---

¹⁶ Though he reported that he had only recently begun selling cannabis regularly to support his brothers, on another occasion he reported that he had worked as a dealer for more than thirteen years, and consequently had thirteen years of experience negotiating with the police to ensure his freedom.

¹⁷ Large quantities of cannabis are sold this way every day in Dar es Salaam. On one occasion I was invited to observe activities in one of the main cannabis markets, which was located in an open field near the city centre. Enormous bales were cut into smaller parcels with machetes and these were wrapped in brown paper and then stuffed into the backpacks and plastic bags that dealers had brought with them. Market times and sites change constantly but are easy enough to locate for those seriously interested in buying.

loitering if they refuse to pay a minimal bribe and inform on thieves. Spencer and the others we talked to at Uwanjani reported that police harassment had increased dramatically in recent years and that it made little difference whether one was committing a crime or not.

Since so many of those who live in Uwanja are engaged in marginally illegal activities like selling cannabis, *gongo* or prostitution, they are fairly easily coerced into becoming police informants in exchange for being permitted to continue operating their businesses without going to jail. When people talk about hyenas, they often use the word *mpambe*, a term used to describe someone or something that benefits from associating with someone or something else in a position of power. Hyenas are said to have an *mpambe* relationship with lions, stealing and eating their food. Similar comparisons are made between the police and petty criminals, though in such comparisons it is not always clear who is playing the role of the hyena and who is playing the role of the lion. Spencer admitted that he had been a police informant for years and that, as a result, many of his neighbours did not like him. He reported being on good terms with the chief of the local police station, a man thoroughly despised by nearly everyone interviewed. The Tandale police station was considered the most corrupt in Dar es Salaam, forcing the residents of the area to go to other police stations when they wished to press legitimate charges against someone.[18] Even filing a charge cost money in Tandale, as did any attempt to get someone to follow up on the charges. Many people described police activities with the word *mradi*, or project, associating bribery with any other money-making scheme. Routine and petty harassment were the norm. All officers were expected to collect bribes that would be split amongst everyone all the way up

---

[18] The Tandale police station opened in 1995, just prior to the national election, as part of the 1993 initiative sponsored by the then Minister of Internal Affairs, Augustine Mrema, to increase the number of local police posts with community-collected funds. Though few residents of Tandale contributed to this fund, the state provided funds for the building of the station. Residents of Tandale with whom I spoke suggested that, prior to the opening of the station, there had been a great deal of crime in the area but also that crime had not diminished since it opened. Before 1995 the closest police station was in Magomeni and there was little police harassment in Tandale. The irony is that Mrema, who eventually broke away from the CCM and ran for president in 2000, is best known for fighting corruption. A great majority of the young men I asked reported voting for Mrema in the 2000 elections. Generally, people see his programme of opening more police stations and an initiative he sponsored in the late 1980s to encourage the development of a nationwide neighbourhood watch programme (*sungusungu*) as constructive efforts in the fight against crime. Those I interviewed in Tandale seemed to think that the reason the experiment had failed in their community was that the police station was initially built without the local community's support.

to the police chief. Several of those we interviewed reported seeing this with their own eyes.

It is no surprise that most of the police in Tandale are hated and that, when an opportunity to retaliate presented itself, people actively pursued it. I heard several stories of police being beaten up in local drinking establishments when they became too drunk to defend themselves. A story that Ester told me, however, stands out. A uniformed police officer was beaten by a crowd in broad daylight after attempting to solicit a bribe from a thief already under attack from the crowd. The police officer had intervened, no doubt saving the thief's life, but when the crowd realized he did not intend to arrest the thief they began beating up both of them.

The beating and burning of thieves in Tanzania is not uncommon. The mob mentality that ensues on such occasions is truly horrifying. As Esther chillingly observed, people with almost no money for food and other basic necessities will quickly hand over whatever cash they happen to have when a collection is made for kerosene to douse an accused thief. People I have met who have participated in such beatings defend them by claiming that they are left with no other recourse since the police will not prosecute a thief if offered even the smallest of bribes. Such reasoning was particularly disconcerting given that it was often put forth by itinerant thieves.

The police also commonly demand sexual favours from the women they arrest, as was made evident in the example above from Athumani. Esther offered the following in a discussion about police harassment.

> Police use their position to force women to have sex with them. Sometimes they make women who can't pay bribes with money pay with their bodies. Other times they may just ask a woman outright for sex and if she refuses, they threaten to arrest her, to bring charges against her. They often go after bar girls, *gongo* sellers and *mama ntilie* (food vendors) because they are easy to target. Because they are engaged in illegal activities it is easy for the police to harass them. They harass the people who work in the places where the police go every day to eat and drink. The police do terrible things to women once they are in jail. I've seen them threaten girls who refuse to confess, telling them they will be put in a cell with male prisoners. Sometimes they force women to undress and stand in front of male jail cells. Once when I was being held in jail I watched them beat a young girl to make her confess that she stole money from her stepmother. The girl said she only did it to pay for school supplies and that it was money her father had left for her anyway. The police didn't care. They just kept beating her. Everything they do is for money. The law has become blind. They don't attempt to bring justice, to represent the truth. I've seen them dividing up the money they've collected through bribes at the end of their shift. It's based on hierarchy and those at the top get the most money.

From this example, it is clear that the police commonly target women who are working informally in bars and eating establishments, threatening them with arrest if they refuse to sleep with them. Women who engage in sex work, who in many circumstances also work as bar girls and/or *gongo* sellers, are in a doubly precarious position, as many of them also have boyfriends who are known thieves. When the police want to reach a thief, they will often put pressure on his girlfriend. In this no-win situation, women are forced to choose between turning in their boyfriends or being sexually abused by the police.

Trust, transactional sex and domestic unions

Despite the dangers of police harassment in Uwanja wa Fisi, not to mention more generalized threats of violence and disease, every day women make the decision to sell their bodies to earn money to support themselves and those closest to them. Most of those engaging in transactional sex who I interviewed did not identify themselves as prostitutes, even though everyone around them did. Different words are used in Kiswahili to refer to different types of transactional sex.[19] *Malaya* is the word most readily translated as prostitute and is used to refer to women (and sometimes men) who openly engage in prostitution. The words most often used in Uwanja wa Fisi and at Maskani were *changudoa* and *dada poa*.[20] A more lengthy discussion on these terms is offered elsewhere but it is important to note that while these terms certainly implied engagement in transactional sex, they also implied that it was only undertaken out of necessity, as a way of making ends meet (Moyer 2003a). Most of the women who engaged in transactional sex in Uwanja wa Fisi also had boyfriends, though it was often suggested by men from Uwanja and Maskani that they were only able to establish such relationships with thieves and people who did not otherwise have a home. Young men with minimal resources were considered more likely to accept that their girlfriends also slept with other men for money because they knew they could not afford to support a woman on their own. Despite this, however, they still longed for some semblance of domesticity and thus sought out women who would be willing to support themselves and to

---

[19] For an extensive overview of the various terms used in Dar es Salaam, see Kamazima (1995). See White (1990) on prostitution in Nairobi and Bujra (1977) for comparative purposes.

[20] *Changudoa* is a type of small spotted fish and it was a term originally used to refer to young boys working in the fish market who were willing to do anything to make a little money. Now it is almost exclusively used to refer to women who engage in low-profit sex work. *Dada poa* literally means 'cool sister'. Those working at Maskani seemed to think this was a more polite term to use to refer to sex workers.

accept a boyfriend with very little money. Through such an arrangement, the women are able to gain some degree of respectability and the men a place they can call home, even if only temporarily.

There were others engaged in transactional sex living in Uwanjani who identified themselves as prostitutes, but as they were not the women with whom most Wamaskani formed domestic unions, I did not focus on them. Most of those with whom I did speak however came to Dar es Salaam specifically to be a prostitute and save money. As in many other cities in eastern Africa, they were often Bahaya women from around the Bukoba region of the country (Kaijage 1993, Kamazima 1995, Swantz 1985, White 1990). Bukoba is also the informal name given to the street in Tandale where they live and work. Though they openly acknowledged their profession and charged relatively low rates for sex (Tsh 500, or about US$ 0.75), they were respected because they insisted that every customer use a condom. Most other women involved in transactional sex rarely insisted on condoms, but this was not because they lacked information.

Those I interviewed on the subject demonstrated in-depth knowledge of the ways HIV could be contracted and prevented. Everyone I spoke to in Uwanja wa Fisi claimed that they observed the public-health demonstrations on sexually transmitted diseases, AIDS and the use of condoms that were regularly organized by NGOs.[21] Both male and female condoms were readily and cheaply available, and information on how to use them was abundant. It was not unusual to see Salama condom posters plastered to the walls on guest house rooms and dispenser-size boxes of condoms in women's rooms. All of the women I interviewed reported using condoms regularly with paying customers, but only rarely with boyfriends. Of course, most of their boyfriends had once been customers and, as far as I could ascertain, the decision not to use condoms was never tied to any evidence showing that they were disease free.

Several of the young women reported wanting to become pregnant by their boyfriends in the hope that this would cement the bonds between them. They saw pregnancy as one of the only ways to escape the stigma that marked their lives in Uwanja wa Fisi. For them, it would not have made sense to use condoms even in instances when their partners might have suggested it. Since many men reported they were more likely to marry a woman after she had a child by him and had proved that she was fertile, the thinking of the young women in Uwanjani seemed to make perfect sense. The only hitch, of course, was the very real risk of HIV. Sheldrake (2002) has suggested that young

---

[21] It is worth noting that they were often critical of these shows. They were frequently described as distasteful and embarrassing. More than one interviewee reported leaving such shows early because they found it inappropriate to discuss AIDS and sex in mixed company.

people may choose not to use condoms as a way of demonstrating their trust for one another. The young men in Dar es Salaam with whom she worked reported they would only use condoms with women they did not trust, women who they believed were likely to be engaged in sexual relations with other men. Those with whom I worked, however, *knew* their girlfriends had other lovers, if only in the form of customers. Yet, they also reported not using condoms with women with whom they had set up house.[22] For them, not using condoms signalled the special quality of their relationship with individual women. Their girlfriends may have had to resort to sex work to support themselves (and their boyfriends) but they were expected to do so discreetly and to use condoms. The boyfriends trusted the women to protect them both from AIDS despite evidence that such trust was not deserved.

Though none of those with whom I worked had ever taken an AIDS test, many reported having contracted various sexually transmitted diseases (STDs), both from prostitutes and from their girlfriends, illustrating that trust had been broken on both sides. In cases where a man or woman knows who was responsible for infecting him or her, he or she will most likely denounce the other party in public. The shame is not so much in having these diseases but in having so dishonourably passed it on to someone with whom a bond of trust had been established. Esther suggested that often women do not know they are infected as the signs are less visible in women but said that in many cases a woman will not tell her boyfriend even if she does know for fear of being publicly humiliated and of losing future customers. She said that women also talk about the untrustworthiness of men who pass on STDs, but that they do it more secretly than risk a public confrontation. She thought this might be because they wanted to keep their own infection a secret, again for fear of scaring away customers.

I was inclined to interpret the choices made by many of the young women in Uwanja wa Fisi in empathetic terms, recognizing the difficulties they faced as a result of being economically dependent on men while being disconnected from their families. Others who have conducted research among young marginalized women in urban Tanzania uniformly argue that sex work is the only option many of them have for earning money (e.g. Kamazima 1995, Lugalla & Mbwambo 1999, Masawe 2000, Tesha 2000, Tungaraza 2000). It is also the most profitable. One study suggested that young women were likely to make four to five times as much money through sex work as young men working on

---

[22] Mgalla & Pool (1996) present similar data from their research among female bar workers in northwestern Tanzania, though they also examine men's reasons for not using condoms. Ng'weshemi *et al.* (1995) offer supporting data but suggest that men are more likely to use condoms with women they suspect of being sex workers. See also Pool *et al.* (1996).

the streets (Masawe 2000: 11). This seems excessive for those from Maskani (who seem to be comparatively better-off than a lot of other young men struggling to get by on the streets) and Uwanja wa Fisi (where women seem to make less than commercial sex workers who target customers in the city centre) who were involved in this study. Many of the young men who were the customers and partners of the women in Uwanja, however, seemed to think most of the women were motivated by *tamaa*, an excessive desire for material goods (see Moyer 2003a, especially Chapter 8). There was definitely a degree of resentment towards them based on the belief that they were making money 'freely' (*ya bure*), with no recourse to the types of hard physical labour most of the men claimed to engage in. As a result, most of them did not think the women deserved much sympathy. They quickly countered any economic arguments I might put forward in the young women's defence, arguing that had they been willing to settle for less material wealth, they would have been able to establish a permanent monogamous relationship with a man. Instead, the young women constantly demanded new clothes, shoes and make-up from their boyfriends, and the longer they were in Uwanja the greater their wishes and demands became. The men pointed out that many of the young women working in Uwanja were actually from good families and had chosen to come to Dar es Salaam in search of quick money and a good time. Some had originally come with the intention of saving money to start a business of their own but most would eventually decide to spend their money on beauty products and clothing intended to make them look more appealing and to increase the amount of money they could earn.

Though women tried to save money they would usually spend it on beautifying themselves to attract better customers who would pay more. This cycle never ends, however, and life in Uwanja is hard, with people aging fast. Most women who end up there leave within a few months, either ill, pregnant or disheartened. Some settle into more permanent relationships, while others return to their home villages. It is primarily for these reasons that long-term residents of Uwanja wa Fisi reported rarely seeing anyone die of AIDS in their midst. Most people would leave long before they began to exhibit signs of infection. In most cases, news of AIDS deaths only reached Uwanjani by word of mouth, though in some cases it was suspected that certain people had been infected. A story I heard in various versions on several different occasions was about a young woman who agreed to take a large sum of money (Tsh 45,000, or about US$ 50) from a man who was visibly sick and suspected of having AIDS in exchange for having unprotected sex with him. Afterwards, the other women spread rumours about her and, when they got angry with her, they would publicly accuse her of having AIDS, both shaming her and greatly reducing her earning potential. She eventually decided to leave Uwanjani but maintained contact with a few friends there, one of whom brought news of her AIDS-related death a few years later after she had been with numerous other men from other parts of the city, the last of whom was an army officer notorious for his promiscuity.[23]

Most of the young men I worked with thought that they could determine whether a woman was HIV positive based on her appearance and character (*tabia*). Those with excessive *tamaa*, appearing too thin or too desperate were always subjected to AIDS accusations. It is believed that when people become sick they begin to lose weight rapidly, a condition they will commonly try to conceal by wearing several layers of clothing. Thus women dressed as such were often suspected of having AIDS. Likewise women who spent too much time in bars drinking alcohol were not to be trusted as most agreed that women were much easier to cajole into having unprotected sex when they were drunk. They would carefully choose the women with whom they decided to establish domestic relations based on their observations of their behaviour and character, combined with information obtained from friends and neighbours who knew her. The young men felt they were greatly reducing their risk of contracting AIDS in this way. Such logic, while always argued convincingly, is faulty on numerous accounts but most men (and women, for that matter) seemed to feel that they had no other recourse. In their minds it was impossible to know for sure if someone had AIDS. At the time of my research, very few people were being tested for AIDS, and most agreed that they would not trust anyone who reported having tested negative anyway.[24] None of those I worked with have yet developed HIV-related symptoms; however, many contracted other STDs, illustrating that their calculations regarding who was and who was not a safe partner were frequently wrong.

One method of reducing risk employed by young men like Spencer, his brother Abu, and Maatata was to establish serially monogamous domestic

---

[23] That these and other similar stories might be considered urban myths is certainly a suggestion worth exploring further, but one on which I will pass for now. See de Boeck & Plissart (2004) for an interesting discussion of the importance of urban myths for reflecting urban anxieties that arise from operating in circumstances difficult to fully analyze.

[24] Late in 2001 efforts were stepped up by both the Tanzanian state and various NGOs to encourage testing in Tanzania, after preliminary evidence suggested that it was one of the most important reasons for lower HIV infection rates in neighbouring Uganda. When I returned to Tanzania in 2002, many more people were talking about the possibility of testing, though none of those I worked with had seriously considered it. The possibility of HIV testing has come to the fore again more recently in the context of the growing availability of highly active antiretroviral treatment (HAART) for HIV, though, since few Wamaskani or residents of Uwanja are likely to have access to such treatment, it is unlikely they will be sufficiently motivated to get tested.

relations with women who had just come to Uwanja wa Fisi from the rural areas of Tanzania. It was imagined that such women, who seemed to embody tradition and the past for them, had better manners, worked harder around the house, had yet to be spoiled by city life, had less *tamaa* and, therefore, were less likely to be HIV positive. In most cases, they would stay with such women for several months until they became 'used to life in the city' (*kuzoea*) and began demanding gifts and money. When this happened they would quickly be replaced by another recent migrant to the city eager for the security of domesticity. As the supply of women was seemingly endless, they argued, it seemed a fairly good way of ensuring their own good health.

For the most part, people are able to avoid dwelling on the subject of AIDS in Uwanja wa Fisi, and in Dar es Salaam in general, by convincing themselves that their social ties are sufficient to allow them to determine who might already be infected. When I pressed them, something I rarely did, most would admit that in all likelihood they had been exposed to HIV. In such instances people usually resorted to religious discourses, claiming that only God could protect them from HIV. On one occasion Esther told me that she thought God must be protecting people in Uwanja wa Fisi from AIDS. 'If God brings AIDS to Uwanja,' she said, 'all of us girls will be finished'. I conclude with a story that forced many of those with whom I worked at both Uwanja wa Fisi and at Maskani to confront the likelihood that they might have been exposed to HIV.

The story of Rehema[25]

It was during the last formal interview of my research that I discovered that several people from Maskani and Uwanja wa Fisi with whom I had worked most closely had been directly exposed to HIV. At a subconscious level, I had already realized this, but, like them, I was hoping they might have actually succeeded in determining who had AIDS or that they might have been miraculously lucky. I began to fully recognize the allure of denial because, like them, I found it too difficult to live with the obvious likelihood that my friends had either already been infected or would soon be and that, as a result, they would die. I did not actually attend this interview but listened to the audiotapes later with my research assistant, Mbelwa, who had conducted it at Uwanja wa Fisi in my absence, something which was highly unusual. In the entire time I was in Tanzania there were only two occasions when I was not present during interviews and I continue to wonder to what degree my absence that day made a

---

[25] Rehema was not the name she was known by in Dar es Salaam. I use a pseudonym here to protect the memory of a young woman who I never had the privilege of meeting.

difference to people's willingness to discuss AIDS in such an open and unguarded way.

When he arrived at Uwanja wa Fisi to conduct the interview, he found people strangely reflective. Formally in attendance were Spencer and Abu, Haji who had recently been released from jail, and a young man named Adam, who joined the group to replace Esther when she was taken away by her father. There were also several others gathered together for the purpose of informal mourning. News had just come that afternoon that Rehema, a girl who used to live and work in the area, had swallowed a handful of chloroquine tablets, taking her own life to escape the shame of AIDS when she began showing physical symptoms of the disease.[26] She had left Uwanja wa Fisi about a year earlier when rumours started spreading that she had been with a man who had AIDS, but a good friend of hers who still lived in Uwanjani had kept in contact with her and had brought news of her death that day. Adam, one of the young men who regularly participated in our group discussions in Uwanja, had been her boyfriend in 1998, which he claims was prior to the time she was infected. He repeatedly insisted that he had been with her when she first came to Uwanjani, but I could not help but wonder who he was trying to convince. Mbelwa told me that Adam seem stunned throughout the interview, perhaps coming to grips with his own mortality, or perhaps just realizing what a close call it had been for him.

It was commonly known that at one time Rehema had been Maatata's girlfriend too. At the time of her death, he was in Arusha hiding from the police. She had also regularly had sex with Dixon, who was in jail when she died, and several other young men from Maskani. She was reportedly a kind and beautiful girl. On hearing the story from Mbelwa, I recognized Rehema's name at once. On different occasions I had heard at least three different boys talk about Rehema as a girl who seemed to hold a special place in their hearts. Though she was a prostitute, she had always accorded her boyfriends the greatest respect and made sure that they never came into contact with her clients. From what I

---

[26] Chloroquine tablets were a common treatment for malaria in 2000 and were readily available over the counter in Dar es Salaam pharmacies. Suicide was not an uncommon choice among those inflicted with AIDS and the use of chloroquine seemed to be particularly popular among young women. This may be so because most young women readily recognize excessive chloroquine ingestion as a way of inducing abortion and ending unwanted pregnancies (see Kamazima 1995: 52, Tesha 2000: 120, and Mpangile et al. 1993). Unfortunately, the line between inducing abortion and inducing maternal death is a thin one and young women often make mistakes. In 2002 international treatment protocols for malaria changed in Tanzania and it became difficult to get chloroquine, though I was informed that mefloquin, the new drug of choice, was equally suitable for bringing on an early death.

understand, she was also a good cook and would not hesitate to invite her boyfriend's friends for food, creating a relaxing and enjoyable home environment.

Although AIDS was obviously central to the discussion that day, those present in the interview were less upset about what she died of (AIDS), or how she died (a lonely suicide), than they were about the fact that no one knew her last name, where she came from, or even what religion she was. Since many young women change their names when they come to the city, the first name Rehema did not necessarily mean she was Muslim. The essence of the problem was that no one knew how to bury her properly.[27] Her body had been lying in the morgue at Muhimbili hospital for two days and it was now assumed that she was going to be buried by the city in a pauper's grave. For the young men at Uwanjani that day, this seemed to bring home just how marginal their existence in Dar es Salaam was. It showed them the transient existence their lifestyles produced and the potential meaninglessness that marked their lives and deaths. How relevant is the cause or mode of one's death when one's identity is effaced by insignificance in all the ways usually considered important? Without a home, a family, a community, how can one live? How can one die? Among many of the people I knew, individual status is constituted by the number and quality of social ties one has. If one's worth at death is best measured by such relational connections, then by most accounts Rehema was worthless. But she had been someone's girlfriend, someone's friend, and someone else's fictive cousin. Had her friends at Uwanjani known where she was from, they would have raised enough money between them to send her body back home, or at least to send a message about her death.

The tone of the discussion that day was highly reflective. It was nearly impossible for anyone present to deny the similarities between Rehema's situation and their own. In facing her death, they were facing theirs. Although all the signs were there before, it was not until this interview that I realized how strong the connections were between AIDS and death in the minds of many Tanzanians. In many ways they are synonymous. Popular songs, city murals, dramatic performances on stage, as well as TV, repeatedly lamented *UKIMWI ni Kifo*, 'AIDS is death'. I had always thought of this as a metaphorical expression most likely invented by some public-health official as a reworking of the Silence = Death slogan made famous by artist and AIDS activist Keith

---

[27] Tesha (2000: 10) reports that this is not uncommon among young women who engage in sex work in Dar es Salaam. 'They bear different identities in order to hide their actual names. ... We have witnessed the unfortunate ones being buried by the city officials after failing to trace their families ... some have both Christian and Moslem names, it is hard to judge their religious denomination when such sad events occur.' Also see Kilonzo & Hogan (1999) for an examination of the way mourning practices have been affected by the AIDS epidemic in Tanzania.

Haring in the United States. On that day I began to see just how real the equation was for most people. In many people's minds, the inevitability of AIDS was as real as the inevitability of death. The fact that so many of them struggled to fashion meaningful lives in the face of such knowledge shows the strength and determination of their character more than ignorance or denial.

One of the reasons that Rehema's story became so significant for me is that it brought me face to face with my own denial about the mortality of people I was working with, people who had become my friends. At times, I found it difficult to continue working and building close relationships among people with such uncertain futures. A few days before I left, Shida, a young food vendor from Maskani who had worked closely with us, laughingly teased me saying, 'when you come back, we'll all be dead'. Between the time we recorded the story of Rehema's death and the time I left Tanzania, Mbelwa and I had already become increasingly aware of the likelihood of this uncomfortable vision of the future, but as he repeatedly reminded me, 'at least you get to leave, I have to stay here and watch all of my friends die'. The last few weeks comprised the most psychologically challenging period of my research, but I think in many ways they were also the most productive. It was only after several discussions that Mbelwa and I began to comprehend just how difficult the reality was that we had been asking people to face. Not only were we asking them to confront their own deaths – a task that is difficult enough – but we were also asking them to confront the possible meaninglessness of their deaths. Young, marginal and on the move, most had fractured their ties with their birth communities and were still avidly pursuing new relational ties. My own discomfort regarding the probable deaths of those I had come to know could be explained by saying that death is always an uncomfortable thing to face, but I think there was something else at stake as well. To a certain extent, I think, I resented their deaths. I wanted to establish life-long friendships with those who cared enough to help me, and it was difficult to accept how short a time 'life-long' might be. Had I been unable or unwilling to look closely at the causes of my own emotional discomfort, I undoubtedly would have missed this all-important fact in understanding how denial – the bane of AIDS prevention and treatment – continues to function, not in spite of the unbounded evidence that 'AIDS is death', but precisely because of it. AIDS, taking the lives of so many young people, tearing families asunder, and wiping out entire generations denies the potency of relations, denies the power of locality. It unsettles. It uproots.

The roots laid by those I came to know were rarely deep, but they were extensive. Like the roots of the mangroves that once clogged Dar es Salaam's harbour, they take hold where they can, adding shape to an otherwise continually shifting landscape, wandering endlessly in search of life, occasionally but relentlessly popping their heads up for air. Their very entanglement requires them to support one another in an effort to survive. But above all, they must remain focused on their own survival.

References

Augé, M. 1995, *Non-Places: Introduction to an Anthropology of Supermodernity*, London: Verso.
Bakhtin, M. 1984 (1968), *Rabelais and His World*, Bloomington: Indiana University Press.
de Boeck, F. & M.-F. Plissart 2004, *Kinshasa: Tales of the Invisible City*, Brussels: Ludion.
Caldeira, T.P.R. 1996, 'Fortified Enclaves: The New Urban Segregation', *Public Culture* (8): 303-28.
Caldeira, T.P.R. 2000, *City of Walls: Crime, Segregation, and Citizenship in Sao Paulo*, Berkeley: University of California Press.
de Certeau, M. 1984, *The Practice of Everyday Life*, Berkeley: University of California Press.
Davis, M. 1992 (1990), *City of Quartz: Excavating the Future in Los Angeles*, New York: Vintage Books.
Harvey, D. 1990, *The Condition of Postmodernity: An Enquiry into the Origins of Cultural Change*, Cambridge: Blackwell.
Harvey, D. 2000, *Spaces of Hope*, Berkeley: University of California Press.
Kaijage, F.J. 1993, 'AIDS Control and the Burden of History in Northwestern Tanzania', *Population and Development* 14 (3).
Kamazima, S.R. 1995, 'Existence and Implications of Female Commercial Sex Workers in Urban Centres: A Case of Female Streetwalkers in the City of Dar es Salaam, Tanzania', Masters Thesis. University of Dar es Salaam.
Kilonzo, G.P. & N.M. Hogan 1999, 'Traditional African Mourning Practices Are Abridged in Response to the AIDS Epidemic: Implications for Mental Health', *Transcultural Psychiatry* 36 (3): 259-83.
Kuppinger, P. 2002, 'Exclusive Greenery: New Gated Communities in Cairo', Paper presented at the American Anthropological Association meeting.
Low, S. 2001, 'The Edge and the Center: Gated Communities and the Discourse of Urban Fear', *American Anthropologist* 103 (1): 45-58.
Lugalla, J. & J. Mbwambo 1999, 'Street Children and Street Life in Urban Tanzania: The Culture of Surviving and its Implications for Children's Health', *International Journal of Urban and Regional Research* 23 (2): 329-43.
Masawe, S. 2000, 'The Politics Surrounding Street Children's Life: How to Best Tackle the Problem in Tanzania', Unpublished report, International Conference of Street Children and Street Children's Health, Dar es Salaam.
Mgalla, Z. & R. Pool 1996, 'Sexual Relationships, Condom Use and Risk Perception among Female Bar Workers in North-West Tanzania', TANESA Working Paper, no. 11, Mwanza.
Mitchell, T. 1995, 'Orientalism and the Exhibitionary Other', in: N. Dirks (ed.), *Colonialism and Culture*, Ann Arbor: University of Michigan Press, pp. 289-318.

Moyer, E. 2003a, 'In the Shadow of the Sheraton: Imagining Localities in Global Spaces in Dar es Salaam, Tanzania', Dissertation manuscript. University of Amsterdam.

Moyer, E. 2003b, 'Keeping Up Appearances: Fashion and Function among Dar es Salaam Street Youth', *Etnofoor* 16 (2): 88-106.

Mpangile, G.S., M.T. Leshabari & D.J. Kihwele 1993, 'Factors Associated with Induced Abortion in Public Hospitals in Dar es Salaam, Tanzania', *Reproductive Health Matters* 2 (November): 21-31.

Mwasanga, P. 1998, 'The Spectacular Rise of Edward Saidi Tingatinga', in: Tingatinga Cooperative Society (ed.), *Tingatinga*, Dar es Salaam: Mture Educational Publishers Limited, pp. 30-32.

Mwidadi, A. & S. Chilamboni 1998, 'Development of Tingatinga Arts Cooperative Society Limited', in: Tingatinga Cooperative Society (ed.), *Tingatinga*, Dar es Salaam: Mture Educational Publishers Limited, pp. 33-36.

Ng'weshemi, J., T. Boerma, L. Barongo, K. Senkoro, R. Isingo & M. Borgdorf 1995, 'Changes in Male Sexual Behaviour in Response to the AIDS Epidemic: Quantitative Evidence from a Cohort Study in Urban Tanzania', TANESA Working Paper, no. 6. Mwanza.

Pool, R., M. Masawe, J.T. Boerma & S. Nnko 1996, 'The Price of Promiscuity: Why Urban Males in Tanzania Are Changing their Sexual Behaviour', *Health Transition Review* (6): 203-21.

Roberts, A.F. 1995, *Animals in African Art: From the Familiar to the Marvellous*, Munich: Prestel.

Sassen, S. 2003, 'The Repositioning of Citizenship: Emergent Subjects and Spaces for Politics', *Berkeley Journal of Sociology* (1): 4-25.

Sheldrake, M. 2002, '*Bongo Noma*: The Urban Experience and its Impact on Young Men's Identity and Sexual Health', Unpublished report. Key Centre for Women's Health, University of Melbourne.

Swantz, M.-L. 1985, *Women in Development: A Creative Role Denied?*, London: C. Hurst.

Tadele, G. 2005, 'Bleak Prospects: Young Men, Sexuality and AIDS in and Ethiopian Town', Dissertation manuscript, University of Amsterdam.

Tesha, F.P. 2000, 'The Hardships that Street Girls Experience: Their Coping Mechanisms and their Impact on Street Girls' Health', Unpublished report, International Conference of Street Children and Street Children's Health, Dar es Salaam.

Tingatinga Cooperative Society 1998, *Tingatinga*, Dar es Salaam: Mture Educational Publishers Limited.

Tripp, A.M. 1997, *Changing the Rules: The Politics of Liberalization and the Urban Informal Economy in Tanzania*, Berkeley: University of California Press.

Tungaraza, F.S.K. 2000, 'Networking among Street Children as a Strategy for Surviving and Coping with Urban Life: A Case Study of Kisutu-Gerezani Streets, Dar es Salaam', Unpublished report, International Conference of Street Children and Street Children's Health, Dar es Salaam.

Waldrop, A. 2002, 'Fortification and Class Relations: The Case of a New Delhi Colony', Paper presented at the American Anthropological Association meetings. New Orleans, Louisiana.

White, L. 1990, *The Comforts of Home: Prostitution in Colonial Nairobi*, Chicago: University of Chicago Press.

9

Togolese cartographies: Re-mapping space in a post-Cold War city

Charles Piot

> *This chapter explores the remaking and re-mapping of Togo's capital, Lomé, from the 1990s onwards. The end of the Cold War brought an economic and political crisis that left a deep imprint on the everyday lives and neighbourhood practices of Togolese citizens. As the developmental state of the 1980s was transformed into an increasingly militarized post-Cold War state, and as political and economic exile for Togolese citizens became more norm than exception, spatial practice shifted in significant ways to adjust to the new realities. Drawing inspiration from Lefebvre and de Certeau, this chapter tracks these shifts in place-making practices, suggesting that while space may be remade by historical process, it also actively affects and orders spatializing practice itself.*

Introduction

I conceive of the concept 'neighbourhood' in the broadest Lefebvrian (1991) sense – as the spatialization of social relations or, put otherwise, as space that is saturated with social relations, and thus that can only be understood through and in terms of the social. In that the social is always in history, and thus always site of transformation, I read the making and remaking of the spatial as forever indexed to historical process. But the reverse is true as well. Since the social is forever em-placed, it gets spatialized and embodied in highly specific ways, ways that must also conform to territorializing logics. Space, in this view, is no *tabula rasa* on which history unproblematically inscribes its colonizing agendas. The embodied spatial – place, city, neighbourhood, road network – must be seen as asserting its own agency, actively shaping power's imperatives.

In this chapter, I examine shifts in spatializing practices in post-Cold War Togo at a time when the country entered a prolonged political and economic crisis. During the Cold War, and because of its pro-West political leanings, Togo was relatively flush with foreign aid money. Thus despite the presence of a repressive military regime, both France and the United States had large aid missions to Togo and annually channelled millions of francs and dollars into Togolese development and the state apparatus. With the end of the Cold War, however, and because of the Togolese government's resistance to democratization, the money spigot was turned off and the state apparatus became a shadow of its former self. The 1990s were also a time of intense ethnic conflict, when decades of simmering resentment by southern Togolese of northern political overlordship bubbled to the surface, exacerbated by the northern government's theft of three consecutive presidential elections. As a result, this decade of economic and political crisis spawned large communities of Togolese exiles in Europe and the United States, and turned the homeland into a remittance magnet, with monies from the diaspora filling the gap left by an eviscerated state.

I focus here on the effects of this moment of crisis on Togolese place-making practices, and the political-economic shifts that accompanied the crisis. I am thus interested in ways in which the capital of Lomé was spatially reconfigured during the 1990s – and in those ways in which neighbourhoods and centres of congregation were remade and re-signified in response to the upheavals of this period. I am also interested in the consequences for place-making practices at home of the diasporization of the Togolese population – and in the effects on neighbourhoods, neighbourliness, family ties and national belonging of the virtualization of sociality. My argument is that city and neighbourhood space in Lomé during this period was, on the one hand, militarized, and, on the other, evacuated and virtualized, with profound consequences for the life of the nation and its citizens.

Togo after the Cold War

The ending of the Cold War affected this small nation as much as any other in West Africa. Surrounded throughout the early independence period by three countries with Soviet leanings, and occupying (during the early 1980s) the one at-large seat on the United Nations Security Council, Togo was of more than passing strategic interest to France and the United States. Thus, not only were Togolese state coffers, and the pockets of the political elite, lined with money, but also the international community turned a blind eye to General Gnassingbé Eyadéma's repressive state apparatus. With the collapse of the Soviet Union and the end of the Cold War, however, much of the money disappeared and Eyadéma's regime came under attack from below as well as above. Street protests in the early 1990s were accompanied by the cutting of United States and European Union aid to Togo, and the foreign embassies supported the political opposition in calling for Eyadéma's departure. While Eyadéma remained in power throughout this period – through a mix of cunning, ruthlessness, election fraud, and what Mbembe (2003) has called 'necropolitics' – the Togolese state nevertheless became a shell of its former self. It was (and remains) a state that, to cite Mbembe (1992, 2001) again, has been little more than a 'simulacral regime', subsisting on 'performance' and the staging of dramatic events – false coup attempts, hyperbolic celebrations of national holidays – as much as anything substantial. It is also a state that responded to its increasing evisceration with paranoia and surveillance.

The crisis for Eyadéma's subjects was of course worse still, but it was also enormously 'productive' (in the Foucauldian sense), spawning a new round of extraordinarily inventive bricolage – of cycling and re-cycling, of dividing the seemingly indivisible, of surviving on nothing – and raised the art of the scam (the invention of false identities, the manufacture of papers and visas) to a new level. It also produced a culture and an imaginary of exile – and, indeed, one might say, an entire nation in exile. Witness the northern town of Sokodé, for instance. This sprawling gathering of rusted tin roofs – the sleepy seat of bygone colonial power in Togo's hinterland – has in the last ten years undergone a dramatic makeover. Today phone booths dot virtually every street corner and new Western Union stations go up every few months – conduits for information and money from the tens of thousands of Kotokoli who fled the country for Germany (and received political asylum there) after opposing Eyadéma during the early 1990s. It is said of Kotokoli that no Togolese group has as pure a collective fantasy as they, a dream that they will one day all live in Germany.

But fantasies of exile are by no means the provenance of Kotokoli alone. One could say the same of residents of Lomé, where cybercafés sprout like mushrooms, filled night and day with people connecting to various elsewheres, and where playing the US State Department's green card lottery has become a national pastime.[1] (I was told by a US embassy official that there are more green card lottery visa applications per capita in Togo than in any other African

---

[1] The United States government's 'Diversity Visa Lottery' annually awards up to 50,000 permanent residency visas to those from countries with low rates of immigration to the US, especially those in the global south. Applicants apply online (www.travel.state.gov/visa/immigrants/types/types_1322.html) and are randomly selected by a lottery system, before then submitting themselves to a lengthy process of medical examinations and embassy interviews. If they successfully jump through all these hoops, they receive a green card.

country, and that in 2004 Togo had ten times as many applicants as Benin, the similarly-sized country next door.) It would not be exaggerating too much to say that everyone in Togo is trying to leave – by playing the lottery, by trying to get into European or American universities, by arranging fictitious marriages with foreigners, by hoping to be signed on by a European soccer team or by joining churches that might take them overseas. A friend of mine whose 'wife' (a female friend he married expressly to obtain a visa) won the green card lottery a year ago but failed the embassy interview last November – after he had spent the better part of a year and all his resources preparing her for the interview – emailed me a week later to see whether I could get him a medical visa to come to the States to get a prosthetic arm! But while many, like my friend, fail in their attempts to leave (while nevertheless spending all their time trying, and therefore enacting a sort of virtual exile), many others have succeeded. Thus, today as much as 50% of Togo's GNP comes from the diaspora.[2]

If Togo in the 1990s was characterized by the crisis of the state and its effects on imaginaries of exile, it also saw the emergence of a set of powerful new non-state actors. Despite the fact that Eyadéma and his cronies nominally held onto power, they capitulated to international pressures to liberalize Togo's economic and public spheres, opening the floodgates to a host of novel agents and agencies, most importantly NGOs and the Pentecostal Church. NGOs were given free rein to bypass the state and operate on their own, effectively disengaging the developmental apparatus from the state apparatus. So, too, was the religious sphere liberalized for the first time – during the Cold War years, only Catholics and Presbyterians (churches with deep colonial roots in this area of West Africa) were permitted to evangelize in the country – and a host of new Pentecostal/charismatic churches emerged on the scene. Within only a few years, these churches – Assemblies of God, Church of the Pentecost, Baptist – became wildly popular and are today found in virtually every neighbourhood and village throughout the country, preaching strict codes of conduct, promising this-worldly success, and trafficking in End Times eschatology.

New urban mappings

How were these shifts in Togolese politics and political-economy reflected in spatial practice? I focus here on the Togolese capital, Lomé.

---

[2] It is worth noting here that it is not at all easy to differentiate the economic from the political as motive for exile. In the Togolese case at least, they are intimately related and intertwined: 'I have to leave because I can't make a living in Togo' always bears the tag line 'because of Eyadéma', and vice versa.

A dusty border-town which abuts the Atlantic Ocean, Lomé is home to half a million people. The core of the city is ringed by a lagoon and by the semi-circular Boulevard Circulaire, which meets the ocean in the west near the border with Ghana and in the east near the port. These bookends – the Aflao border and the port – are cities within the city, sites of congregation and commerce that have undergone dramatic expansion in the last ten years. Most of Lomé's government offices and the foreign embassies are found within the loop of the Boulevard, as is the Grand Marché, home to the largest textile market in West Africa. Beyond the Boulevard are sprawling suburbs, the university and the military camp. Two major roads lead out of the capital to the north – the Rue de Kpalimé on the western side of the Boulevard, and the Rue d'Atakpamé on the eastern side. The road to Atakpamé, which extends all the way to the northern border with Burkina Faso, has recently become a major conduit for large trucks travelling from the port of Lomé to the Sahelian countries to the north (Burkina Faso, Mali, Niger) and today boasts one of the best pavements in all of West Africa, thanks to a large grant from the World Bank, one of the few aid gifts to Togo during the post-Cold War period.

One of the principal effects of the 1990s moment of political crisis was an increasing militarization of this city by the sea. The city's major roundabouts and central points of entry – the border at Aflao and the two roads entering the city from the north – became sites of increased surveillance (as well as of bribery).[3] At these points of circulation and entry, cars and taxis were routinely fleeced by gun-toting soldiers in camouflage, in performances that staged military presence as much as anything else and indexed the rising paranoia of the Eyadéma regime. Even more indicative of the martial makeover of the city during this period was the construction of a new military camp just beyond the lagoon, off the Rue d'Atakpamé. Called 'Lomé II', the name alone suggesting a collapse of the distinction between city and camp, this barracks became Eyadéma's residence and also the seat of government during the 1990s. In this way, the post-Cold War merging of government and military was written into the life of the country and the space of its capital. Note, too, that while power thus transforms the space of the city, it must also conform to, and work through, a spatializing logic – here, a logic of roadways and points of entry, and grids on a modernist map. An oblique example of this point: Eyadéma's government's withdrawal from the city centre to the suburban barracks was in part motivated by his desire to avoid the twice-daily motorcade through Lomé's streets from his residence to the government building where he worked – a journey he felt was vulnerable to ambush.

---

[3] Virtually unheard of in the 1980s, the police bribe became standard by the late 1990s – another effect of the crisis.

Lomé's other intensely militarized space was (and remains) the *quartier* of Bè in the northeast, the site of fierce anti-regime street protests during the mid-1990s and again in February 2005 when, following Eyadéma's sudden death, the generals abrogated the constitution and installed his son in power. At this time, pictures streamed across the world's media of marches, blockades, and tire and car burnings in Bè, as well as of government retaliation and the killing of protesters. Since the mid-1990s, police checkpoints have been more numerous in Bè than anywhere else in the city, and heavily-armed olive vehicles circulate day and night throughout the *quartier*'s sandy streets. As one such vehicle – with semi-automatic weapons on its roof – slowly drove by a bar where I was sitting with friends one evening in summer 2004, a companion remarked, 'They

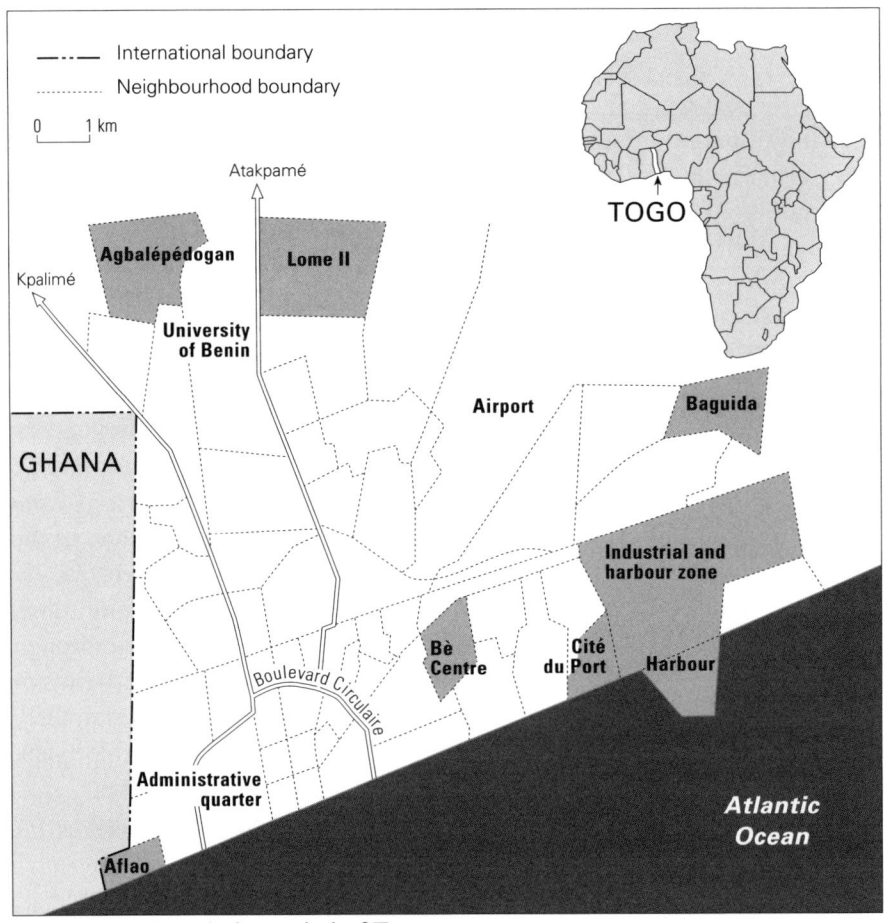

Map 9.1   Lomé, the capital of Togo

do this to let us know that they are watching and that the iron fist is right around the corner. ... It's pure intimidation.' As a site of anti-government opposition, Bè has become a neighbourhood of protest and death.[4]

Another neighbourhood, Agbalépédogan, a sort of inverse-Bè, has sprung up in the last few years due north of the central part of the city. The sudden appearance and rapid growth of this neighbourhood of northerners, many from Eyadéma's own Kabiyé ethnic group, is directly tied to the moment in the mid-1990s when relations between southerners and northerners heated up and many northerners were evicted by their southern landlords. Fearing an uncertain political future, many of Lomé's northern residents decided to buy their own land and have turned Agbalépédogan into an ethnic enclave within the city.[5] Here, northern languages are the *lingua franca*, and northern food and beer are the currency of the streets. These two examples – Bè and Agbalépédogan – of course also index an increasing ethnicization of the Lomé neighbourhood during the 1990s.

The afore-mentioned 'cities within the city' – the border with Ghana and the port – have been sites of bustling activity for decades. But their current size – the port extends for miles and has swallowed up all of the neighbourhoods around it, as has the border at Aflao – and their prominence in the commercial and imaginative life of Lomé are recent. As the post-Cold War economic crisis deepened, the port became the main gateway for foreign, especially second-hand, goods. And, as the Togolese expatriate community in Europe grew during the 1990s – especially in Germany where many of those opposed to Eyadéma were granted political asylum – supplier networks also grew. Increased supply in turn generated vast informal commercial networks. Today, virtually everyone in Lomé has ties to someone – a family member or friend – who works at the port.

The growth of the port was also spurred by a fortuitous event beyond Togo's borders. The start of the civil war in Cote d'Ivoire in 1999 sent ocean traffic scrambling to find a new point of disembarkation for European goods bound for the 'enclave' countries of the West African interior, and Lomé became their port of choice. Needless to say, this has been a godsend for the cash-starved

---

[4] Another symptom of the recent militarization of Lomé, and a highly visible one at that, involves the barricading of the foreign embassies in the wake of the embassy bombings in Kenya and Tanzania, and the 9/11 attack on the World Trade Center. Until the late 1990s, for example, anyone could walk unimpeded right up to the front door of the US embassy or the US Cultural Center. Today, there are newly-erected walls and security checkpoints a block away.

[5] Other similar recently-emergent northern *quartiers* in Lomé include Lossosimé, Agoé and Avedji.

post-Cold War Togolese state, which by all accounts has supported itself over the last five years almost exclusively from taxes on goods arriving at the port.

The border at Aflao is a conduit for not only people but also goods – particularly second-hand European merchandise entering the port. Again, the traffic – and the size of this city on the border – has increased exponentially during the post-Cold War period, not only because it is the portal for goods travelling west from Togo's port but also because the tens of thousands of Togolese who temporarily fled to Ghana during the mid-1990s moment of violent ethnic conflict have maintained ongoing ties, both familial and commercial, with family and friends on the other side of the border. The sprawl of both the border zone and the port has utterly transformed those neighbourhoods they abut. These proximate spaces now also cater to the food, lodging and entertainment needs of those travellers, merchants, money changers, hawkers and scam artists who frequent these borderland spaces.

Perhaps the largest single effect of the 1990s political and economic crisis, and certainly the one with the most significant financial consequences for a majority of Togolese, has been the creation of a sizeable Togolese exile community in Europe and the United States. During the past ten years, hundreds of thousands of Togolese have migrated overseas in search of jobs and money, in flight from the oppressive political order at home. While obtaining a visa has become increasingly difficult, there are nevertheless today entire cottage industries, both in Lomé and throughout the diaspora, of Togolese devoted to helping others obtain visas (student, green card lottery, political asylum, tourist 'multi-entry')[6] – thus feeding more and more Togolese into the diaspora. Most

---

[6] Local inventiveness surrounding the US State Department's annual green card lottery ('lotto visa') system is quite extraordinary, and in some ways reconstitutes kinship and neighbourliness by other means. Once someone has been selected (by a lottery system in Lexington, KY), and before he/she goes for the obligatory interview at the US embassy in Lomé, they will often attempt to add 'dependants' to their dossier. Sometimes these are legitimate relatives but usually not. (Indeed, they are often relatives of those already in the diaspora – who can more easily afford the quid pro quo: payment of the visa winner's embassy interview fee of US$ 435 and purchase of his/her plane ticket to the US.) Since US immigration rules only permit the visa winner to be accompanied by a spouse and children, the winner must then 'marry' his sponsor's wife (or sister or cousin) and 'adopt' any children before the interview – and present proof that they are indeed his/her dependants. This in turn requires producing a file of documents – marriage papers, wedding photos, birth certificates. One somewhat atypical but nevertheless revealing example: a friend's wife recently arrived in the US as the 'wife' of a friend of her brother. Three years ago, the brother and the friend both received political asylum in the US (needless to say, under false pretences) and entered into a 'sister-exchange' arrangement, whereby each would 'marry' the other's sister and pay her way to the States. As part of the agreement, my friend's wife's 'husband' recently spent over US$ 2500 returning to Togo to take wedding photos with his friend's sister – for her to

importantly for the homeland, these exiles continue to send money back home. Whereas ten years ago expatriate remittances constituted only 10-20% of the Togolese GNP, today they are at least double that, with some estimates as high as 50%.

What effects do these exiles, and their remittances, have on the space of the city? For one, like many West Africans abroad, they build houses back home. Thus, another set of virgin *quartiers* – Baguida, Adamavo and Kagomé – have sprung up in the last few years to the east of Lomé near the border with Benin. These are ghost neighbourhoods, like those found in capitals all over West Africa (in Accra's East Legon, in Abidjan, in Lagos), filled with largely uninhabited houses still under construction. (And they will remain so for years. Since the banks do not offer mortgage loans, the owner must build on a pay-as-he-can basis, starting with a wall around the property, then later – often several years later – adding the foundations and walls, and finally, topping the structure off with a roof.) These expatriates may never return, or if they do it is only rarely and for short stays, but they want their mark left on the skin of the city, so that others will know that they succeeded abroad and that they have not forgotten those they left behind. (There is an irony in this display of wealth-from-abroad, of course, for many in the diaspora are working unbearably long hours and make barely enough money to live on, to say nothing of the loneliness and alienation that attend their lives in such faraway places. Still, while their wages may not earn them much of a living in the US or Europe, a small amount of savings goes a long way back home.) It is, then, through these

---

present at the embassy as proof that she was married to him. However, the 'husband' could not fly to Lomé itself – for fear that if US authorities discovered that he had been back in Togo it might jeopardize his asylum status. Instead, he flew to Accra, took a bus to the border – where they only check passports of non-West Africans – and crossed into Togo on foot.

A cottage industry of lotto visa entrepreneurs has grown up around these practices – of those who help others with the online visa registration, of those who know who to bribe to get false marriage or adoption or job papers, of those who arrange the taking of marriage photos, and especially of those who serve as brokers between those in the diaspora and those at home. Another friend of mine – the one whose 'wife' failed her interview and then enquired whether he might get a medical visa for an arm replacement – signed up 300 people, mostly women, for the lotto visa last fall. He is currently in the process of 'marrying' one of those who won, paying for her apprenticeship (as a maker of batik), and saving money for the embassy interview.

As one telling sign of the importance the lotto visa is assuming in the cultural life of Lomé today, I have heard repeatedly from Togolese that the consular official who conducts the visa interviews at the embassy is far better known than the ambassador. 'We don't even know who the ambassador is,' a friend said. 'But Mme Johnson, we know her well. She's a celebrity here. We study her every move – for she's the one who will decide whether we have a life beyond Togo or not.'

proxy structures – structures that at once mark their owners' nostalgic desire for the homeland, while simultaneously fuelling a desire to leave in those who remain – that they make themselves ongoingly present in the life of the city.

Another effect of this community of exiles on life back home has been to re-centre – to 'de-' and 're-territorialize', in Deleuze and Guattari's terms (1983, 1987) – the hubs and conduits of information and money flow that are so important to the life of the city. Whereas in the 1980s and early 1990s, Lomé's main post office was a centre of coming and going, and of access to the world beyond the nation, today it is little more than a sleepy backwater with a trickle of daily visitors. Instead, it is the ubiquitous Internet cafés (over 200 in this small capital) and the money-transfer stations (Western Union, MoneyGram) that buzz with activity, and that have become new sites of congregation. It is noteworthy too that the Internet cafés are used for much more than simple (email) letter-writing. Most denizens of Lomé's cyber parlours spend much of their time exploring the Internet's proliferating websites, thus stirring the imagination about various elsewheres and producing, in yet another register, fantasies of escape.

Another striking feature of the post-Cold War Lomé landscape, like that of Lagos, Cotonou, Accra and Abidjan, is the proliferation of the new charismatic churches. Their congregations often run into the thousands, and their sites of worship – large open-air buildings in residential neighbourhoods – are much more than simple structures with four walls. Their Sunday services – and Friday 'all-nights', Thursday prayer meetings, and so on – spill over into the life of the neighbourhood, redefining its sounds and sensibilities, its temporalities and modes of belonging. Thus, neighbourhood space is imagined as no longer simply local but rather as annexed to something larger and higher, and its neighbour-citizens are redefined as global Christian subjects. Many of the new churches also attempt to reconstitute social and familial relations – and the neighbourhood network – within the congregation itself. Thus, churchgoers periodically break up into 'neighbourhood' groups to establish support and prayer networks. Marriage is also tightly controlled by these churches, with a mandate to marry within the ranks of believers or else suffer excommunication. Finally, through their End Times eschatology, these reconstituted urban 'neighbourhoods' (whose members nevertheless see themselves as trans-urban members of a global evangelical community) also enact a form of imaginary exile – which complements those other forms of exile, both real and virtual, that characterize the post-Cold War Togolese landscape more generally.

Virtualizing the nation

Before concluding, I would like to briefly discuss the way in which the empty nation, the nation-in-exile, has stretched the boundaries of national belonging and spawned new senses of attachment and neighbourliness – thus also re-spatializing the territory of the nation.

I begin with an anecdote from the presidential election of June 2003. During the run-up to the election, I was in contact with a Togolese friend who was living in the United States (after winning the State Department's green card lottery two years previously). He was driving a baggage van at Newark airport and living in a crowded apartment in downtown Newark with seven other Togolese. During the weeks leading up to the election, this friend would return home from working double (16-hour) shifts at the airport and go online to read the latest postings on the half dozen websites that Togo's various political parties run (out of Paris, Toronto, New York), sometimes posting his own e-messages as well, adding his own opinion to the arguments circling around the various candidates. He would then call friends in Lomé on his cell phone to get the latest local news on the election, and to convey information to them from those sites that were blocked by government censors.

One of the things that intrigued me the most in my discussions with Kodjo was his insistence that the outcome of the election would be decided not by those at home but by those in the diaspora: that if the right deals were made by the opposition leaders in exile – especially Gilchrist Olympio, the leader of the main opposition party who lives in Paris – they could defeat Eyadéma at the polls. When I asked how, from afar, they would marshal the votes back home, not only in Lomé but also in the villages, he said that it would be easy: there were people in the diaspora from every village and from most extended families throughout Togo, and that a single call to a cell or pay phone in the village would instruct people how to vote and could throw the election one way or the other. 'But why would the whole village follow your advice?' I asked. 'Because they're beholden to us – we send money back – and because we know more about politics than they do.' Here then is a 30-year-old Togolese exile, a proletarian with a laptop and cell phone (and thus someone whose profile defies many of the conventional categories), but also someone who, from his small apartment in North America, felt he was not only a full participant in, but was also able to play a role in influencing, an election back home.

What then of Togolese national belonging today? What does it mean to have a virtual nation – a nation of exiles, both real and imaginary? To have a diasporic longing within the space of the nation itself but also – the flip side – a desire for the nation within the diaspora? And what does it mean to have the nation now constituted through this doubled gaze – of those who are away looking home, and those who are home looking elsewhere?

As my friend's example makes plain – and I could offer many others like it – many of those who leave remain intensely involved in politics back home. In some cases, they are even more engaged than before – or at least more passionately or libidinally engaged. Kodjo told me, for instance, that during the run-up to the 2003 election, he could think of nothing else, whether he was at home or delivering bags at the airport. There was only one thing for which he lived, and that was to see Eyadéma removed from office.

Some of those in exile also operate with greater cachet than before, as illustrated by Kodjo's ability to access news from the diaspora and its websites and relay it back to those in Lomé. Indeed, he told me at one point that this was an 'Internet election', an election driven by information posted on the various party websites by those in exile. As someone with greater (and cheaper) access to those sites, he was thus able to command considerable cultural capital at home.

If the Internet provided Kodjo with a source of prestige, it also provided a new site of sociality. He made many virtual friends in the weeks leading up to the election – Togolese in Paris and Toronto and Cary, North Carolina – who were as passionately engaged in the politics of the moment as he was, and with whom he continues to communicate. Moreover, many were from ethnic groups other than his own, and from groups with which he had had very little contact at home. What Kodjo missed, of course, was the tactility of everyday politics in Lomé, the endless chatter and banter with others, the familiar streets and meeting grounds, the embodied fears and anxieties of the lumpen, the nation all moving to a single (albeit agonistic) beat – a far cry from his surfing the web in his room in Newark. But these tactile pleasures are now being replaced with other pleasures – those pleasures of the virtual – which, with time, will be no less real than those of the everyday in the neighbourhoods back home.

While identification with the nation is thus reaffirmed, and even strengthened, it has also shifted. Not only is it virtualized and mediated through informational proxies of various sorts, it has also been shot through with the ambivalence of diasporic identification/disidentification. The sign of Togo as homeland is now also a site of disavowal. Identification with the homeland, of course, also competes with those other identities and regimes of governmentality that mark the figure of the 'refugee', the 'green card holder', the raced post-colonial subject. But a similar set of shifts is true as well for those who remain at home. In seeking an elsewhere, and in inscribing that desire into their identity, they too can never return home again. 'Every child who grew up in the 1990s', a friend in Lomé told me in July 2004, 'wants to leave – and will keep trying to leave until he gets a visa. There is nothing for us here anymore. No jobs, no future. Imagining going to the US or to Europe enables us to dream again, and until then our only dream is of leaving.'

I offer one final example to underscore the increasing importance of the cyber nation and its virtualized citizenry – and thus also of the way in which the Internet has become a mediator of Togolese identity today, in the process refiguring what we mean by the term 'neighbourhood'. In the hours after Eyadéma's sudden death in February 2005, amidst the uncertainty that ensued as the generals ignored the Constitution and placed the dictator's son in power, all of the main Togolese websites continued to post hourly commentary on what was happening on the streets. (This was quite extraordinary, and was clearly directed at the overseas audience, for the electricity in Lomé was down and all the cybercafés were closed.) The unfolding events of this 'military coup', as the opposition labelled it, were thus immediately available to diasporics abroad, among whom the news of Eyadéma's death spread like wildfire. A Togolese friend I know in North Carolina received over 50 calls on his cell phone within hours of the breaking news, from points all over the United States and Canada, as well as from Germany, Spain, France and Lomé. Needless to say, government web postings attempted to reassure its citizenry-in-exile that things were calm and the transition was proceeding apace, while opposition websites maintained the opposite – that the streets were far from quiescent and that protests were already underway. This episode thus provides clear recognition of the fact that both the opposition and the government know that today its constituents lie beyond the nation's borders as much as within, and that political fortunes at home very much depend on marshalling its citizenry abroad.

Coda

My argument has been that the Togolese social and political landscape has been dramatically transformed by the changes of the post-Cold War moment, and that these changes are inscribed in place-making practices. As the old colonial and early post-colonial structures of authority that defined relations between metropole and colony, and within the colony between state and local, have been replaced by new transnational structures of power and sovereignty, so too are those spatial structures and urban spaces that were indexed to the modernizing, developmental Cold War state apparatus being remade. Moreover, as an eviscerated Togolese state – itself a product of the neoliberal moment – has reinvented itself, and as a disaffected exilic population has come into being, new spatial practices and urban cartographies have emerged.

It is nevertheless important to bear in mind, as de Certeau (1984) and Lefebvre (1991) have so powerfully shown, that as power is em-placed, it is also inflected and colonized by territorializing logics, logics that are nevertheless always themselves historically produced. Thus, modernist – and now transnational – modes of sovereignty may seek to shape and transform the space of the city, but so too must they always come to terms with and work through the specific logics of an already-emplaced city space. This dialectic is certainly at work in the post-Cold War moment, wherein new forms of sovereignty run up against earlier (modernist) modes of spatial organization, at once necessarily adapting themselves to those modes while also seeking to transform them.

It remains to be seen what effect the recent death of Eyadéma, Togo's military dictator of 38 years, will have on the body politic and the space of the city. Will the militarization of the city – with its checkpoints and surveillance practices – become a thing of the past? Will the presidential palace and seat of government become disengaged from the military barracks? Will the return of international aid diminish the importance of the port? Will more Togolese choose to stay at home rather than enter the diaspora? Will the virtualization of the polity and its citizens – yes, a product of today's informational age, but also, and even more so, of life in a dictatorial post-Cold War state – shift? In short, how will the space of the nation – a nation whose spaces have been so much the product of Eyadéma's presence – change now that he has gone? My guess is that, as with the dreaded paternal signifier, his effects will remain long after the moment of his passing.

References

de Certeau, M. 1984, *The Practice of Everyday Life*, Berkeley: University of California Press.
Deleuze, G. & F. Guattari 1983, *Anti-Oedipus: Capitalism and Schizophrenia*, Minneapolis: University of Minnesota Press.
Deleuze, G. & F. Guattari 1987, *A Thousand Plateaus*, Minneapolis: University of Minnesota Press.
Lefebvre, H. 1991, *The Production of Space*, Cambridge: Blackwell.
Mbembe, A. 1992, 'The Banality of Power and the Aesthetics of Vulgarity in the Postcolony', *Public Culture* 4 (2): 1-30.
Mbembe, A. 2001, *On the Postcolony*. Berkeley: University of California Press.
Mbembe, A. 2003, 'Necropolitics', *Public Culture* 15 (1): 11-40.

10

Neighbours on the fringes of a small city in post-war Chad

Mirjam de Bruijn

> *Drought and war are important reasons for migration to small urban centres in Chad, and those who are forced to migrate are often the poor who find they can no longer survive in their villages. The central question in this chapter is whether these people group together once in town and form a distinct neighbourhood. Such a neighbourhood can hardly be based on exchanges of material goods because these people have virtually nothing to share. What does in fact bind them? Are a shared history of misery and emotions of hardship a basis for developing a feeling of belonging? In the last few decades, Chad has experienced severe droughts and extensive violence, with a civil war that heavily influenced mobility patterns in the countryside. The case study presented here is from the migrant quarter of the small town of Mongo in central Chad,* Secteur 4, *where people have settled as a result of drought and war. Not only people from outside Mongo have found shelter here but also impoverished families from Mongo town itself. The majority of the inhabitants of* Secteur 4 *are women who share a common history and emotions.*

Urbanization in Africa is a result of both migration and the internal growth of the population of a city itself. In rural areas of Africa however, the growth of small towns is mainly due to migration and results from people's inability to make a living in the rural countryside. Poverty and insecurity influence their decisions to move to town. This form of forced migration, which in international jargon is labelled 'internal displacement', is common in the Sahel where climate variability is always present and people move with the rhythm of the seasons or in response to a crisis like drought.[1] War and conflict – like the rebellion of the Tamacheck in the 1990s and the Mauritanian border conflicts in the 1980s – have erupted regularly in the Sahel and have influenced population mobility there. This chapter considers the formation of new quarters in small towns which have sprung up as a consequence of forced migration and questions whether this crisis-induced migration influences the character of the new neighbourhoods. Who are the migrating people? How do their personal histories influence their urban lifestyle? How much of a common background do they have? Do these people indeed unite in a neighbourhood or do they simply become urban squatters?

Neighbourhood is a geographical interpretation of a quarter in a city but also indicates that the people who live there share a material, social and emotional life.[2] A neighbourhood has characteristics that go beyond the indication of place, implying feelings of being connected and a feeling of belonging that is linked to a shared history. When people move to town in situations such as those described above, one wonders what these people do in fact share. They often arrive in town in dire poverty and have nothing to share but their poverty. If sharing of material goods is not possible what then keeps these people together? Platteau (1991) introduced the term 'co-variance of risk' to indicate that people who have nothing cannot share and will thus not create social security arrangements. This may be true but do people only share in a material sense? Feelings of belonging may be very non-material and be based on the sharing of history, on shared emotions or on moral support.

The case study presented in this chapter is from central Chad. Chad's post-colonial history contains all the elements that contribute to patterns of forced migration: civil war (1965-1990) and its ensuing insecurity, recurrent droughts and ever-increasing rainfall variability. The civil war officially ended in 1990 when President Idriss Deby came to power and installed a government that subscribed to the development of a democratic republic.[3] However the Chadian

---

[1] This variability in climate and its consequences for society are extensively described for the Sahel. In this literature a link is made between society and the ecological environment (Raynaut 1997, Dietz et al. 2004, de Bruijn 2000, de Bruijn & Van Dijk 2003, de Bruijn et al. 2005).

[2] Neighbourhood means neighbours, people of a district; especially one forming a community within a town or city. But it also means neighbourly feelings or conduct and a sense of nearness (*Concise Oxford Dictionary*, 6th edition, 1980).

[3] Although the history of Chad's civil war is well described (Buijtenhuijs 1978, 1987), very little is known about what the war has meant for the people in the country side. The only exceptions are the reports by Pairault (1994) who revisited his research area after the war around Lac d'Iro, Doornbos (1982) who was in eastern Chad during the war, and de Bruijn & Van Dijk (2005) who started research on this topic in 2002. It

state still resembles the models of a patrimonial and authoritarian state, with a substantial proportion of its population living in dire poverty.[4]

The area around Mongo is Sahelian and does not escape the droughts and increasing rainfall variations that have been described for other parts of the Sahel.[5] Although there are hardly any rainfall figures for central Chad, people's stories, observations of the landscape and the scarce statistics that do exist all confirm the Sahelian pattern for central Chad. Analysis of archival material shows that this is not a new pattern and that Chad experienced frequent droughts and famines throughout the twentieth century.[6] However, people indicate that the droughts in the last few decades have struck much harder, one of the main reasons being the long civil war when people had limited access to markets, agricultural production decreased, and no technological advances were made. After the war, state intervention in the rural areas has been of a more exploitative than developmental nature and has prevented people from building prosperous livelihoods (Van Dijk 2003).

New mobility patterns have developed in response to the changes brought about by environmental uncertainty and the civil war: economic migration, forced migration because of violence, migration in desperation by old women looking for work, etc. One of the most visible results has been a growth in the size of provincial capitals, although few concrete figures concerning this growth are available. Statistics relating to the growth of N'djamena, the capital of Chad, indicate rapid urbanization during and after the war. The population of N'djamena increased from 88,160 inhabitants in 1961 (Courtier & Gosselin 1961) to 835,000 in 1997. Today it surpasses one million, with an annual growth rate of 7.8%.

This chapter investigates the mobility and settlement patterns of the people who fled various crises in central Chad. More specifically, it looks at how these people settled in one of the peripheral neighbourhoods of Mongo town and the kind of neighbourhood that developed. The chapter is descriptive and presents the first results of on-going research into the urban dynamics of Mongo town.

---

would seem fair to conclude that Chad's development has been very badly hit by the civil war.
[4] See for a discussion of recent developments of the Chadian state, Eriksson & Hagstromer (2005) and de Bruijn & Van Dijk (2005).
[5] The case study presented in this chapter is part of a larger research project that is looking into the consequences of drought and war in Chad. The main researchers in this programme are Han van Dijk and Mirjam de Bruijn from the Africa Studies Centre in Leiden, the Netherlands.
[6] Part of the project is the reconstruction of the colonial area of this specific region (Rense forthcoming).

The Guera and Mongo in central Chad

The Guera is a mountainous area in central Chad that people used in the past as a refuge during raids by the Waddai, Baguirmi and Bornou Empires. It was then an area on the margins of these empires and its inhabitants were seen as potential slaves. Mongo town did not exist until 1911 when the French, who colonized Chad, set up their administrative headquarters near the Mongo Mountain, thus creating the centre of the town. The Daadjo, who were dominant in the region before the French arrived, had a chiefdom just three kilometres from the site and became the local leaders under the French. Even today Mongo's *Chef de Canton* is a Daadjo. The other ethnic groups living in and around Mongo include the Dangaleat, Migaame and Bidio, who are collectively called the Hadjerai (the 'inhabitants of the rocks' in Arabic). The largest group after the Hadjerai are the Arabs, the Guera's former nomadic livestock herders who have settled and established their own villages.

The Guera was an important region during the civil war that dominated Chadian politics and the daily lives of the people from 1965 to 1990 and coincided with severe Sahelian droughts that ruined many people's livelihoods. Poverty has become widespread in the Guera[7] and an important effect has been that the people became very mobile as they sought places of refuge. The small towns in the region offered refuge, especially in the first decade of the civil war, with stories revealing that many people from the villages in the Guera lived as refugees in and around Mongo. Later, in the 1980s, when the rebels took over in Mongo, people themselves then left the town because of the violence and repression. The influx of people seeking refuge was also related to droughts, bad harvests and political unrest. Thus the size of the town appears to have fluctuated significantly, although statistics are non-existent because the war meant that demographic figures were not recorded and, if they did exist, the rebels destroyed them by burning the town's archives.

---

[7] Life expectancy at birth for the Salamat is 40 years. The Human Poverty Index of Chad is 0.403 (or 57%) which means that 6 out of every 10 Chadians suffer deprivation. However there is a big differentiation between the zones. In 2000 the Human Development Index for the Guera was 0.350 and in adjacent zones Salamat was 0.259 and Ouaddai was 0.395. These have all become zones of chronic poverty (PRSP 2003: 32, based on UNDP Report).

Research in poverty

The Mongo quarter, where this recent research has been done, is one of the poorest in town. Undertaking research among people who are hungry, who have no food for their children and who are constantly short of every basic need is not easy. It is especially difficult for a white female researcher who, however gentle and friendly she may be, is of course astonishingly rich in the eyes of these people. I was also quickly confused with Geeske, called Riskje, a Dutch woman who worked at the Protestant mission for many years helping blind children and coordinating the leprosy programme in central and eastern Chad. She also visited this sector, where leprosy is still common and where many people are blind. As a result, I became associated with this charity work, which made interviewing even less easy. People accepted a first round of short talks but by the second time they started asking for money and help. They simply could not understand why I did not provide aid. Some women were different and accepted my constant questioning. However, to get an impression of the people living in this sector I needed a more systematic overview. This interviewing was done by a man and a woman – both barefoot doctors who had been educated by the Red Cross. The two assistants considered *Secteur Quatre*, as it was called by the people in town, as one of the poorest quarters of town and also as one of the most diverse, most recent and most fluctuating as it was where migrants from the rural hinterland tended to settle. As the interviewing progressed, they could not avoid getting involved in treating people's illnesses and in giving money to those in need and to those who wanted to send their children to school. They were at a certain point as depressed as I was about the situation, and for them interviewing in this sector became an intriguing insight into the poverty and misery of so many Chadian people and the failure of the state to organize its economy better.

Secteur Quatre and Mongo

Today Mongo, the country's fifth largest town, officially has an estimated 20,000 inhabitants. It is the capital of the northern Guera in central Chad (see Map 10.1) where the offices of the prefecture, the military and the gendarmerie are vested in old buildings that remind the town of its colonial past. As the area's administrative headquarters, the town has an important regional market on Wednesdays, some shops, a cattle market, a Catholic mission, a Protestant mission, two big mosques and numerous smaller ones. Most of the inhabitants are Muslim. Being wealthy in Mongo is the privilege of a few – most people just have enough money to get by and to feed their families. Mongo is in appearance and in reality a poor town but the different quarters do not experience this poverty to the same extent; it depends partly on their histories.

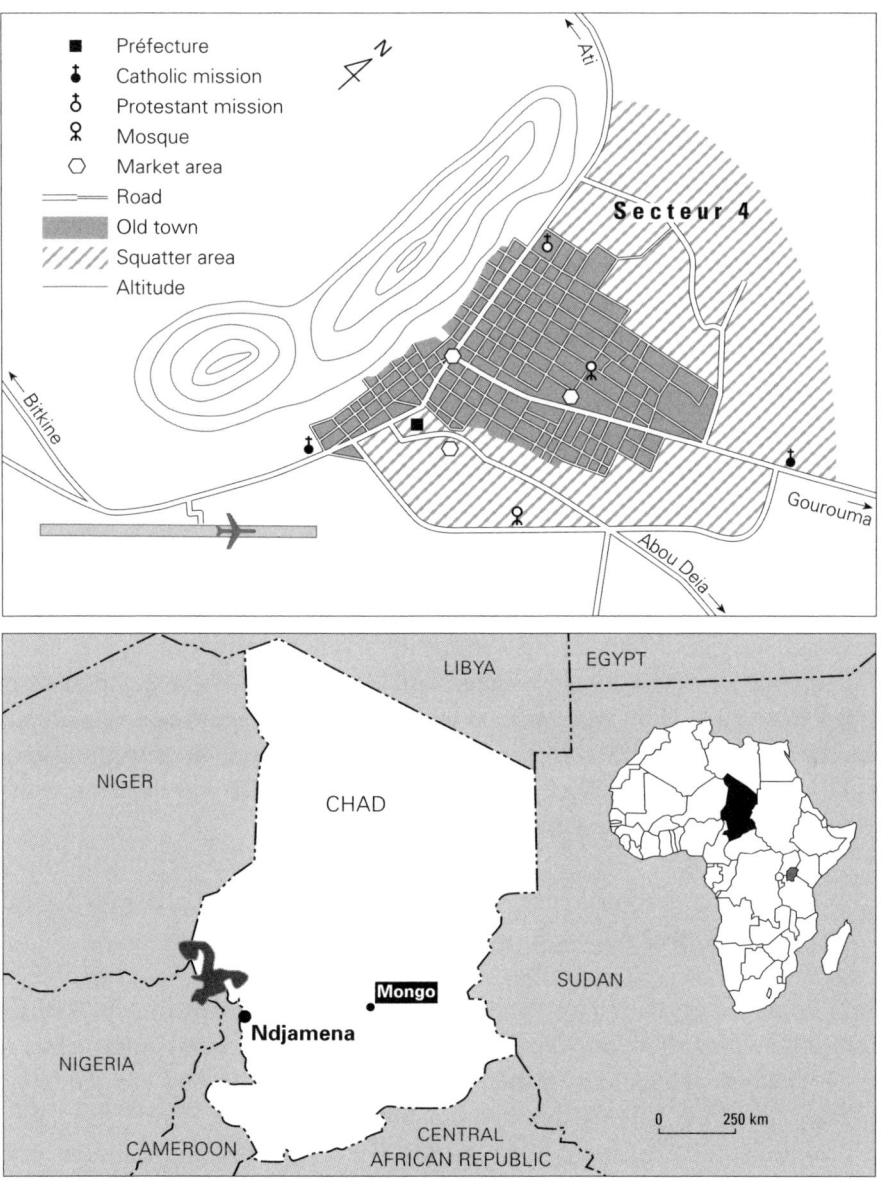

Map 10.1   Secteur Quatre in Mongo

In the administrative centre, the old buildings from the French colonial period are still in use by the Chadian administration, housing the *sous-préfet* and the *préfet*, various government services, the hospital, the secondary school, etc. South of this is Sector 1 where many old people live: it is the oldest sector and predominantly inhabited by Daadjo. It is also home to the *Chef de Canton*. Sector 8, to the north of the centre, is an old quarter where the Hausa- and Fulani-speaking businessmen live: it is one of the richer quarters and is the centre of commerce. Another distinct quarter is Sector 9 on the southern fringes of town where big houses are being built by military and police personnel, and other high-ranking civil servants. These are the people who are able to buy land and build expensive houses, and who have access to the government elite in town who provide them with the land on which to build. The military camp is located in this sector. On the other side of town towards the north is Sector 4 that forms, together with Sectors 6 and 7, the poorest part of town. Among the three, Sector 4 is considered the poorest. It borders Sector 3 where I lived with my family from October 2002 to May 2003 and to where I have returned every year since.

We lived in the old mission house belonging to the Protestant mission on the edge of Sector 4, a house that is a reflection of Mongo in the twentieth century. It was built in the 1950s when the Protestant mission was first establishing itself in Mongo. They have never had a lot of followers but their presence has always been significant and one of their important contributions to Mongo was the setting up of a boarding school for blind children. When the school was built in the 1950s it was on the edge of a forest. People still remember the fruit trees there and refer to it as the Forest Barbaza. Today the forest has disappeared and the area has become incorporated in Mongo town.

Mongo was a stronghold of the Chadian government during the civil war until 1979 when violence broke out throughout the country and led to the fall of N'djamena. Mongo's *Chef de Canton* left the town with rebel troops to occupy N'djamena and Mongo fell into the hands of one of the rebel factions[8] who then set up their headquarters in Barbaza. The mission house where we lived was the commander's house, and the church and the boarding school were occupied by troops. According to old people still living in Sector 4, the forest that was still left was used by these troops as a source of wood for construction and fuel.

This was also the period that many people remember as a period of extreme violence and crime. The people who lived in Mongo at that time and even the few who now live in Sector 4 said that it was almost impossible to live in

---

[8] I will not go into the details of the civil war. This faction was part of the CDR. For a history of the civil war, see Buijtenhuijs (1978, 1987).

Photo 10.1 Children are often left alone during the day to fend for themselves

Photo 10.2 A typical street in Mongo
(Photos: Mirjam de Bruijn)

Mongo then. The rebels left Mongo when Habre took over in 1982, leaving behind dilapidated buildings that were rebuilt in 1987 and a large open space north of Mongo where people could settle. The stories of the people who fled in this period are numerous, with most returning after a few years when calm had returned to Mongo. They settled then in what is now called *Secteur Quatre*.

At first sight *Secteur Quatre* has the appearance of a chaotic village, with the predominant colours being yellow and brown. Huts are made of mud bricks and straw and millet stalks, and have been erected at random over the foot of the mountain. Most of them have no fence around them, and roofs that do not leak are a luxury. Household equipment in the huts is minimal, there are no latrines, and water comes from wells outside Mongo. The small paths people have walked along to go from their huts to the bush every morning before sunrise form the only permanent infrastructure. A few goats nibble at the huts and chickens pick at the herbs. Trees are scattered and scarce. This sector has no school or other government-related services. The few better houses are the one belonging to a Malian immigrant whose father was an *ancien combattant* and those of a few civil servants and the widows of rich traders. There are two farms in the sector that are owned by fathers and sons. At one, the cattle return to their stalls every evening and two big oil mills turn for hours every day to extract the oil from the sesame and peanuts harvested just outside Mongo.

Who are the other people living in this sector? On our initial visit, we simply started at the house closest to our house. There we only made the acquaintance of the children as their mother had left for work. When we asked them what they had eaten, they said they were waiting for their mother to come home. My assistant asked if they went to school or not. These children did not. The next produced the same story. Then we came to a hut that had a large fence made out of thorny branches around it. It seemed at first that there was nobody at home but when we entered we found two old people in the house. Both were blind. After a while a child came in who appeared to be in charge. It was their niece. They told me that their only son had left for N'djamena and I would probably be able to find him there when I was doing my interviews among street children.[9] A few huts further we met an old blind lady who lived with her daughter, whose husband had beaten her in such a way that it had left a deep scar on her neck. The old mother left every morning to see if the people in town had something for her. I also knew her from her visits to our home where she would come with her elderly husband and they would both sit on the doorstep waiting for us to give them some money. Her husband had died by the time I

---

[9] In N'djamena we did indeed find a group of street children who had left the Guera. I did not find this specific boy but other children from Mongo do live on the streets of N'djamena (see de Bruijn & Djindil forthcoming).

visited them again in 2004. We came across many elderly women and young mothers with children in other huts. It was really striking how few men there were in this sector. For most of the year the inhabitants of Sector 4 earn their living by working for others in town, in the household, working in the fields, or watering their gardens. They also have their own fields, mostly in the bush a long way from town. These fields are owned by relatives, or the people have just taken them over as it was considered bush land. Gathering wood for fuel and leaves from different nutritional trees are other major occupations. The revenue from all these activities hardly sustains them, but they may also have access to social networks which they can fall back on when times are even harder.

Settling histories

From the 68 short interviews we did in this sector, it is possible to reconstruct the occupation history of the sector. Twenty-seven of those interviewed referred explicitly to drought as a reason for settling in Mongo. They related this to hunger and one woman explicitly said, 'if I had stayed in my village I would have died of famine like the others'.[10] Five of them, three old ladies and two women of about 40 years of age, recounted the story of the refugee camp that was set up in Barbaza. They had come to Mongo because of the distribution of food by the Red Cross. This was at the beginning of the 1980s when the Guera experienced a hard time after the outbreak of violence and war, and several poor rainy seasons. A few years later the big Sahelian famine shook the world. Due to the war, the country's infrastructure was terrible and NGOs had little or no access to people living in the countryside. Nevertheless, under the dictator Habre, relative calm returned to Chad and food aid was organized. The Red Cross was then the only international aid organization to come to Mongo to help the local people.[11] They refer to themselves as 'refugees' and even talked in interviews about a camp where they lived. The Red Cross did not stay in the area for a long period of time but after they left the people they had attracted to Mongo did not leave Sector 4. As one woman told us, she could buy a piece of land in the sector for FCFA 1500. Another said that land was available in the

---

[10] This old Migaame lady of about 60 had come to Mongo from Gourbiti, 60 km to the east.
[11] Interview with the *Chef de Canton* Baro, April 2003, KRO, 'Brandpunt', a documentary on the situation in Chad in 1982: Archives Beeld & Geluid NOS, Videotape 12207, 2-10-1982.

part of town that was considered bush. These people did not go back to their villages.

A few old women came to town in the 1970s just after a period when rebellion in the Guera was at its height: villages were attacked by rebels and government troops, huts were burnt, and rebels moved into the villages where they exploited the villagers and restricted their freedom of movement. The Guera became a zone of insecurity. This insecurity went hand in hand with the irregular rainfall patterns at the end of the 1960s and in the early 1970s. When drought finally hit the region many people decided to leave their villages and try their luck in Mongo.

Mongo was not only a place of refuge for those in need but was also attractive as a centre with its hospital and possibilities for work. There are numerous accounts of migrants who came to Mongo to find a cure for illnesses that could not be treated by local doctors. People sold their assets and arrived in town to settle in Sector 4 with family members who had migrated before them. Others who moved to Sector 4 already lived in Mongo in one of the better-off quarters but had had to sell off their land and house in order to be able to pay hospital bills.

Other women claimed to have come to town because they followed their husbands. In many cases these husbands have died or the women have got divorced, and today male-headed households are rare in this sector of Mongo. I interviewed 15 men, among whom three were young men (aged 15-25) who still lived with their mothers. Three of these men were divorced. The others were among the wealthiest in this sector. They had come with their fathers who were either an *ancien combatant*, or had a job as a civil servant. Two men came with their family during a period of drought and food scarcity, but they started a big farm that today is in the middle of Sector 4 and they lived there as they would have lived in the village. One of them was also a healer. He said that the big advantage of living in town was that there were always people to buy your products and services. He and his son were big producers of sesame and peanut oil, and they also assisted deprived family members who lived in the same sector.

The timing of people's settlement in Mongo is often part of a history of being mobile. As I discovered in the longer interviews and with the few people I came to know better, their life histories are full of displacement. Either they have moved frequently themselves, or their relatives, partners or children have moved.

Khadame Saleh
Khadame Saleh married a man from her village and had two children by him. He worked for the military and was based in Harras-Margai near Am Timan.

They went there together but he turned into a real womaniser and they had many fights before she decided to leave. She took her son and left on foot to go back to her home village. However her husband followed her and took her children who he entrusted to the care of his girlfriend at that time. Apparently it did not go well. He asked Khadame to return to him but in the meantime she had given birth to another son. She decided to return to her husband but only for her children's sake; with the idea of taking them back with her. Finally she stayed with her husband for a longer period of time, again getting pregnant with a fourth child, her second daughter. She had this daughter on her back (i.e. still a baby) when they had another fight. This time she went to the gendarmerie and reported the incident. She went back to her village where she stayed with her parents. Her first son then died, as did her second son. She kept her two daughters and a second husband came to ask her to marry him in the village. Later they went to Mongo but her second husband was always drunk and she could not live with him. That was also the time when she produced distilled alcohol (*argui*) but stopped because of non-payment by her clients. After five years and having given birth to three children, she decided to leave her second husband. He still lives in Mongo in this sector. She moved into her present hut – without a fence – that was given to her by two old women who had been living there for 30 years. Her eldest daughter is now 23 years old, is married and lives in the village. Her second daughter is 11 and helps her to cultivate, to look for fuel wood and leaves to sell at the market. Her three youngest children are too small to be of any help and during the day they are often at home alone. Khadame realizes that her life is not easy, but at least in town she can be independent. She took the initiative to organize the women in a *tontine*, where they put some money together and every month one of them receives the whole amount of FCFA 500, which can make a big difference to a small household economy. Khadame does not expect any help from her neighbours but at the same time she recognizes that at some crucial times they have helped her, i.e. by giving her a hut, and sometimes when someone is ill they give her moral support. Her *tontine* has made her a central point of reference for women in this sector and she is lucky, as she herself said, to be in good health. She considers her village to be her main anchor but it was not possible for her to go back. She could not expect support from her elderly parents and she admits that village life is not easy either. It is better to be in town!

Settled

It is clear from people's stories that most of those living in the sector found an easy way to get land to live off. The early settlers bought their land or occupied it when it was still considered as bush. They have all lived in huts or mud-brick houses, as life in this sector did not allow them to accumulate enough capital to invest in better housing. Furthermore, the majority have come from the villages and do not aspire to owning a big house. Because the area was not considered an urban zone but a forest, it was not incorporated in town plans. Town planning has never in any case been a top priority of the Mongo municipality and it is only now that discussions are starting on how to improve Sector 4. These discussions are clearly an off-shoot of recent reforms in government policy that delegate responsibilities to the region in a form of decentralization. For now the area is not organized: there are no water points, no roads and no schools, with the exception of the Koranic schools.

Except for those living on the few richer farms and people with a basic salary, everyone lives off cultivation and gathering in the bush. Most of those interviewed were women who live on their own, having been divorced or widowed. In many cases the stories about their menfolk were not very encouraging: they were always drunk, had other women, or left and never returned.

Once in town, women discovered that they could earn money and that even if harvests were bad they could still survive. These work-related opportunities were at the bottom end of the urban economy; work that would only attract desperate people. But this did not bother them. As they said, it was better than in the villages where in times of scarcity nobody would help and nobody would buy their products. These women all gathered fuel wood, and leaves to sell at the market. They earned at most FCFA 200 a day, with which they could buy a bowl of millet and some ingredients for a sauce, which in its most luxurious variant would contain roasted grasshoppers or some dried fish. All the women had to do this kind of work because harvests failed frequently, and even if they were able to harvest, it never sustained them for a whole year simply because they could not work sufficient land. Other women made and sold alcohol (*argui*). One of the producers said that she was fed up with drunken men who never paid her and who always wanted credit. However, most of the women in Sector 4 enjoy their independence, despite the poverty and marginality of their lives, and prefer it to village life or to life with a husband who does not take care of them.

Mongo is a Muslim town. All the inhabitants present themselves as Muslim, though they may still adhere to the animistic margay cult in secret.[12] In general however, this cult is considered as being 'from the village'. Mongo's Islamic character is expressed in the town's atmosphere: its numerous mosques, the

---

[12] Margay is the mountain spirit that each village in the Guera has. This spirit has many related spirits who can become one's own personal spirit. Women in particular are specialists in this cult (Fuchs 1970).

Koranic teachers with their students and the clothes people wear are all visible manifestations of Islam. Another more hidden aspect is the mentality of the people, where the Islamic ideology of sharing and caring for the poor and deprived is expressed in the custom of *zakat* and *sadaqa*, i.e. sharing one's wealth with the poor. Asking for gifts when one is in need is accepted and people do indeed give to the elderly and to Koranic students. For the people in Sector 4 this has become an important element of their daily existence. Old women, some of whom are blind, beg at least on Fridays at the mosques and some also on Sundays at the churches. They roam through town during the week going to the market, and from house to house, receiving a substantial part of their family's food from others. They were always happy to show me the results of their begging activities.

The women all consider their lives hard and difficult, but at the same time they are very accepting. 'Isn't life in the village worse?' Many have health problems but no means to pay for treatment. They all have to care for their children, either their own or those of their migrated or deceased children. Most women had lost at least 30% of their children at a young age. A nutrition survey undertaken among them showed that 70% of the children were malnourished. This is an indicator of the difficult and harsh conditions these women live in.

Support networks need a basis of material wealth, which is what Platteau (1991) meant by the term 'co-variance of risk': it is impossible to share nothing. Interviews and observations showed that in this sector neighbours do try to help each other. Support networks often involve direct neighbours but more so children or family members. However these support groups are very small. Probably the most important element is the moral support they offer. They share the same lives, and by sharing your life with others it becomes bearable. These relations may also be *ad hoc*. New people come in, others move out. Their existence became clear to me when a person died and the women all visited her house, or when a baby was born and they all came with small gifts. Sector 4 in that sense has become a social neighbourhood and this sociality is not primarily linked to ethnicity or village relations, but rather to sharing the same life and, of course, being family. In two cases, sisters lived together. In another case, a woman lived with her brother who is the owner of one of the big farms. Her story however shows that caring for another person is a limited affair and that it is finally the individual who has to take care for him/herself.

Adama Hassanabi

Adama Hassanabi is from Korlongo, a relatively rich village in the area. In 2003, she was 31 years old. She came to Mongo with her first husband, who is from the same family. They decided to move because of the suffering in the village but their life in Mongo was not happy. She separated from her husband about 8 years ago. He did not work, being a cultivator, and she was fed up with him, especially after he hit her so hard that she lost the child she was carrying at the time, resulting in her being hospitalized. He now sometimes visits her; she is pregnant by him with her fifth child but she does not want to live with him any more. She has had three children so far: two live with her and one of her sons died of an illness. After separating from her husband, she stayed with her cousin who has a farm in Sector 4. He gave her a hut but does not help in any other way according to Adama, although her cousin told me that he does. Adama feels ashamed living on this big farm but her hut opens off the centre so she has some privacy even though it indicates her low status. She said that she prepares her own sauce and eats alone. Her sauce is bad because she has no money to buy good ingredients so she does not offer it to the other women in the household. She works a field and gathers wood and leaves and although the land is owned by her husband, he did not take it away from her. In the past she cultivated a large field but an accident a few years ago means that this is no longer possible. She fell out of a tree while gathering leaves and broke her left arm in two places. It did not heal properly and her arm is now deformed and she cannot use it as she used to. However this does not prevent her leaving home at 4 a.m. every morning to gather wood and to work her land.

In 2004 I revisited Sector 4 and tried to find Adama who was no longer living in her cousin's house. I was told that she had returned to Korlongo and her cousin was happy for her. I went to see her and indeed she was married to a man from the village. He was not the richest man and their hut on the edge of the village. Adama said that she had less support there than in Mongo but, more importantly, she had no income. Even if she could find wood she would not be able to sell it at the market. This marriage probably made her decent in the eyes of her family but she preferred her life in Mongo where she was a relatively independent woman.

Formation of neighbourhoods in small towns rooted in the histories of war and drought

The question at the start of this chapter was whether urbanization as a consequence of drought and war, as is the case in Chad, leads to the formation of specific urban quarters, and whether these can be labelled neighbourhoods in a geographical, social and emotional sense. On the basis of one case study it is not possible to generalize, nevertheless I think this case study does not stand on its own. The case of Mongo is comparable with situations in Mali where after the droughts many people left the rural areas to settle elsewhere (see de Bruijn & Van Dijk 2003, Zondag 2005), or the case of Niamey (Gado forthcoming,

Broekhuis *et al.* 2004). It seems obvious that conflict and war create such crises and situations of insecurity that people flee to town. These situations lead to increasing numbers of urban people who are forced to create new quarters in town. Mongo's *Secteur Quatre* is a geographically located area with a population that has its own specificities.

Secteur Quatre is considered by the inhabitants of Mongo to be where immigrants and the poor live, and it was indeed here that there used to be a food distribution centre, which still marks the area. Although people no longer live in such extreme misery, the inhabitants of this sector have not been able to rebuild prosperous lives. Appalling poverty is a very visible characteristic of the quarter: housing is rudimentary; there is no water, and roads and other services are non-existent. People do not wear nice clothes and their bodies speak for themselves – children are malnourished and illness is an accepted state of being. However this is an outsider's view.

In this view, the history of their poverty is overlooked. Many of the inhabitants fled the droughts and came to Mongo without any possessions. Others were not merely driven by drought, but had also had a previous life of bad luck and missed chances, as Khadame's and Adama's stories illustrate. In interviews, the women stressed that they had a chance in town. They had also made deliberate decisions, foreseeing a better life in town and not expecting any support from their village. People in this Mongo neighbourhood share the same fate, a fate linked to poverty. If women are ill and their children have problems, they mention their poverty, but on other occasions they stress the fact that at least they can live their own lives here. Although they were forced to migrate out of poverty there was a certain voluntarity in their decision. The attraction of an urban centre is an important element in migration histories.

Secteur Quatre's inhabitants are primarily women: old women who have outlived their husbands, and many young women who have been divorced or whose husbands have left for N'djamena. It seems that the women prefer to stay with their children and are more reluctant to move to faraway destinations. It is also clear from the different stories that the women do not expect much from their husbands, who are often drunk, lousy workers and womanizers. These women have often taken the initiative and become independent of their husbands. This is an important characteristic of the neighbourhood. Its inhabitants share being female, and the fact that they can do without men. With this attitude, they challenge gender relations as they existed back in their village of origin, where women were expected to be married. However the pressure of the family – as in the case of Adama – can reverse this immediately, but only because she could no longer be independent because of her physical handicap and the birth of her third child.

The women and few men share in their materiality and have developed a basic form of mutual help in times of need. They share their belongings if there is a pressing need to do so and, of course, only if there is something to share. As the stories about housing reveal, newcomers always find a place: people who live in the area share their space with others and they visit each other on ritual occasions. An explicit example is the *tontine* organized by Khadame. There is a certain solidarity among those living there but this is not a wide network covering the whole quarter although it unites small groups of neighbours, or people from the same village. Often these are various individual help relations based on reciprocity but at least they give the neighbourhood sociability.

Everyone in Sector 4 claims to be a Muslim and their inspiration for action is based on the morality described in the Muslim rules of sharing: *zakat* and *sadaqa*, i.e. sharing one's wealth with the poor. This provides the motivation to visit each other and to help when a person is ill. But it also explains the way people reason and talk about the asking for gifts on ritual occasions and begging. 'It is through the believers that I live,' an old woman explained. In Sector 4 there is always space for another *fakih* (Islamic scholar) with his students: they will never be denied a place. So we can speak of a shared morality in this sense.

This notion of 'being Muslim' is mainly an urban phenomenon for the people in Sector 4. Many of them converted in town, while others became fervent Muslims there. For the old women this is not easy: they are often forced to convert by their own children who threaten not to care for them if they continue to adhere to the Margay-cult. The women have realized that it is in Islam that they can escape starvation as help relations are inspired by it, but they regret having abandoning their personal spirit and feel they have lost their sight or are ill. Yet they had no choice! And these stories unite the old ladies.

To conclude what in fact makes the neighbourhood *Secteur Quatre*. Is there a feeling of belonging? I think this does exist, especially among the old and young women who share a history of misery, who share emotions related to their gender and their position in society, who share their status of being single, who share their expectations of town. On the other hand, they all live their individual lives and do not depend on each other in a material sense. They cannot. Thus it is a neighbourhood of shared misery, shared history and shared ideas about the chances town can offer.

As the insights of Alex de Waal (1997) and many others have shown, poverty and famine do not exist on their own. Poverty is related to rules of access and denial of access to resources that are contained in local and national politics. The above-mentioned research into the situation of the people living in Sector 4 and the very existence of the sector as it is should also consider the politics and relations of power related to access to all kind of resources. The answer to this question cannot yet be fully answered. Chadian politics are complicated. One investigation is at village level. Why did these people move? Was it their own will and individual decision, or were they pushed to leave? Where do 'village social security arrangements' come in? Why do the villages let these people go? The other angle of this investigation is why these people live in the conditions they live in on the periphery of town. Why is there no assistance at all to help them create a better life? At the municipal level, it would seem that interest is mostly focused on the richer parts of town, with investments in Sector 9 where the civil servants and military personnel live. This part of town is new, but also well registered, while Sector 4 has not yet even been divided into plots. During my final discussions with the *Chef du Quartier*, it emerged that Mongo did have plans to re-organize Sector 4. Mongo is increasingly the centre of a developing Guera and land is becoming scarcer as the number of people who want to live in town increases. Sector 4's inhabitants are at the bottom of Chad's modern political hierarchy. As a result, the people there who do not have the correct papers to convince the municipality of their rights to the land they have claimed as their own will have to move. They may well again become displaced people though not recognized as such, living on the fringes of our world.

References

Broekhuis, A., M. de Bruijn & A. de Jong 2004, 'Urban-rural Linkages and Climatic Variability', in: T. Dietz, R. Ruben & A. Verhagen (eds), *The Impact of Climate Change on Drylands, With a Focus on West Africa*, Dordrecht/Boston/London: Kluwer Academic Publishers, pp. 301-23.

de Bruijn, M. 2000, 'Poverty and Mobility in Arid Lands: The Case of Sahelian Pastoralists', in: Wil Pansters *et al.* (eds), *Rethinking Poverty, Comparative Perspectives from Below*, Assen: Van Gorcum, pp. 136-49.

de Bruijn, M. & H. van Dijk 2003, 'Changing Population Mobility in West Africa: Fulbe Pastoralists in Central and South Mali', *African Affairs* 102: 285-307.

de Bruijn, M. & H. van Dijk 2005, 'Chad', in: A. Mehler, H. Melber & K. van Walraven (eds), *Africa Yearbook 2004*, Leiden: Brill.

de Bruijn, M., H. van Dijk, M. Kaag & K. van Til (eds) 2005, *Sahelian Pathways, Climate Change and Society in Central and South Mali*, Leiden: African Studies Centre..

de Bruijn, M., R. van Dijk & D. Foeken (eds) 2001, *Mobile Africa, Changing Patterns of Movement in Africa and Beyond*, Leiden: Brill.

de Bruijn, M. & N. Djindil forthcoming, 'Etat Nutritionnel et Histoire de Vie des Enfants de la Rue de la Ville de N'djamena, Tchad', *Psychopathologie Africaine*.

Buijtenhuijs, R. 1978, *Le Frolinat et les Révoltes Populaires du Tchad (1965-1976)*, The Hague/Paris/New York: Mouton Publishers.

Buijtenhuijs, R. 1987, *Le Frolinat et les Guerres Civiles du Tchad (1977-1984), la Révolution Introuvable*, Paris: Karthala.
Courtier M. & M. Gosselin 1961, 'Etude sur l'Urbanisation et l'Amélioration de l'Habitation dans les Quartiers Africains de Fort-lamy', Paris: Sécrétariat des Missions d'Urbanisme et d'Habitat.
Dietz, T., R. Ruben & A. Verhagen (eds) 2004, *The Impact of Climate Change on Drylands, With a Focus on West Africa*, Dordrecht/Boston/London: Kluwer Academic Publishers.
Doornbos, P. 1982, 'La Révolution Dérapée. La Violence dans l'Est du Tchad (1978-1981)', *Politique Africaine* 2 (7): 5-13.
Eriksson, H. & B. Hagstromer 2005, 'Chad-Towards Democratisation or Petro-Dictatorship?', Uppsala: Nordiska Afrikainstitutet, Discussion Paper 29.
Fuchs, P. 1970, *Kult und Autorität, die Religion der Hadjerai*, Berlin: Dietrich Reimer Verlag.
Gado, B. forthcoming, 'Paupérisation, Marginalisation et Exclusion en Milieu Urbain, le Cas d'un Quartier Périphérique de Niamey', in: M. de Bruijn & G. Hesseling (eds), *Urban Dynamics and Climate Change*, Leiden: African Studies Centre.
Pairault, C. 1994, *Retour au Pays d'Iro, Chronique d'un Village au Tchad*, Paris: Karthala.
Platteau, J.P. 1991, 'Traditional Systems of Social Security and Hunger Insurance: Past Achievements and Moderns Challenges', in: E. Ahmad *et al.* (eds), *Social Security in Developing Countries*, Oxford: Clarendon Press, pp. 112-71.
PRSP 2003, 'National Poverty Reduction Strategy Paper', Ndjamena: Ministry of Planning, Development and Cooperation.
Raynaut, C. 1997, *Sahels, Diversité et Dynamiques des Relations Sociétés-Nature*, Paris: Karthala.
Rense, M. forthcoming, 'Koloniale Geschiedenis van de Guera, Centraal Tsjaad', Leiden/Amsterdam, Masters Thesis.
Van Dijk, H. 2003, 'Decentralisation in Post War Chad', paper presented at the Vrije Universiteit, Amsterdam.
Van Dijk, H., D. Foeken & K. van Til 2001, 'Population Mobility in Africa: An Overview', in: M. de Bruijn, R. van Dijk & D. Foeken (eds), *Mobile Africa, Changing Patterns of Movement in Africa and Beyond*, Leiden: Brill.
de Waal, A. 1997, *Famine Crimes, Politics and the Disaster Relief Industry in Africa*, Oxford: James Currey.
Zondag, R. 2005, 'Douentza, the Dynamics of a Rural Centre in the Semi-arid Sahel', in: M. de Bruijn *et al.* (eds), *Sahelian Pathways Climate Change and Society in Central and South Mali*, Leiden: African Studies Centre, pp. 168-89.

11

Neighbourhood (re)construction and changing identities in Mauritania from a small town perspective

Kiky van Til

> *In the last forty years Mauritania's nomadic and pastoral Moorish society has undergone radical changes due to rural-urban migration, sedentarization and rapid urbanization. The transition to a more sedentary and urban mode of life has affected almost every aspect of economic and social daily life. This chapter focuses on identity transformations due to the challenges that rapid urbanization has brought. People's struggles to uphold old norms and values or, on the contrary, to liberate themselves from conservative values by trying to integrate modern ones demonstrate how they are maintaining or recreating their identities. They participate and manoeuvre in divergent neighbourhoods that determine to a certain extent their norms, ideas and identity, but through their participation they also (re)construct these fields or neighbourhoods leading to social change. Two case studies illustrate the identity problems people are confronted with in the process of rural to urban transition.*

Introduction

Forty years ago, Mauritania was one of the world's least urbanized countries. The majority of its people were Moorish nomadic pastoralists who roamed the country's immense plains, only venturing into the few established cities to exchange their pastoral products for grains and other commodities. However various events, the most important being the droughts in the 1970s and 1980s, caused an accelerated process of sedentarization, rural-urban migration and urbanization. The transition from a nomadic pastoral way of life to sedentary and urban livelihoods has brought many changes to Moorish society.

This chapter focuses on identity change and people's quest for a new identity in this (formerly) nomadic society. To study these processes of identity transformation, the fieldwork on which it is based aimed to gain insight into the active construction of relationships, meanings, patterns and systems by individuals participating in both social and economic domains, but also into recent transformations in these relationships and meanings due to the challenges that rapid urbanization has brought. In the midst of such urban dynamics where the modern and traditional, and nomadic and sedentary aspects of culture coexist, people are struggling to position themselves between their current aspirations and their traditional customs and values. This struggle to uphold old norms and values or, on the contrary, to liberate themselves from conservative values by integrating modern ideas indicates how local people are maintaining, restyling or creating their identities. The intention here is to identify 'changes-in-the-making' or indications of future history that the present is currently revealing (cf. Moore 1987, 1994).

A specific understanding of 'neighbourhoods' to schematise social and economic domains in an urban setting is essential. People participate and manoeuvre in these various social fields that determine to a certain extent their norms, ideas and identity but at the same time through their participation they can also (re)construct these fields or neighbourhoods, a process that leads to social change. A distinction between social and economic neighbourhoods serves to facilitate the analysis. However in reality, the social and economic aspects of neighbourhoods are closely intertwined.

Individual case studies are used here to illustrate the transition from a rural, nomadic and pastoral context to an urban and sedentary one based on multiple – and often multi-spatial – livelihoods. I show how inhabitants of a small town in Mauritania are managing to participate in various social and economic neighbourhoods simultaneously and the extent to which these neighbourhoods determine how people identify themselves. This also reveals the ways in which people are trying to keep up with the changes in their urban lives and how neighbourhoods determine people's options and choices regarding economic activities. The examples are drawn from stories of inhabitants[140] of Aioun el Atrouss, a small town in southeastern Mauritania. The fieldwork on which this chapter is based was conducted there from January to December 2002 and from October to December 2004. as part of a PhD project.[141]

---

[140] Their names have been changed to ensure privacy.
[141] I gratefully acknowledge the Netherlands Foundation for the Advancement of Tropical Research (WOTRO) for financing this project.

Social and economic neighbourhoods and transformation processes

Moore (1973: 720) articulated the concept of 'semi-autonomous social fields' that generate rules, customs and symbols internally but that are also vulnerable to rules, decisions and forces emanating from the wider world by which they are surrounded. Although I mainly follow the ideas of Moore and consider social and economic neighbourhoods to be semi-autonomous social fields, I should stress that the concept of 'neighbourhood' used here also touches on the spatial notions of the 'rural' and 'urban' in order to illustrate the process of transition from a rural to an urban setting.

The economic activities in Mauritania in which individuals are involved are primarily determined by the position they occupy in society. The boundaries of economic neighbourhoods are more or less determined by socio-cultural factors (customs, norms and values). Economic neighbourhoods are thus semi-autonomous social fields in which people conduct their economic activities.

Neighbourhoods give meaning to people's lives and people affect and shape the neighbourhood they feel they belong to. Their neighbourhood determines their frame of reference and their frame of reference in turn influences the neighbourhood's norms and values.

Not infrequently, people operate in several neighbourhoods simultaneously. These neighbourhoods are often closely intertwined, although geographically they may be far apart. In societies undergoing a process of rapid transformation, the social and economic fields of interaction in which people operate are frequently characterized by a wide divergence of views, beliefs, ideals and codes of conduct. To move between different neighbourhoods and to play continuously in different *voisinages* requires a measure of patience, flexibility and compliancy. To hold their own in a society that is undergoing rapid change, people develop the skills required to manoeuvre in these semi-autonomous fields and to constantly adapt.

When operating in a certain neighbourhood, people will accentuate those features of identity representative of that specific neighbourhood. These may concern social, religious or economic identities or be based on principles of class differences. In this way people manage to manoeuvre in different social and economic neighbourhoods, adopting a different identity when necessary, or emphasizing diverse facets of their identity. Through people's participation in divergent social and economic neighbourhoods they manage to maintain, develop, create or restyle identities, thus bringing about social change.

Such a concept of neighbourhood lends itself well to a study of change-in-the-making. How do people combine a rural nomadic history with the urban present? How do they link modern aspirations with traditional ones? How do they negotiate different neighbourhoods? How and when do they present different facets of their identity to the outside world? In fact, people are constantly struggling to negotiate their position between their aspirations of today and the traditional customs and values being lived in the present.

In Aioun el Atrouss, most of the Moorish inhabitants grew up with nomadic traditions. Older people still recall their former mobile lifestyles centred on their cattle. Others have heard their parents' and grandparents' stories of an unclouded existence with an abundance of milk and meat for everyone. Today's reality is quite different due to migration, sedentarization and urbanization and nowadays almost all Aiounians live a sedentary and urban lifestyle, having adopted new livelihoods in which livestock no longer provide the sole source of income. Their economic survival is now dependent on multiple activities, and their urban interactions differ significantly from those of their nomadic ancestors.

Although the Moors, especially the nobles, are endeavouring to preserve their traditions, norms, values and perceptions, these too will change over time. Tradition is, after all, a subjective construction. What people remember of their ancestors' past is often romanticized and unreliable. Pre-colonial material is scarce, it is difficult to access, and colonial accounts are often biased with ethnocentric points of view as to what is 'normal'. What one comes across today and what local people may present or perceive as 'traditional' may in fact have been recently invented (cf. Hobsbawm & Ranger 1983). People tend to emphasize the value of the cultural continuity of traditions although they may now live in a different socio-political and economic environment. What is described and perceived as traditional in the present is not the same as the traditional lived in the past (Moore 1987). By analyzing people's struggles to position themselves in several different social and economic neighbourhoods in a rapid urbanizing context I want to identify social change in a daily urban setting.

Aioun el Atrouss

Aioun el Atrouss is a small town in the southeast of Mauritania situated more than 800 km east of the capital Nouakchott, in the province (*wilaya*) of Hodh el Gharbi. This is a zone suitable for pastoralism *par excellence*, with extensive pastures and relatively abundant water sources. The town is located along the 'Route de l'Espoir' (the Road of Hope), an 1100-km tarred road that winds like a black carpet between the yellowy-white sand dunes from Nouakchott in the southwest to Néma in the southeast.

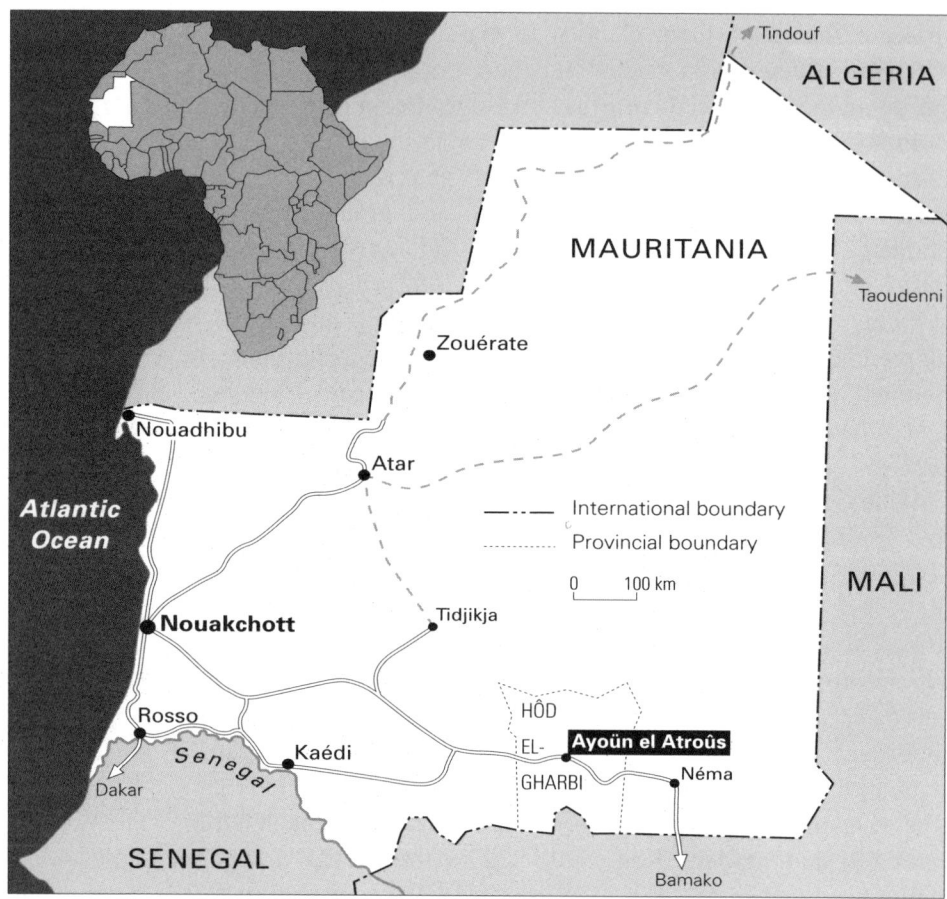

Map 11.1   Mauritania

Today, Aioun has almost 13,000 inhabitants[142] (ONS 2004) and a recent regional census carried out to assess the charging of property and excise taxes recorded a total of 2,500 households and 560 shops.[143] The small population figure does not do justice to either the importance of the town from a historical point of view or to the important position it occupies nowadays as a focal point of regional and national commerce.

---

[142] Aioun el Atrouss is the centre of the so-called *Moughata* (comparable with a municipality) of Aioun el Atrouss. The *Moughata* of Aioun has 45,000 inhabitants (ONS, 2004).

[143] However, this data is not very reliable because in the census every entrance is assumed to be a household. This leads to a disproportionately high number of households and a disproportionately low number of shops because many residences accommodate one or more small shops with their own separate access.

Mauritania used to be one of the world's least urbanized countries but nevertheless had (and still has) a few famous ancient cities – such as Shinguetti, Walata, Atar, Wadane, Koumbi Saleh and Rachid – that played a vital comercial role in the seventeenth and eighteenth centuries in the age of the trans-Saharan caravan trade. While some of the newer towns in Mauritania have developed from villages, Aioun occupies an unusual and unique position and is called *dešra shadida* (the new town). Established by the French colonial regime in collaboration with the local leader of one of the Moorish *qaba'il*,[144] the Oulad an Nacer Aioun was founded in 1940[145] near the water source that bears its name and on a spot where no one had previously lived. In the mid-1940s, Aioun already had a hospital, a primary and secondary school, a market and was well on its way to becoming a major commercial centre. The town attracted pastoral nomads from miles around, offering the prospect of abandoning the harsh nomadic way of life and the possibility of a new lifestyle.

Aioun is, however, essentially still a pastoral town in which not so long ago the majority of the inhabitants continued to live as nomads. Its foundation coincided with a series of droughts at the beginning of the 1940s, which provided small-scale herdsmen with a stepping stone from nomadic pastoralism to a more commercial livelihood of cattle breeding, and the raising of sheep and goats (Koita 1994). Aioun, the regional capital of the Hodh,[146] consequently became a commercial centre for these new traders.

Cattle raising still forms an essential economic pillar of Aioun's economy, with milk and meat sales providing an essential element in trade. In the past, many people settled on the outskirts of town with their herds of cows, camels or small ruminants. From there the animals have easy access to the surrounding pastures during the day and at dusk they return to the compound to be milked. Larger herds of animals are usually sent to remote pastures accompanied by professional herdsmen.

However much is changing and today, a small elite of officials and businessmen now own the greater part of the national cattle herd. These are rich urbanites who do not often have the slightest idea as to what the daily life of a nomadic pastoralist involves. They leave their cattle in the care of professionals

---

[144] In French the term *tribu* is commonly used. In English the term 'tribe' would be the obvious translation but it has a pejorative connotation. I prefer to use therefore the local Hassaniyya terms *qabila* (sing.) and *qaba'il* (pl.).

[145] In some early documents and on old maps, for example in Marty (1920) and in British Foreign Office files (1920), the name of Aioun el Atrouss (or Aiun Latrus) already occurred to indicate the water source in the area after which the town was named.

[146] Later in 1948, the Hodh was further divided into the Hodh el Chargi and the Hodh el Gharbi. Aioun is the capital of the former and Néma the capital of the latter.

in exchange for a monthly salary (cf. Ould Cheikh & Bonte 1982), while average families in the town keep one or two milk cows or a few goats, which roam around their compounds.

Photo 11.1   A pastoral-urban mix with camels travelling in a 4x4 along a typical Aioun street
(Photo: Kiky van Til)

Aioun is a Moorish or Bidan town and contrasts markedly with towns along the Senegal River, for example Boghé, Kaedi or Selibaby, which are mainly inhabited by black African communities such as Halpulaar, Wolof, Bambara and Soninké. These social groups live predominantly off agriculture, use their own languages in addition to the *lingua franca*, and wear typical African caftans and *boubous*.

There is also a clear distinction between the so-called *Djambur* (or *Jembour*) towns, such as Kiffa and Timbedhra, whose inhabitants are known to be ex-slaves who challenged slavery and fought to obtain their freedom from their (white) Moorish masters (cf. Brhane 1997). Strained relations continue to exist between these two parties.

What does 'Moorish' or 'Bidan' signify? Moors are a people of Arabo-Berber origin, influenced by and mixed with Sanhadja Berbers, Almoravids and

Banu Hassan, an Arabic ethnic group that invaded the territory of Mauritania from before the seventh century to after the fourteenth century. The latter imposed their Arabic dialect, *Hassaniyya*, which is – even today – the main language in Mauritania. Frequent interactions between Berber, Arab and African ethnic groups led to a high degree of miscegenation (Marchesin 1992, Taylor 1996).

A strict hierarchy, in which nobles, non-nobles, freed slaves and slaves are all distinguishable, characterizes the Moorish social structure. Nowadays, and especially in urban areas, people commonly distinguish between Black Moors[147] and White Moors, which implicitly refers to an important difference between the nobles and those descended from slave families. The former are called Bidan and the latter are Haratin. Black Moors or Haratin have virtually adopted the Arab-Berber culture and language. Within Moorish society, both culturally and religiously, the existence of different social categories and thus class differences between people is largely accepted.[148] A more visual marker of Bidan culture[149] is their style of clothing. Men wear a white or blue robe called a *derra'a* over a pair of baggy trousers buckled up to keep them in place with an extremely long belt, and women wear *malefas*, (semi-)transparent veils that cover their heads and are worn over a dress.

Aioun can also be characterized as a 'small town'. The process of urbanization in small towns takes on a different form to that seen in the big cities of Nouakchott and Nouadhibou. In small towns, rural and urban links are closely intertwined and traditions easily coexist alongside modern ideas, customs, norms and values. Aioun is a dynamic focal point: it forms the commercial centre for the whole region, offers an outlet for rural products, arts and crafts, and provides an ample job market. Customs related to the pastoral economy still find their application in the urban setting and the influence of *qabila* and family traditions extends through nearly every aspect of socio-cultural, political and economic life. Various forms of social security based on membership of a *qabila* or one of its sub-divisions continue to exist in Aioun,

---

[147] According to Brhane (1997), some people in the capital favour other terms to denote a dark skin colour such as *sudan* (black) or *jil a'khal* (black skin). *Sudan* is exclusively used to refer to Black Moors. People of other African communities are called *kwar*. The term *jil a'khal* is becoming ever more popular and is used to designate all dark-skinned people.
[148] This is also the essential difference with the Djambur, who definitely do not accept an inferior social position because of their servile descent.
[149] The term 'Bidan' is ambiguous. It is often used in the Bidan versus Haratin dichotomy to refer to the nobles as opposed to their liberated slaves. But when Bidan is used in Bidan culture, it merely refers to the whole set of cultural understandings in which both Bidan and Haratin take part.

whereas in the major cities forms of *entre-aide* or mutual assistance have become rare.

At the same time, people in Aioun are developing modern urban habits: they take taxis to go shopping or to work; they keep in touch with friends and family through frequent mobile-phone calls; they have daily access to at least forty international television channels especially Arabic ones via satellite, and many make use of the Internet.

Work ethic

Individuals are not free to choose a profession in Mauritania. One's economic occupation is closely linked to one's social status. The ideology concerning labour, which includes a strict division of labour between the various social strata of Moorish society, explains why social and economic fields of interaction are closely linked.

This ideology results from the way the society's social and economic life was traditionally organized. A class of nobility occupies centre stage and is made up of warriors and *marabouts* who are engaged respectively in armed warfare to protect the community and in religious affairs, including Koranic education. This includes people belonging to the professional castes who favour the reproduction of the pastoral economy: *mualimīn*, blacksmiths who make metal tools, leather and jewellery, and *igawīn*, griots or itinerant singers that praise the heroic courage and history of the *qabila*, who are indispensable in the preparations for war and during marriage ceremonies. The *znaga* are free herdsmen who often play an important role in tending the herds and in the medical care of animals. The nobles coexist with their servile families who tend, water and milk the animals, work at the oasis or cultivate sorghum after the rainy season, and are responsible for all household work. As the property of the nobles, the large herds of camels and small ruminants guarantee milk, meat and other nutritional requirements for an entire group (Marchesin 1992). In the past, the hierarchical social structures that characterize Moorish society were functional to the nomadic way of life.

The loss of nomadic pastoralism, the impoverishment of nobles who could no longer take care of their subordinates, the sedentarization of former nomads, and the high degree of urbanization brought many changes to society. But the notion that certain occupations ought to be done by people of a corresponding social position continues to exist. For example, any form of manual labour is still considered unsuited to nobles. The choice of income-generating activities that might be acceptable for them is therefore limited to cattle breeding, commerce, or work in the public service. Due to the impoverishment of the noble class, only a few have the means to live off their cattle.[150] Also, few of them have obtained the required level of education to enter the public service. Consequently, most of the noble urbanites have been relegated to living off commercial activities.

Photo 11.2 Grass being brought to town by a local Haratin
(Photo: Kiky van Til)

Griots and blacksmiths living in towns usually still perform their professsional tasks, but on a more commercial basis. The Haratin continue to be the moving force in town where many are retailers, butchers or bakers, while others work in transport or construction. In fact, they are to be found in all kinds of labour. Senegalese and Malinese mainly perform specific crafts such as welding, furniture making and car mechanics.

---

[150] After the droughts of the 1970s and 1980s only a few people tried to or succeeded in reconstituting their herds. On the contrary, the majority of people sold their remaining animals to finance their installation in town.

An emic view of neighbourhoods: Two cases

The cases of two Moors in Aioun with significantly differing circumstances and their interactions in specific social and economic neighbourhoods will show the transformation processes in the day-to-day life of people, or some of the changes-in-the-making. In the analysis, the neighbourhoods of economic interactions and those of social interactions have been separated but in reality both fields are interlinked and divisions are barely discernible.

Case 1: Nourdin
Nourdin is a forty-year-old White Moor who has lived and worked in Aioun for over ten years. He was born into the noble *Zawaya* (*marabout*) family of Mohammed Ould Saleh of the Abd ould Wahab faction, a sub-division of the *qabila* Oulad an Nacer.

Nourdin's grandfather was an important *qadi* (Islamic magistrate) in the region and a good friend of the famous leader of the Oulad an Nacer: Ethman ould Bakar. During the 1940s, when the colonial regime considered the sedentarization of nomads necessary, Ethman ould Bakar assigned territory to all his *qabila* factions to facilitate his subjects' settlement. The Abd ould Wahab people were allocated the depressions and the then-swampy forests of Sawana. A dam was constructed in 1948 to assist with irrigation and the place was called Leglik (literally: the dam). It was not until the early 1960s that the Abd ould Wahab started to finally become settled in Leglik. The village is situated about 45 km from Aioun and, like other villages in the area, is heavily dependent on Aioun.

Nourdin moves between various neighbourhoods. The first is the social neighbourhood associated with his family and acquaintances in Leglik, the village where he was born and grew up. His father is the village chief and teaches the Koran to boys and girls in the village, and the family plays a prominent role in village politics. They manage the water supply and land for the entire Abd ould Wahab faction. Such an influential position also has its downside: they share the territory with a large number of people who used to depend on the noble family of Ould Saleh. Although today they live an autonomous life – they work plots that they own personally and they have no obligation *vis-à-vis* their former masters in the sense of payment or contributions – they are nevertheless a much more vulnerable group than the nobles. They have no one to turn to in times of need other than the families they used to depend on. According to Moorish customs, as well as Islamic tradition, people in need cannot be turned down and appeals are frequently made to Nourdin's family. However, the more people one can provide for, the greater the power and respect one will gain.

Zawaya families apply more stringent behaviour precepts *vis-à-vis* each other than for example noble warrior families do. As the village chief's son, Nourdin is obliged to show respect to his father, which includes, for instance, not speaking about his relationship with his wife and children in the presence of his father. He may not even show affection to his children in front of his father, nor can he smoke. His wife cannot show her face to her father-in-law and covers it with a veil when she has to be in the same room. It is essential to refrain from any behaviour that could possibly damage the family's honour.

His position brings with it restrictions on the social and economic activities he can engage in in Aioun. For a long time he has been the black sheep of the family because he tried to earn his living from jobs not fitting to his family's social status. During a four-year period of unemployment after leaving university, he earned his keep by making charcoal from wood. Blacksmiths or others at the bottom of the social ladder should typically carry out such work and his family saw their son's activities as degrading and a disgrace to the family name. Nourdin's behaviour resulted in tensions within the family and led to a difficult relationship with his father.

The second neighbourhood Nourdin is involved in is the social neighbourhood in Aioun. He lives with his second wife and baby son on a hill near the town centre. His second wife, like his first wife, is a *Zawaya* from a noble *marabout* family. Instead of living with members of his extended family, he prefers to be independent as far as possible and to distance himself from the social interference and control of his own and his wife's family. His first marriage ended in divorce because he could no longer tolerate the meddling of his parents-in-law and the fact that his wife could not live separately from her mother. However his second wife is still young and also has difficulties being away from her parental home. Almost every day she and the baby visit them. Nourdin is disappointed by the fact that his wife discusses their private affairs with her mother, things that, according to Nourdin, concern only him and his wife. He recognizes the opinions, hopes and fears of his in-laws in his wife's words.

The friends with whom he has frequent contacts are mainly of the same social status: fellow students from the past, other *Zawaya*, and officials in the civil service. He receives visitors every day, often in his atelier but also at home, usually family or friends who stay over for dinner and for the night but also people that have some sort of relationship with the Ould Saleh family come to visit him. With some of them he or his parents maintain 'milk' ties: people who shared the same mother's milk. A milk tie socially brings people of different social ranking together as if they were biologically related. The most important consequence of milk kinship is that milk relatives cannot intermarry. Nowadays fewer people are entering into milk relations but already established relations may remain for a few generations until nobody is left to testify to their existence (Cleaveland 2000, Fortier 2001).[151] Nourdin's milk relatives pay frequent visits and often ask for financial support for reasons as varied as a son who is getting married, to help with paying a big bill for medical care.

It is very often in this area that traditional values start to diverge from modern opinions. In general, it is considered *mal vu* to send away empty-handed someone who comes for help. This may be partly explained by the harsh circumstances in which nomads used to live and their constant mobility: when a stranger arrived at someone's camp, the hospitality offered to him could be of vital importance. Many Moors have internalized the belief that helping other people might be a matter of life and death and therefore one could not possibly ignore a person in need.

Should these people address Nourdin's father in Leglik they would never be turned away, but Nourdin often finds himself financially cornered. He is living an urban life with all its related costs and many people appeal to him for money: his parents, relatives and acquaintances in Leglik, his ex-wife and their three children, his present wife and their baby and his present wife's family in Aioun.

Nourdin has developed an attitude that does not fit with Moorish society. For example, he would rather live in poverty than ask anyone for a favour. He wants to earn his own livelihood, even if he has to engage in work that does not fit his social position and it will result in his family rejecting him for it. This attitude contrasts sharply with that of his colleagues in the civil service, who would feel that it is generally better to be a thief or a beggar than to do work that is considered inferior to one's social status.

Nourdin prefers an independent life, both socially and financially, and it annoys him that all and sundry request money from him, especially when it is people he does not know personally but who just know him to be a son of the Ould Saleh family. He sometimes sends people away empty-handed. This attitude has started to emerge relatively recently in Aioun and is generating bad-feeling and resistance. Time and again, Nourdin finds himself in an awkward position: if he does meet someone's wishes, he himself risks having to borrow afterwards, but if he is not conciliatory he risks the rejected persons speaking badly of him and his family.

There are two separate economic neighbourhoods that Nourdin participates in, namely, the civil service and the open market. The civil service is a privileged neighbourhood of officials, a field dominated by White Moors. Officials are underpaid but participation in this economic neighbourhood at least ensures a regular income and also guarantees a certain degree of access to national

---

[151] For further details about the complex system of milk kinship, see, for example, Altorki (1980); Héritier (1994) and Ensel (2002).

funds. In other words, it offers a good opportunity for *tcheb-tchib*, a set of transactions that can be characterized as the art of seizing opportunities. People engaged in such transactions are usually ready to do whatever is required to earn money. This often involves embezzlement and/or the illegal distribution of state or other funds (cf. Ould Ahmed Salem 2001). It is an environment in which descent and relations are extremely important, and where success is achieved in the first instance through connections, favouritism, haggling and 'arrangements', and not by one's own efforts or abilities. The moment Nourdin succeeded in obtaining a post as a radio-aerial engineer in Aioun, relations with his family improved slightly since holding office in the public service is in accordance with his social position, and such officials are generally highly esteemed. His professional position confirms his social status and allows him the free use of a property with electricity since he needs to install radio equipment. The position and the benefits that go with it thus emphasize his status as a White Moor.

Unlike in the civil service, personal capacity and effort form causal factors for success in the commercial sector. The installation of a mobile-phone network in Aioun in mid-2002 made Nourdin focus on the repair and sale of mobile phones but the salary he earns as the state's radio engineer is in no way sufficient to allow him to support his family. However, carrying out such repairs is considered *forgeronnage* (labour associated with blacksmiths). When he started this work, he equipped a studio in a backroom of his own home in order to be able to receive customers discreetly, and out of the inquisitive glaze of acquaintances of his family in Leglik. Fear of causing further resentment among his family members prevented him from exposing his business but it did not prevent him from running it. He preferred to risk being disparaged by his family than to not follow his own career. Every year he has made a little headway: he moved from his backroom to a bench in a friend's grocery shop, and finally to his own workshop in the market place.

Now his family has accepted his new source of income and it would seem that the repair of electronic items such as mobile phones or other status symbols is less associated with manual, and thus inferior, labour. Radiotelephony forms an important means of communication, a status symbol, even a means of reserve capital[152] and is far from being the preserve of the upper class only. Nourdin has acquired a reputation among all classes due to his technical know-how and his attention to detail, making him one of the few highly respected technicians in

---

[152] A brisk trade in the purchase and sale of mobile phones has developed. In the past, one or more animals in the herd used to be sold when a cattle owner was pressed for money, but nowadays status symbols are purchased when sufficient means are available and sold the moment the owner has a cash-flow problem.

town. This is how he has gained the prestige he enjoys today in this neighbourhood.

Case 2: Yacoub
Yacoub is a tall, strong man with a dark skin and distinct African features that set him apart physically at least from the White Moors. His family is well known and respected in Aioun due to the achievements of his father as a military policeman and their close ties with the general chief's family as a result of milk ties.

But his family is of slave descent. His father and grandfather were born slaves in the royal encampment, the *hella* of the *qabila* Oulad an Nacer, Ethman ould Bakar's camp. The *hella* used to be mobile, just like all the nomadic camps and it was not until the 1960s that it became permanent in Vougous, a village about 15 km from Aioun.

Because their grandmother, a slave of Ethman's brother, gave her mother's milk to Ethman's cousin, the latter and her son (Yacoub's father) became milk relatives. Not only do these relationships continue to exist, but Yacoub's sister also renewed milk ties with the same family by nursing the daughters of Ethman's son and successor Mohammed el Moctar. Mohammed Moctar's son is also named Ethman and he is likely to succeed his father as the general leader of the Oulad an Nacer.[153]

Because of these milk ties, the future chief Ethman is a regular visitor in Yacoub's house and through these frequent contacts Yacoub's family is socially and politically associated with the Oulad an Nacer leaders. They obviously derive much status from this and if there is any trouble, everyone in Aioun knows that Ethman will do whatever is in his power to help his milk relatives. This provides them with a degree of social and economic security, a certain political power and, above all, earns them a good deal of respect. Participating in his family's social neighbourhood stresses aspects of Yacoub's identity such as self-awareness and self-respect and he enjoys a good reputation.

If another of Yacoub's social neighbourhoods – the social group of friends with whom he regularly interacts – is considered, a different side of his identity can be seen. Yacoub is divorced and at the moment is a bachelor. He is attractive to women because of his physical looks, his reputation and the fact

---

[153] Descendants of the royal family reside not only in Vougous but also in Terenni and Kobenni. A dispute over a successor's rights is the reason why the Oulad an Nacer do not have a general chief today. They are dispersed over three zones and all claim the right to succeed the last leader Mohammed el Moctar ould Ethman, the son of Ethman ould Bakar. The son of the last leader, Ethman ould Mohammed el Moctar, is the leader in Vougous and seems to be supported by the majority of the Oulad an Nacer concerning succession.

that he owns his own business and is considered to be quite well-off. The latter is a particularly important factor. Whereas it used to be impossible for a Haratin man like Yacoub to date White Moorish women, today women themselves decide who they go out with. The determining factors have become property and financial success instead of descent and skin colour. Yacoub has many girlfriends, including several White Moors. Among his friends it is prestigious to be seen with a white lady as it marks him out as being 'successful'. However, the reason that a White Moorish woman would go out with a Haratin is purely financial: she wants to benefit from the relationship financially. Generally, a family will gain directly from their daughters' engagements. Yacoub knows what women expect of him; being with women requires the constant offering of indulgences and the giving of presents. Dating many girls proffers status but at the same time incurs significant costs. Squandering money to please women is typical of Haratin men who struggle to be respected by nobles. Likewise, they try to copy the behaviour of wealthy Bidan to present to the outside world a favourable image of their status.

Yet there is a difference. When a Bidan girl courts a Bidan man, and especially when it is a close relative, they do not spend much money during their meetings, preferring to keep their means within the family. Once married, the wife and her family will legitimately obtain that which is theirs by right.

For Yacoub, love can sometimes be very complicated: when he has money he might support many mistresses, but when his business affairs are disappointing he rarely receives the sympathy he furtively expects. Giving presents wins him the highest praise but when he is temporarily not able to fulfil his social obligations, his social standing topples to a lowly Haratin level, accentuating the antithesis with Bidan.

Finally, Yacoub operates in an economic neighbourhood that underscores his social position as a Haratin: he is a motor mechanic and works in his own service station. His situation here is typical of the Haratin in general. Nowadays, cars abound in Aioun and Yacoub has a lot of clients from all walks of life. Many people depend on his technical know-how and experience and respect him accordingly. He earns enough money to live a comfortable life, like a Bidan. And in spite of the appreciation with which he is met, the fact remains that he walks around in a dirty boiler-suit with greasy smears all over his hands, underlining the fact that he is involved in manual labour. His appearance thus reveals a part of his identity that he is trying very hard to ignore.

Analysis of the case studies

These two case studies show how individuals have been able to make the transition from a nomadic, rural way of life to a sedentary, urban lifestyle. In both, there are the conventional social family circles with a firm rural footing, the social circle of friends and relatives that surrounds them in town, and the urban social fields within which they work.

Within the social and economic neighbourhoods the tendency to focus on Bidan models is striking. Nourdin, who as a Bidan noble is encouraged by his family and friends to behave as such and is reviled when he does not, and Yacoub, who as a Haratin tries his best to act as a Bidan, are both being judged according to Bidan standards. Their behaviour illustrates their identity struggle: they struggle with what they want to do and who they want to be.

For the Bidan, their social life involves a straitjacket with all sorts of regulations, and extricating oneself from these rigid codes of conduct requires profound conviction. When Bidan want to live a life based on other standards, they meet with severe social pressure, as is demonstrated by Nourdin, who has had to overcome serious differences of opinion with his parents.

The Haratin are still struggling with their slave past. For centuries they have assimilated into the Bidan culture but without ever coming close to being considered Bidan. Their relationship with the Bidan continues to be ambiguous: those who have the financial means nowadays copy the typical appearance of the nobles and wear expensive *derra'as* complete with trousers and belt over a French-style dress shirt, they have their beards trimmed according to the latest Arabic fashion and they try to seduce women by spending a lot of money on them.

Although they may have adopted these social and economic fields of interaction that straitjacket and cramp dissidents, the population of Aioun adds to their sense of frustration with their frequent gossiping. A conscious downplaying or spreading of rumours about someone's wayward behaviour can put extra social pressure on an individual. This has happened to both Nourdin and Yacoub.

Within Yacoub's family, nobody – not even the chief of the Oulad an Nacer – would ever refer to his family's servile origins or to a previous master-slave relationship. Nor will his social status ever be explicitly referred to by his friends. But outsiders may make embarrassing remarks about his slave descent behind his back and Yacoub is consequently very concerned with how other people see him. He even keeps a diary in which he notes down how he thinks strangers view him. Nourdin is especially hurt by people who go to his father to speak badly of him or by those who vilify the Ould Saleh family.

It appears that Bidan who are still living a conservative rural life are more prepared to accept former slaves as independent and free people, as is the case of the royal family of the Oulad an Nacer, who see Yacoub and his family as full family members. On the other hand, neo-urbanites and especially those in the big cities tend to emphasize class and racial differences. The superior way some Bidan address Haratin, and equally importantly, the subservient response to this behaviour show how deep-rooted ideas of superiority versus inferiority still are. The case of Yacoub also shows how frustrating and embarrassing it is to always have to work hard in order to be taken seriously and at the same time be exposed to denigration and humiliation.

The process of urbanization plays a significant role in identity transformations. The introduction of innovative technologies, the changing economy, and a kind of emotional alienation of the rural way of life influence the customs, norms and ideas of individuals to a large extent and change the economic alternatives that people have. Social change is making it possible to stretch the boundaries of social and economic neighbourhoods and to create or restyle identities. For example, the rapid spread of television, which encourages Occidental and Middle Eastern ideas and lifestyles, has created the desire in many people to become rich and be able to afford the comfort they see on television. They realize that certain economic activities are not despised in other parts of the world and that it can be considered a virtue to be (financially) independent.

Expatriates from the West working on development projects in Aioun are living a (material) life that many local people wish to imitate. Those who do not depend financially on others are beginning to realize that sharing their income with their extended families is hampering the realization of their dreams.

The town offers a sizeable job market. Opportunities to become financially independent exist for those not restricted by cultural labour taboos. Today, ever more cases like Nourdin are emerging. About fifteen years ago when Nourdin started producing charcoal, he was exceptional. When I met him in 2002 he was still hiding his true business but just two years later he had managed to open his own workshop in the urban centre. This shows that although Bidan society is generally depicted as being rather rigid, it is proving nevertheless to be fairly flexible and willing to adjust and to re-evaluate its own norms and values through the identity changes of individuals. The mobile-phone business has somehow inscribed itself as one of the economic activities suitable for Bidan. The ability of rapid re-adjustment may be partly explained by the fact that nomadic societies have to be flexible to survive in harsh conditions and under erratic circumstances. The acceptance of Nourdin's parents of their son's business illustrate how the various social and economic neighbourhoods in which individuals participate influence and change each other's ideas and identities.

The case of Yacoub demonstrates that it is possible nowadays for a Haratin to maintain relations with a Bidan on a more or less equal footing. Whereas nobles used to consider themselves too superior to associate with lower-class people, today young Bidan have fewer problems in this respect, especially when it comes to dealing with people who have a certain wealth. This demonstrates that there is a growing tendency to overcome setbacks of descent and skin colour through becoming prosperous.

By focusing on individuals who operate in social and economic neighbourhoods we identify indicators for changes-in-the-making: how people in the process of moving between several neighbourhoods in turn construct and reconstruct these neighbourhoods, thereby changing their social identities. The cases show clearly the connection of social and economic aspects of people's lives and the influences on identity.

Conclusion

During the last forty years in Mauritania, processes of migration, sedentarization and urbanization have unfolded at a rapid pace, and the process of urbanization is still in full swing. The transition from a pastoral way of life to sedentary, urban livelihoods has brought many changes to Moorish society.

In the midst of the urban dynamics in which modern and traditional, and nomadic and sedentary aspects of culture coexist, the Bidan and the Haratin – both groups within Moorish society – are struggling to position themselves between their current aspirations and their traditional customs and values. Modern values are being incorporated and traditional norms and values are taking on a new meaning in the changing socio-economic urban setting. These changes shed light on the process of changes-in-the-making or disclose processes of future history.

To analyze this process of changes-in-the-making the concept of neighbourhoods was adapted from the ideas of Moore (1973), who defined the notion of 'semi-autonomous social fields' that generate rules and customs and symbols internally but that are also vulnerable to rules and decisions and other forces that emanate from the larger world they are surrounded by. People participate and manoeuvre in divergent neighbourhoods that determine – to a certain extent – their norms, ideas and identity, but through their participation in them they also (re)construct these fields or neighbourhoods, leading to social change.

In societies that undergo rapid transformation processes, like Mauritania, neighbourhoods are characterized by divergences of views concerning beliefs, ideals, opinions and codes of conduct. While operating in a certain neighbourhood people will usually accentuate those identity features representative of that specific neighbourhood. People are struggling to position themselves between their aspirations of today and their traditional customs and values. To facilitate analysis, a distinction has been made between social and economic neighbourhoods but, in reality, the social and the economic elements of neighbourhoods are closely intertwined.

The examples presented here have been drawn from the small town Aioun el Atrouss that, in spite of its rapid processes of change and modernization, is still mainly influenced by White Moor or Bidan culture. The Haratin, their former slaves, are highly acculturated: they speak the same language and uphold the same customs and values, but twenty-five years after the abolition of slavery they have still not managed to completely disembarrass themselves of their inferior social status. To overcome the burden of slave descent, the Haratin are trying to incorporate the social standards of the nobles. The Bidan, for their part, are seeking to reappraise or to ennoble work once only considered appropriate for the lower social classes. The two case studies demonstrate the identity struggles of people who participate in several neighbourhoods, the continuous switch from one to another underlining different aspects of their identity and showing their aptitude for restyling their identities.

The two case studies upon which this chapter is based may seem somewhat extreme but the subtlety of changes-in-the-making is most easily identified through extreme cases. In fact, both cases are typical examples of the problems with which Moorish society has been confronted over the last forty years in terms of identity, social relations, economic activities and the transition from rural to urban lifestyles.

References

Altorki, S. 1980, 'Milk Kinship in Arab Society: An Unexplored Problem in the Ethnography of Marriage', *Ethnology* 19: 233-44.

Brhane, M. 1997, 'Narratives of the Past, Politics of the Present: Identity, Subordination and the Haratines of Mauritania', PhD Thesis, University of Chicago, UMI: Chicago.

Cleaveland, T. 2000, 'Reproducing Culture and Society: Women, and the Politics of Gender, Age, and Social Rank in Walāta', *Canadian Journal of African Studies* 34 (2): 189-217.

Ensel, R. 2002, 'Colactation and Fictive Kinship Rites of Incorporation and Reversal in Morocco', *The Journal of North African Studies* 7 (4): 83-96.

Fortier, C. 2001, 'Le lait, le Sperme, le Dos. Et le Sang? Représentations Physiologiques de la Filiation et de la Parenté de Lait en Islam Malékite et dans la Société Maure', *Cahiers d'Etudes Africaines* 161 (XLI-I): 97-138.

Héritier, F. 1994, 'Identité de Substance et Parenté de Lait dans le Monde Arabe', in: *Epouser au Plus Proche. Inceste, Prohibitions et Stratégies Matrimoniales autour de la Méditerranée*, Paris: Editions EHESS.

Hobsbawm, E. & T. Ranger 1983, *The Invention of Tradition*, London: Cambridge University Press.

Koita, T. 1994, 'Migrations, Pouvoirs Locaux et Enjeux sur l'Espace Urbain', *Politique Africaine* (55): 101-109.

Marchesin, Ph. 1992, *Tribus, Ethnies et Pouvoir en Mauritanie*, Paris: Karthala.

Marty, P. 1920, 'Les Tribus Maures du Sahel et du Hodh', *Etudes sur l'Islam et les Tribus du Soudan*, vol. 3, Series: Revue du Monde Musulman, Paris: E. Leroux.

Moore, S.F. 1973, 'Law and Social Change: the Semi-autonomous Social Field as an Appropriate Subject of Study', *Law and Society Review* 7 (4): 719-47.

Moore, S.F. 1987, 'Explaining the Present: Theoretical Dilemmas in Processual Ethnography', *American Ethnologis* 14 (4): 727-36.

Moore, S.F. 1994, 'The Ethnography of the Present and the Analysis of Process', in: R. Borofsky (ed.), *Assessing Cultural Anthropology*, New York: McGraw Hill, pp. 362-76.

Office National du Statistique (ONS) 2004, http://www.ons.mr.

Ould Ahmed Salem, Zekeria, 2001, '"Tcheb-tchib" et Compagnie: Lexique de la Survie et Figures de la Réussite en Mauritanie', *Politique Africaine* (82): 78-100.

Ould Cheikh, Abdel Wedoud & P. Bonte 1982, 'Production Pastorale et Production Marchande dans la Société Maure', in: P.C. Salzman (ed.), *Contemporary and Nomadic and Pastoral Peoples: Africa and Latin America*, Studies in Third World Societies, Williamsburg, Virginia, pp. 31-56.

Taylor, R.M. 1996, 'Of Disciples and Sultans: Power, Authority and Society in the 19th Century Mauritanian Gebla', PhD Thesis, University of Illinois, Urbana.

List of authors

Mirjam de Bruijn is an anthropologist at the African Studies Centre in Leiden. Her research has a clear interdisciplinary character and an important theme throughout it is how people manage risk (drought, war, famine, etc.) in both rural and urban areas. She has done fieldwork in Chad and Mali and her fields of interest include nomadism, social (in)security, poverty, marginality/social and economic exclusion, violence, slavery and human rights. In Mali she worked in the Mopti area with the Fulbe and in Menaka with the Tamacheck, while in Chad she has worked in both N'djamena and in Central Chad with Hadjerai and Arab groups.
bruijnm@ascleiden.nl

Rijk van Dijk is an anthropologist at the African Studies Centre in Leiden. He has done extensive research on the rise of Pentecostal movements in urban areas of Malawi and Ghana and is the author of *Young Malawian Puritans* (ISOR Press, 1993). He co-edited *Modernity on a Shoestring* with Richard Fardon and Wim van Binsbergen (EIDOS, 1999), *The Quest for Fruition through Ngoma* with Ria Reis and Marja Spierenberg (James Currey, 2000) and *Situating Globality* with Wim van Binsbergen (Brill, 2004). His current research focuses on the transnational dimensions of Ghanaian Pentecostalism, in particular in relation to the migration of Ghanaians to the Netherlands and Botswana.
DijkR@ascleiden.nl

Dick Foeken is a human geographer and works at the African Studies Centre in Leiden, the Netherlands, where his main research interest is urban agriculture in Africa. He is currently involved in two projects, the 'Nakuru Urban Agriculture Research Project' (NUAP) in Kenya and 'Sustainable Urban Agriculture' in Tanzania. He co-edited, with Jan Hoorweg and R.A. Obudho, the *Kenya Coast Handbook. Culture, Resources and Development in the East African Littoral* (Lit Verlag, 2000).
dfoeken@ascleiden.nl

Piet Konings is a sociologist of development and senior researcher at the African Studies Centre in Leiden. He has carried out extensive research on labour and trade unionism, rural development and political processes in Africa and has published widely on the political economy and labour in Africa, especially in Ghana and Cameroon. His current research focuses on political change and regionalism in Cameroon and the role of civil society in Africa. His

recent publications include *Unilever Estates in Crisis and the Power of Organizations in Cameroon* (Lit Verlag, 1998), *Trajectoires de Libération en Afrique Contemporaine* (Karthala, 2000) and *Negotiating an Anglophone Identity: A Study of the Politics of Recognition and Representation in Cameroon* (Brill, 2003).
Konings@asc.leidenuniv.nl

Eileen Moyer teaches medical anthropology at the University of Amsterdam where she also serves as coordinator of the 'AIDS Medicines in Resource-Poor Settings' action research group. She completed her PhD entitled 'In the Shadow of the Sheraton: Imagining Localities in Global Spaces in Dar es Salaam, Tanzania' in 2003 and continues to conduct fieldwork among street children and youth in Dar es Salaam. Her recent articles include 'Popular Cartographies: Youthful Imagining of the Global in the Streets of Dar es Salaam, Tanzania' (*City and Society* 16 (2):117-43) and 'Keeping Up Appearances: Fashion and Function among Dar es Salaam Street Youth' (*Etnofoor* 16 (2): 88-106).
eileenmoyer@hotmail.com

Basile Ndjio is a research fellow at the Amsterdam School for Social Research, University of Amsterdam. He has published several articles on ethnicity, criminality and sorcery in Cameroon. His recent works, '*Carrefour de la Joie*: Popular Deconstruction of the African Postcolonial Public Sphere' and 'Douala: Inventing Life in an African Necropolis' are due to appear respectively in the journal *Africa* and in Palgrave's volume on cities in contemporary Africa (forthcoming).
bndjio@yahoo.com

Emmanuel Nkurunziza is a land surveyor and urban planner who specializes in urban land policy, development planning and urban poverty in Sub-Saharan Africa, in particular in Uganda. He worked for many years at Makerere University in Uganda as a university lecturer in the fields of surveying and urban planning prior to joining the University of Birmingham where he is currently a staff member in the International Development Department.
E.Nkurunziza@bham.ac.uk

Samuel Owuor is a lecturer at the Department of Geography and Environmental Studies, University of Nairobi, Kenya and has just completed his PhD at the University of Amsterdam entitled 'Bridging the Urban-Rural Divide: Multi-spatial Livelihoods in Nakuru Town, Kenya'. During this research project, he

was seconded to the African Studies Centre in Leiden where he worked in the Economy, Ecology and Exclusion theme group.
samowuor@yahoo.com

Deborah Pellow is Professor of Anthropology in The Maxwell School at Syracuse University. She is an Africanist whose work, primarily in Ghana, is grounded in the roles and relationships enacted by individuals in the urban arena and plural society, under conditions of social change. She is working on a research project on the Dagomba of northern Ghana to explore the phenomenon of highly-educated men (patrons) who live outside Dagbon and are influencing their uneducated followers (clients) as they combine potent Dagomba symbols and rituals with rhetoric from the West to exert influence on local/national power structures.
dpellow@maxwell.syr.edu

Charles Piot is an Associate Professor in the Department of Cultural Anthropology and the Program in African and African American Studies at Duke University. He does research on histories of slavery and colonialism, as well as on contemporary culture and politics in rural West Africa. His recent book, *Remotely Global: Village Modernity in West Africa*, attempts to re-theorize a classic out-of-the-way place as within the modern and the global. He is currently engaged in research on several new projects. One explores the way in which the human-rights discourse, democratization, development and charismatic Christianity are articulating with post-Cold War West African political cultures. Another tracks global discourses about female genital cutting from Western courtrooms and media into the capitals and villages of West Africa, and the third explores Togolese expatriates in Europe and the US, examining the ways in which exile reshapes questions of citizenship, sovereignty and national belonging.
charles.piot@duke.edu

Kiky van Til is an anthropologist and is currently working on her WOTRO-financed PhD on the socio-cultural and economic transformations that are taking place in the east of Mauritania due to small-town urbanization among the Moors there. She is is affiliated to the Agency in Africa theme group at the African Studies Centre in Leiden, the Netherlands for the duration of her PhD project.
vantil@ascleiden.nl

Katja Werthmann is a senior lecturer in the Department of Anthropology and African Studies at the University of Mainz, Germany. She received her MA

from the University of Frankfurt/Main, completed her doctorate at the Free University in Berlin, and did her habilitation thesis at the University of Mainz. She has done fieldwork among Muslim urban women in northern Nigeria, and among gold diggers and peasants in Burkina Faso. Her research interests include urban anthropology, economic anthropology, migration, land rights, gender, and Islam in Africa.
Werthmann@uni-mainz.de

AFRICAN DYNAMICS

ISSN 1568-1777

1. Bruijn, M. de, R. van Dijk and D. Foeken (eds.) *Mobile Africa*. Changing Patterns of Movement in Africa and Beyond. 2001. ISBN 90 04 12072 6
2. Abbink, J., M. de Bruijn and K. van Walraven. *Rethinking Resistance*. Revolt and Violence in African History. 2003. ISBN 90 04 12624 4
3. Van Binsbergen, W. and R. van Dijk. *Situating Globality*. African Agency in the Appropriation of Global Culture. 2004. ISBN 90 04 13133 7
4. Abbink, J. and I. van Kessel. *Vanguard or Vandals*. Youth, Politics and Conflict in Africa. 2005. ISBN 90 04 14275 4
5. Konings, P. and D. Foeken. *Crisis and Creativity*. Exploring the Wealth of the African neighbourhood. 2006. ISBN 90 04 15004 8